Making It Through the Night

Making It Through the Night

How Couples Can Survive a Crisis Together

Pat Quigley with Marilyn Shroyer, Ph.D.

Foreword by Patrick T. Malone, M.D.

Conari Press
Berkeley, CA

Pat's Dedication

To my husband Jack
To my sons, Matthew and Timothy

With great gratitude that each of you came into my life
With appreciation for your diverse gifts and ways of being your
    selves
With love each day and forever

Marilyn's Dedication

I'd like to dedicate this book to the following people:
    Bill, for supporting dynamic risk taking
    Craig and Michelle, for demonstrating courage in the
        shadow of death
    Audrey and Reed, for striving persistently to achieve goals
    Michelle and Rex, for kindness and devotion
    Aimee, for listening with empathy always
    Joanne, for pursuing excellence and her inner child
    Pearl, for steadfast support
    Lyle, for always being there for me
    Wayne, for teaching us to love learning

Copyright © 1992 by Pat Quigley and Marilyn Shroyer. Preface © 1992 by Patrick T. Malone, M.D.

Printed in the United States of America on recycled paper

Cover design by Andrea Sohn Design; cover illustration by Karen Marquardt

ISBN: 0-943233-33-X
Library of Congress Cataloging-in-Publication Data
Quigley, Pat.
        Making it through the night : how couples can survive a crisis together / Pat Quigley with Marilyn Shroyer. — 1st ed.
            p. cm.
        Includes bibliographical references (p.   ) and index.
        ISBN 0-943233-33-X : $12.95
        1. Marriage—United States. 2. Life change events—United States.
I. Shroyer, Marilyn, 1944-   II. Title.
HQ734.Q54 1992
646.7'8—dc20   91-40496
                        CIP
First edition
1 2 3 4 5 6 7 8 9 10

The authors would like to thank the following for permission to reprint the works indicated:

Excerpts from the article "I Thought I was Alone" by Larry Barton (*Parade Magazine*, September 17, 1990), copyright c 1990. Reprinted with permission from Larry Barton and *Parade*.

Excerpts from THE POWER OF MYTH by Joseph Campbell with Bill Moyers, copyright c 1988 by Apostrophe S Productions, Inc. and Bill Moyers and Alfred Van der Mark Editions, Inc., for itself and the estate of Joseph Campbell. Reprinted by permission of Doubleday, a division of Bantam, Doubleday, Dell Publishing Group, Inc.

Excerpts from the article "What a Father Learned From Grief" by Claire Carter (*Parade Magazine*, July 29, 1990) copyright c 1990. Reprinted with permission from Claire Carter and *Parade*.

Excerpts from articles by Leslie Dreyfous, Associated Press (July 22, 1990 and June 9, 1991). Reprinted by permission of Associated Press

Excerpts from OUR APPOINTMENT WITH LIFE: THE BUDDHA'S TEACHING ON LIVING IN THE PRESENT by Thich Nhat Hanh, copyright o 1990 by Thich Nhat Hanh. Reprinted by permission of Parallax Press.

Excerpts from AT RISK by Alice Hoffman, copyright c 1988 by Alice Hoffman. Reprinted by permission of The Putnam Publishing Group.

Excerpts from SECOND BANANA by Dottie Lamm, copyright c 1983 by Dorothy V. Lamm. Reprinted by permission of Johnson Books.

Excerpts from TWO PART INVENTION by Madeleine L'Engle. Copyright c 1988 by Crosswicks Ltd. Reprinted by permission of Farrar, Straus & Giroux, Inc.

Excerpts from DO I HAVE TO GIVE UP ME TO BE LOVED BY YOU? by Jordan Paul, Ph.D., and Margaret Paul, Ph.D., copyright c 1983 by Jordan Paul, Ph.D. and Margaret Paul, Ph.D. Published by CompCare Publishers, Minneapolis, MN. Used with permission.

Excerpts from TURNING POINTS: TREATING FAMILIES IN TRANSITION AND CRISIS by Frank Pittman, III, copyright 1987 by Frank S. Pittman, III. Reprinted by permission of W.W. Norton & Company, Inc., Publisher.

Excerpts from FORGIVE AND FORGET: HEALING THE HURTS WE DON'T DESERVE by Lewis B. Smedes, copyright 1984 by Lewis B. Smedes. Reprinted by permission of HarperCollins Publishers.

Acknowledgements

From Marilyn and Pat:

Our gifted editor Mary Jane Ryan guided us through the challenging process of turning a good idea into a finished manuscript. Always, she offered her astute suggestions to us with tact and respect. For her early confidence, ongoing support, and considerable expertise, we are most grateful.

Each of the books in Chapter 14, "Other Helpful Reading," influenced the writing of *Making It Through the Night*. Many are quoted in these pages. We thank these authors whose ideas are both inspirational and enlightening.

The twelve-step programs in which we both are involved have influenced our lives and these pages. We are grateful for the wisdom and inspiration of the twelve-steps as originally conceived by Alcoholics Anonymous co-founders in 1935. Newer writings and materials about the recovery process have also been invaluable.

We are also grateful that as the two of us wrote this book together, the process of collaboration deepened our friendship and allowed a synergism that expanded our original concepts.

From Pat:

With special appreciation and love to my mother, Mary Anderson, who inspires me with her courage and who, in the midst of several of her own crises, always kept asking, "How's it coming?"

I am grateful to the men and women who shared with me their journeys with their partners through crises. Their experiences, their courage infuse these pages.

I am grateful to the en-couragers, the ones who kept

instilling courage in me over the years that this book took shape. Each of you knows why you're mentioned here. Special thanks to: Philip Anderson, Ramona Benton, Luann Budzianowski, Sally Escamilla, Jane & Merv Dick, Carol and Walt Friesen, Jetta and Larry Feil, Lydia and Bill Hilliard, Dot and Jim Hinson, Nancy and Gene Hinson, Deborah Hinson-Clymer, Jan Hinson-Caughey, Jay Hinson, Faith and Ben Kepler, Dottie Lamm, Scotti and Jim LeMon, Tamera Trojahn-Marsh, Debra Milton, Ellie Rogers, Connie Ning, Naomi Gaede-Penner, Nina and Jerry Spotts, Kathi Tolle, Susan Ulrich, Margaret Wooten, and Cathy Yeargan.

I am grateful to Rocky Mountain Women's Institute for their early affirmation and support which helped me complete my first book and instilled confidence to continue writing about topics that make a difference.

I am grateful to each member of the Tuesday night CoDA group for ongoing support.

I am grateful to the mental health professionals who graciously granted interviews, including Patrick Malone, M.D.; Mike Reagan, M.S.W.; Vange Sandeen, M.S.W.; and Colleen Sundermeyer, Ph.D.

I am grateful to Jack for helping me write this book by insisting I buy a computer, for helping me learn how to use it, and for showing me in countless other ways his caring, love, and support.

I am grateful to Matthew for consistently cheering me on, listening to descriptions of the good and bad writing days, and quietly affirming me again and again.

I am grateful to Timothy for his long-distance encouragement, for reading the manuscript and offering astute suggestions, and for inspiring me to enjoy the journey, not just the destination.

From Marilyn:

I'd like to acknowledge the professors at the University of Denver for instilling in me a deep respect for the research process, especially Dr. Raymond Kleuver, my adviser. I'd also like to thank my pastors Dr. Mark Brewer and Dr. Gary Reddish for their inspirational leadership in my deep and meaningful spiritual growth.

Of greatest importance are my clients. Their willingness to grow, take risks, and work through their pain has been a constant source of inspiration. I admire their courage and persistence.

Contents

Foreword

Crisis has been a frequently used word during the past few decades. From the political Cuban missile crisis to the psychological midlife crisis, we are a society that is very much "crisis" oriented. Such an orientation is exactly what one might expect in a "doing" oriented culture like ours. And, in truth, many of these crises do affect our lives. Usually more personally meaningful, however, are the very personal crises we have in the course of our ordinary lives. They become the focal points of our existence. Too often, we even let them take over our lives. We then begin to see life as a series of problems to overcome and forget that, in reality, it is a journey we travel.

Understanding the origin of the word *crisis* could direct us back toward seeing our lives as journeys. The word comes from Latin and German roots meaning "to sift," as in sifting flour. If we understood crises as times to sift through (that is, redefine) our lives, we would be much closer to understanding the true nature of those lives, much closer to recognizing ourselves and our spouses, lovers, and loved ones as fellow travelers.

Our journeys are our individual living metaphors of the life process. That process, for most scientists, is characterized by three major qualities:

1. Metabolism
2. Replication
3. Self-Repair

It seems clear to me that these qualities are as applicable to ourselves as they are to plants and viruses. I would even say they are as applicable to our marriages, pairings, and families. The connection between our metabolism and our living and being healthy seems obvious. Not only do we all know we must breathe and eat to live, but we also struggle with trying to do so healthily--keeping our weight in a fit range, giving up smoking, and looking for pollution-free environmental conditions; these are all ways in which we must deal daily with our human metabolism. Our marriages, pairings, and families must likewise be nourished, have room to breathe, and exist in healthy environments if they are to remain robust and growing.

Our replication connection seems obvious as well. Despite the fact that our lovemaking and sexuality are areas of frequent concern and dysfunction in the current culture, we all, nevertheless, are aware of their importance and poignancy. If we understand sexuality as including our creativity, animation, and spirituality, it is also clear how these must be integral parts of our marriages, pairings, and families in order to maintain healthy living.

What is not so clear or obvious to most of us is the fact that self-repair is an integral part of life, that *self-healing is an integral part of living*. We tend to forget that such self-healing is necessary not only to ourselves as individuals but also to our pairings, to our marriages, and to our families.

This point is made poetically by Galway Kinnell in his poem *St. Francis and the Sow*, when he says that "all things must be retaught their loveliness." Indeed, such reteaching, such *self-healing*, must be an ongoing process if any of those things would be healthy and whole. We must have self-healing to avoid illness or even death. It must be present and active in our families, in our marriages, in our pairings, and in ourselves at all times. Perhaps, however, at no greater time than in the "sifting out" that comes with crisis is this need for self-healing so manifest.

Self-healing is, in humans, basically a form of self-education. Self-knowledge is the only true form of education. It is the only form useful to the process of life because all things that can *change* us must first be of us. Self-healing thus requires both *discipline* and *diversity*, two characteristics very much at issue during times of crisis. Out of discipline comes the homeostasis which allows us to survive and continue being who we are. It allows us to endure the crisis and maintain our personhood. Out of diversity comes the evolution which allows us to grow and change. It allows us to adapt and cope, reintegrate and renew in times of great change. Thus out of discipline and diversity *we learn who we are.*

From my point of view, our family and pairing *relationships* are the main engine of our self-education—the main engine of our self-healing—and our family or pairing itself the main classroom. The differences among us, the differences we live in and with, are gifts we give to each other to allow self-healing. At no time, are these differences *and their union* more important than at those critical times in life, the times of maximal stress. At those crisis times, we must remember that by giving the gift of self-healing, we give the gift of life.

Sadly, we often do not live with each other in this way. Instead, we deal with our differences as if they were a threat, not an opportunity for self-education. We try to make others like us, instead of learning from them being like themselves. Or we try to make ourselves like others, instead of giving the gift of being like ourselves. Doing so only makes any crisis worse—it blocks any "self-repair."

We reject the gift of the other being different and somehow come to view differing as something the other *does to us* rather than something they *give to us.* We withhold the gift of our difference and instead see the other as "different" or "alien." We lose touch completely with that "sifting" which could lead us further down our path. In these ways we see difference as a negation, not an addition. The most common presentation of this phenomenon, one that comes out so often at times of stress, is the basic conflict acted out as "someone is right, someone is wrong," a position guaranteed to only worsen any crisis.

But we do not move farther down our path by choosing "being right" over love. It is only in the act of loving each other—of participating reciprocally in the process of self-repair—that we become most fully who we are. At times of crisis, we must actively be about this process. That does not necessarily mean *doing* something. It does, however, most assuredly mean *being* something. Being present, accepting, self-responsible, self-disciplined, reciprocal, connected, and full of faith are ways by which we can "sift" through the difficult times of life and become more fully who we are. This book is a way we can start on that journey.

Patrick T. Malone, M.D.
author of *The Art of Intimacy*

Chapter 1

We Never Planned on <u>This</u>

> *The most practical thing that a married*
> *couple can prepare for is change. The effort*
> *to remain the same, to hold things together*
> *as they were in some golden days of recollec-*
> *tion is disastrous.*
> *Eugene C. Kennedy*

When most of us married or chose a special some-one to love, we dreamed of warm starry nights and midnight strolls under a full moon. Or we fantasized about cuddling under the covers on cool eve-nings made for opening up the windows and letting in the night breeze. Though we knew an occasional storm might blow in, we imagined ourselves sitting close together, dining by candlelight until the power came back on. The warm comfort of the two of us against the world is, after all, one of the main reasons for joining two lives. We assumed that together we'd be safe and secure.

Not many of us, however, plan for crisis. Very few of us sit down with our partner and spell out strategies for what we'd do if our child became addicted to drugs, if one of us was diagnosed with cancer, if a tornado demolished our house, or if we were forced to file for bankruptcy. Few of us anticipate that we might not to be able to have children if we wanted to, that a child of ours might die, that our parents in their old age might need our parenting, or that in our golden years our medical and retirement benefits might shrink or disappear. And even if we did plan for any of the above, or other crises entirely different but equally upsetting, often their close-up realities prove more difficult to deal with than we could have imagined.

Consistent estimates are that 75 to 80 percent of couples divorce or separate after a serious life blow. Often one or both partners tries to flee rather than admit a crisis exists, face it, and learn its lessons. Or if flight is not an option, couples remain together feeling both stuck with each other and struck unfairly by tragedy. In short, they endure together but don't grow together. It doesn't have to be that way! We *can* go through these painful times and ultimately discover the deep joy of coming out together on the other side.

Deep in the midst of a crisis, you and your mate may now be uncertain about how or if you'll make it through the darkness together. You may be struggling with fear, anger, or depression. Or perhaps you are telling yourself, "Oh come on, it's not that bad." It may be that while the two of you try to live through a crisis awful beyond your wildest imaginings, those close to you are lecturing, "You've got to pick yourself up now; you must get on with your life." Or the two of you may be suffering all alone, hiding your crisis from family and friends.

If you are feeling disoriented and perplexed, sad and discouraged, or full of rage about what you are going through, we urge you hang on to these thoughts: You don't have to ignore a crisis, deny its existence, or let it consume your lives and shatter your relationship. You have a much better option—you can stick around and face it head-on, together. This book is devoted to helping you exercise that option.

When a crisis strikes, it has the power of a wrecker's ball. *Bam.* It happens quickly, and with one carefully aimed blow, one or all the walls of our lives collapse and we are left standing in the rubble. We may then find ourselves angry that our partner did not prevent this crisis, or enraged because our mate actually helped bring it about. Or we berate and blame ourselves for what we did or didn't do.

In our journey through life, each time we encounter a crisis, whether small or crushingly huge, there's no question—it puts a special kind of strain on our relationship. In addition to coping with the situation itself, many crises cause us to question the very validity of our relationship. Can we learn to trust again the husband who drove the car that killed our daughter? Will we keep on loving our wife during a long series of chemotherapy sessions that leave her irritable and depressed? Can we stop blaming each other for our son's cocaine addiction? When we're out of work or we've had to file for bankruptcy, can we adjust to a simpler lifestyle together?

Marilyn and I firmly believe that when couples have information, that when the crisis process is understood, many of us can say, "Yes I see how hard it is to survive a crisis together, but now I also see some ways to combat the stress and discouragement and fear alongside my mate." We believe that crisis is a part of our journey together; and one of the most tragic mistakes couples in our culture too often make is to run away from instead of toward each other during a crisis. Out of panic and fear, and influenced by our role models—our parents, friends, almost everyone we know—we bolt, leaving behind our best potential ally.

Danger and Opportunity

Crisis can tear us apart, but it can also bring us together. In the Chinese language, we find a poignant and promising definition of crisis in the characters—*danger* and *opportunity*. Of necessity, in a crisis we face danger, but we can also uncover its hidden opportunities. Out of the shock and pain of a crisis, a new relationship can evolve. But first, to survive the chaos, we must begin to pick up the pieces of our individual lives and our couple relationship, and fit them back together into a new shape. This process is scary because we don't know how to do it and nothing we've learned prepares us for it. In our society we are fed the myth through love songs on the radio, TV commercials, and movies—and we want to believe it--that "happily ever after" is where we'll sail, without encountering any major storms, when we fall in love.

In the early part of this century, men and women seemed to know better. In *Tabor College Magazine*, I came across an account of Jacob Grunau and Minnie Hein's wedding ceremony on a September day in 1912. They were married in the bride's parents' Kansas farmyard, and after the ceremony their church put on a program in their honor. Poems were recited and then the couple was handed three special gifts. The first, a loaf of bread, was delivered with the wish that God would provide for their material needs. The second was a rose to wish them an abundance of joy. The third was a handkerchief to warn them that sorrows would come and to assure them that there would be comfort in those sorrows.

Jacob and Minnie's union of laughter and tears lasted seventy years. But whether you're in a new relationship or a seasoned one, we trust this book will be a valuable gift to you, like the ones that couple received.

Marilyn and I wrote this book because we could not find a specific guide for couples caught in crisis. In books about couple relationships often we discovered only a paragraph or two of generalities about how crisis impacts couples' lives. By and large, writers ignored or denied the power of crisis to destroy. Our purpose here is to provide you with with solid survival information. This is the book Marilyn and I wish we'd had when, over the years, crises kept finding us; this is the book I'll use as a reference the next time a crisis comes along.

Looking back, way back to 1959 when I was a nine-teen-year-old bride in Atlanta, Georgia, I recall believing that with effort and planning, no serious crises would intrude into our happily-ever-after life plans. Once Jack and I set the date for our wedding, I signed my name in the brides' registries at the two large department stores downtown on Peachtree Street, then chose a romantic, curved sterling Reed & Barton silver pattern: Tara, named for the white-columned mansion in *Gone With the Wind*, conjured up images of indomitable Scarlett, drawling, "I'll think about that tomorrow."

I thought about a lot of things as a newly married woman. Making love. Learning to expand my culinary skills from hamburgers and pizza to tuna casseroles and pot roast. Finding a job to help pay the rent . . . . But like Scarlett, I pushed aside anything really unpleasant. If anyone had tried to tell the naive young woman I was that a crisis could intrude on her romantic image of marriage, she would have smiled politely and let that thought slide out of her consciousness as easily as raindrops roll down an open umbrella.

Despite our best efforts however, my husband and I have faced a string of crises. To begin with there was the

shock of infertility and the accompanying battery of pro-
cedures and tests involving thermometers and semen samples.
Later, after adopting one son and giving birth to another,
mixed in with the joys of raising them were child-related
crises that included two life-threatening illnesses for our
younger son. Along the way, moving vans pulled up in
front of our house too many times. Some of my husband's
job transfers were so ill-timed, so close together, that they
became crises. And of course emotional crises have been
interspersed. Particularly frightening for me was a midlife
crisis in which I struggled to redefine my values and
priorities, wondering if the new me would still fit into my
old picture of marriage.

Today, thirty-some-odd years later, I would not, on
most days at least, trade our epic adventure for a dozen
predictable, moonlight and roses romance novels. Our
relationship, like old silver, has the patina of thousands of
daily scratches and even a few deeper gouges. But Jack
and I are still gratefully and joyfully "we," not just in spite
of, but also because of the crises that we've survived
together.

As my story shows, couples *can* outlast crisis after
crisis. It's like the old houses in Galveston; some of the
historic homes, glowing in pastel shades of pink, rosy
beige, or blue and encircled by ornate iron fences have
been through a lot. Maybe in one hurricane their shutters
blew off. Maybe a storm ripped away roof shingles and
uprooted trees. Perhaps shrubbery was lost in a rare deep
freeze. But you'd never know it to look at them; many
have been in the hands of loving owners who keep on
repairing them and restoring them, again and again.

In contrast, other old places are falling down. Columns list. Parts of the roof have caved in. Steps leading up

to once gracious porches are rotting. Windows are broken out. The magnolia trees and palms someone planted are hardly noticeable as they stand in the midst of tall, tangled weeds.

Relationships, like houses, need care and maintenance. We, of course, know that. During a long sequence of sunny days we may get by with a little neglect. But let a storm roar through our lives and, like it or not, we see that our efforts are necessary to keep our love intact.

How can we preserve ourselves and our relationship during a life crisis? How can we keep our love alive and well in the middle of one of life's storms? How can we grow closer to each other, not later, when things calm down, but right now? The following pages are organized to help you face a crisis alongside your mate, inch-by-inch.

Marilyn and I both have recent firsthand experience with inching our ways through crises. In fall of 1989, for instance, I wrote in my journal: "The whites of my husband's eyes are the color of egg yolks mixed with a little milk. His skin has that artificially tanned look you get from a tanning lotion with too much yellow dye. He sleeps off and on all day. All this, because he ate a platter of tainted raw oysters, and now the diagnosis, type-A hepatitis. I fix him nutritious meals—zucchini and squash sauteed in olive oil, black-eyed peas, seven-grain bread. And I worry, then wallow in the unfairness of it all. Wasn't it just a week ago that our second son, our last child at home, slammed the door and left for college? Wasn't it just a week ago that I dreamed of getting reacquainted with this man I've shared thirty hectic years with? Finally, this is *our* time. Now, I wonder, will he be okay? And it's not just the fear, I'm tired—I'd expected maybe at least a short break, an easy stress-free time, in celebration of completing twenty-two years of parenting."

That entry was followed two weeks later by another: "Jack is still weak, ill. And now, Hurricane Jerry is coming our direction. Jerry is going to be a baby as hurricanes go, a category one, okay to sit through in our high-rise condo. But it's scary anyway. Waves crash over the seawall in front of our place. Galveston area residents are being interviewed on the noon news. `I'll be okay, I got lunch meat and bread,' says one older woman. `My puppy and me will just sit in the closet and wait.'"

Wait. Late that same afternoon Jerry blew in with winds up to one-hundred miles per hour, sticking around long enough to snuff out the lives of two Coast Guardsmen, along with a two-year-old, a daughter of one of the young men. They drowned when their vehicle was swept over the seawall into the Gulf like a matchbox toy. Jerry also ruined $8.25 million of property. Our condominium withstood the hurricane intact only to catch the fury of a post-Jerry tornado that ripped a long vertical tear up the side of our twelve-story building. We were lucky. Our apartment, on the opposite side, was dry and undamaged.

Wait. My husband, an airline captain, waited out his illness uneasily. "I wondered if I'd ever feel normal again," Jack remembers. I was concerned too about his returning to work. His job requires excellent health and we weren't sure he'd be able to go back to flying.

We waited this period out, together. It took six months for Jack to recover, but finally he was back in the cockpit. During those months while he was home, we had the opportunity to get to know each other better. It was not exactly the way we had imagined, but it turned out okay. During his recuperation, we reflected on the past, straightening out some unfinished business, issues we'd put aside in the busyness of raising kids and working. We began thinking too about what kind of life we'd like to fashion with just the two of us at home again.

About that same time, Marilyn found herself in the middle of an entirely different drama. In her words, "I got a devastating call from my twenty-six-year-old daughter in California, one I'll never forget. She had been experiencing kidney problems, but now she was in renal failure. She was telling me, from now on, she had to be hooked up to a dialysis machine three times a week, four hours per time. This was hardly a great future for an active cheerleader-type with tons of energy.

"It didn't take long for me to make the decision to move out to California. I had to be close to her. At the least, I could help take care of her. And at best, I could give her one of my kidneys. So I closed my therapy practice and quit my job as a psychologist in a Denver high school. My fiance Bill also rearranged his life to go along with me.

"Once out there, I began the tests to see if I was a compatible donor. I was! Today I have an incision halfway around my body, but my daughter has my healthy kidney which is being retained and functioning well. Bill nursed my daughter and me back to health during the six weeks it took for us to recover.

"By the time we got married last summer, Bill and I had already survived relocating once, that major operation and recovery, plus moving back to Denver to reestablish our careers."

Some of the ideas in this book are grounded in our personal encounters with crises like these. Others spring from three years' research. During that time, I poked around libraries and bookstores, consulting over 150 written sources, interviewing mental health professionals, and talking with men and women who've survived crises with a partner.

It took courage for those I talked with to relive and review a crisis. Again and again, they emphasized they were willing to "if what we went through can help somebody else." They star in these pages. Though none of them are composites, we did change their names, transfer them to different states, supply them with fictitious jobs, and do extensive altering of identifying details. We attempted to protect their privacy as we'd promised without changing the essential truth of their experiences.

Also interwoven throughout these pages are Marilyn's perspectives based on her training and experience as a psychotherapist in private practice for ten years. In counseling couples caught in life crises, she's developed practical, empathetic approaches. She shares those here, along with many of her clients' stories. As we did with those I interviewed, we've also disguised their identities.

A Pathway Through These Pages

Making It Through the Night has one central purpose—to help you survive a crisis with your mate. It aims to assist you in learning how to stay together instead of allowing a crisis to break your relationship apart. Some of you may find the most comfort and assistance in reading through these pages from beginning to end. That way you'll gain a thorough knowledge of how crises impact a relationship and what you can do to combat the multiple stresses accompanying a crisis.

Others of you, however, may be caught in a place of such acute panic, guilt, blame, or raw pain that one particular chapter leaps out at you. You may know, for instance, that getting through the next moment is your one and only goal right now and so may go straight to Chapter 5. Let this book be your guide wherever you are in the complex crisis process. And take note—a chapter that has little relevance today may three weeks or three months from now suddenly command your undivided attention.

Why have you picked up this book? What kind of crisis is happening in your life? What do you fear might happen to you and to your relationship? What are your most pressing needs RIGHT NOW? Here's where we'll take you. Come along for all or any of the stops.

Read Chapter 2 when you're wondering why a crisis has exacted such a heavy toll on you and your relationship. You are not weak or inadequate because a crisis has gotten you down. *Stress* nibbles at us, but *crisis* has the potential to devour us. Most of us underestimate the power of a crisis; understanding its devastating potential will better equip you to deal with it.

Chapter 3 helps you to identify the crisis you're in. Crises come in four basic varieties. Which one has landed in your lives? Putting what has happened to you into a concrete category can help you and your mate go on.

Is a crisis causing you to do or say things that just aren't like you? Is the crisis affecting your partner's actions and attitudes? Chapter 4 sheds light on what's happening. No doubt both of you are in the throes of the crisis process. What the process involves—its series of adjustments and feeling—are surveyed here.

Read Chapter 5 when you and/or your partner have hit bottom and are wondering how you're going to make it through the next day, hour, or moment. The remedies and ideas presented are not designed to help you go forward, but rather to help you hold your own. Some are just for you. Others are to use to help a mate when she or he is down.

When "Why me? Why us?" questions are waking you in the middle of the night, turn to Chapter 6. You are not alone. When you ask those questions, you are joining a great company of sufferers throughout time. Examining your beliefs about why crises occur, singly and together, is a starting point for finding comfort and acceptance if you are willing to face that the two of you might do it differently and in your own time and way.

Chapter 7 is for readers who are wondering about their couple commitment. A crisis, in its pain and un-pleasantness, can make us want to run for the nearest exit. Is your relationship a for-pleasure-only affair, or is it a sturdy for-better-or-worse partnership? Most of us won't make it through a crisis without some form of commit-ment. Making your decision to commit or not, is this chapter's topic.

Chapter 8 examines what to do when your partner's way of handling a crisis is so different from yours that it's driving you crazy, making you mad, or puzzling you greatly. Are you wondering, How could he be acting like this? or What ever could she be thinking now? You are two different people; you can learn to comfort—not change—each other during a crisis.

Read Chapter 9 when you are feeling guilty about your part in a crisis. Until we forgive ourselves and un-load our guilt, we're not very good company; we're apt to make ourselves and our partner miserable. Even though we cannot change the past, by entering into the self-for-giveness process, we can go on to live fully in the present.

If you are blaming your partner, read Chapter 10. Do you think your partner caused this crisis? Unless your partner did something you deem permanently unforgivable, you need to stop blaming and start forgiving. This difficult but rewarding process is outlined here.

Read Chapter 11 when you are having difficulty accepting the ways a crisis has altered your lives. After a tragic or upsetting turn of events, you may be longing to go back to the good old pre-crisis days. When you can't, you can choose to run from the pain; let a crisis take over your life; or move toward accepting the altered situation. Specific ways of finding the strength to make the choice to become an acceptor are explored here.

In Chapter 12 you'll find out what traits couples who've survived crises together share. When you are wondering how or if you're going to make it through this together, these traits can inspire you. They are not the traits of supermen or superwomen. They're attainable for all of us.

Chapter 13 invites you, after facing harsh realities and making many adjustments, to begin to reconstruct your relationship. You're not the same people you were before. You've been broken by a crisis, not to be repaired, but to be transformed. This is a joyful chapter, one that gives you ideas for communicating and comforting each other and suggests ways to celebrate your survival.

Chapter 14 is "Other Helpful Reading." In consulting 150 written sources to research this book, we picked the ones that had the most solid content and relevance for couples in a crisis. Read the brief descriptions to see which ones suit your needs.

Marilyn's "Reflection Opportunities" at the end of each chapter include questions and insights to help readers focus on the possibilities for growth that often go unnoticed during a crisis. These are written for the two of you. If your partner isn't available or interested in this approach, doing them alone will still be helpful. Share your answers or insights if your partner is open to the idea.

Is This Book for You?

This book is not an all-purpose wonder product like one of Gary Larson's *Far Side* comics: Spray "STOPPIT" on a leaky faucet and it stops dripping; spray it in the direction of a charging elephant and the elephant stops dead in its tracks; spray it standing at a street corner and the taxi zooming by stops to pick you up. You'll find no such magic here. Instead you'll find specific practical strategies for getting through a crisis.

Our survival techniques and suggestions for cultivating your love in the midst of a crisis will work, not simply by taking mental note of them, but by doing the demanding work of love, which requires daily attention and acting on the insights you'll be collecting.

We need to point out too that this book will not be tackling certain "structural" crises many couples are facing. "Some families," as psychiatrist Frank S. Pittman III points out in *Turning Points: Treating Families in Transition and Crisis*, "live from crisis to crisis, going through a predictable pattern of crisis behavior at irregular intervals, whatever the stage of a family's development, whether or not there is some external stress."

In other words, some couple relationships resemble an active volcano. Bad things don't happen *to* them, but rather they invent and concoct their own red-hot situations. Crises keep erupting from within, spewing out molten lava, that, over and over, destroys the landscape of their lives.

In such wounded pairings one or both persons may be addicted to substances and still using; continually threatening suicide or divorce; having habitual affairs; getting into trouble with the law; constantly complaining of imaginary illnesses; or physically, sexually, or verbally abusing a family member—a partner, child, or both. More subtle, but disturbing, one or both may be incapable of any intimacy. Or one or both may be so enmeshed with the other that they function as half-persons, with little sense of separate identities.

This book is not designed for people in such situations. The ideas in these pages will make the most sense to couples with relationships which, though far from perfect, are not because of their very nature constantly in crisis. If your relationship itself is habitually deeply troubled, we encourage you to seek help in therapy or through a support group.

You are Not Alone

"What kind of book are you writing?" During my recent annual physical exam the nurse was making pleasant conversation.

After explaining that Marilyn and I were writing about how couples can survive a crisis together, her manner switched abruptly from friendly chitchat to a serious, please-listen-to-me tone.

"My husband had a stroke last year and I had no idea what he was going through—the doctor filled me in on his physical problems but never warned about the depression he'd go through. I didn't know. I just thought he didn't love me. We got a divorce."

"I'm so sorry," I said.

"We need to be educated," she said as I left.

So many times what we don't know can hurt us. So many times what we do know can save us. Come along with us now and learn how it's possible for you and your mate to survive crisis together.

In truth you probably know already, at some level,

most of the suggestions you'll find in these pages. We're simply offering you reminders. Take what fits you and your situation and use it in joy. Reject any parts you sense don't apply. We write this book not as lofty teachers, but as fellow students, who day by day are learning more about the art and practice of loving our partners during both easy and hard times. Though at times you may, as we have, feel helpless or hopeless during a crisis, we're cheering for you as you try to face it together. Your courage will grow along with your knowledge and awareness of the crisis process.

Reflection Opportunities

1. Think back to the time when you first became a couple. What were your expectations of your relationship? Of life? Write them down. Be honest with yourself as you recall, "I expected our relationship would ____"; "I expected life to ____." What were your partner's expectations? Is he or she willing to talk or write about them too?

2. Sometimes our unspoken expectations create a deepseated resentment when they go unmet. Is there anything that remains hidden from even your own awareness, something that is putting a wedge between you and your mate? Can you pinpoint it and talk about it together? (For instance: "Honey I never dreamed we'd end up living in a small town"; "I just assumed I'd get pregnant a few months after we started trying to have a baby"; "I never thought you'd quit law school. I thought by now you'd be in practice and I could quit work and launch my art career.")

3. After beginning to face your losses, can you be patient with yourself, admitting that this crisis is not easy and that instant adjustment is not possible? Can you give youself and your partner permission to take one small step at a time?

Chapter 2

Crises: Mountains Not Molehills

> *Crisis: . . . an emotionally significant event*
> *or radical change of status in a person's life.*
> *Webster's Ninth*
> *New Collegiate Dictionary*

The word *crisis* has been trivialized in modern usage. Spaghetti is boiling over on the stove and suddenly there's a crisis in the kitchen. The washing machine quit spinning and getting a repairperson out to fix it turns into the crisis of the week. We joke about these mini-crises. We moan about them. They are the irritations and inconveniences that are the bane of day-to-day life. They are not, however, critical turning points in our lives. They are not dangerous junctures that threaten us and our relationship with our mate. They are not really crises.

Chances are you are deep in the middle of a real crisis. You're used to handling the stress we casually dub crisis. But this? This crisis may be scary or seem insurmountable. This crisis may be so heartbreaking that you can't speak about it without breaking into tears. This crisis may be wearing you out and making you wonder if you and/or your relationship is going to get through it intact.

If you are feeling inadequate about your individual ability to cope with a crisis, if you are wondering whether you and your partner can handle it together, you are experiencing the doubts that a crisis initially plants in the minds of all of us. It's just that we don't talk as freely about real crises as we do about life's trivial irritants. That's one of the reasons why a crisis takes us so by storm. In our culture, it's more acceptable to rant and rave about a pseudo-crisis than to openly grieve and share deeper losses. This scene I witnessed illustrates this point.

It was 11:17 A.M. at O'Hare International Airport and a Boeing 737 bound for Denver had just departed, exactly on time. As the jet was taxiing out to the runway, a man rushed up to the agent still behind the podium. "That's my flight and I'm on time," he shouted, "Can you get the plane back?"

"I'm sorry sir, it left right on the minute," she answered.

"Here's what happened," he went on not seeming to hear. "My sister let me off out front, only she dropped me off at the wrong airline. So I had to walk a block. Then when I got to the right baggage check-in area, the skycaps had four or five other people to take care of first. And then, when I went through security, they stopped me. They've never examined my video camera before, but this time they did, and . . . "

About this time, his ten-year-old daughter rushed up, tears running down her cheeks. Close behind, his wife, seeing the empty gate area, started crying too. "We'll never fly this airline again," she said, glaring at the agent. "Now I won't get back home in time to rest before work tomorrow," the husband moaned, sounding like a little boy who needed a nap but had been deprived of his bed and blankie. "Now I can't play with Susie tonight," the daughter sobbed, burying her face in her mother's long skirt.

This family was upset, stressed-out. Damned airports with their interminably long concourses! Dumb sisters who couldn't even drive up to the right curb area! Inconsiderate airline agent who wouldn't call that captain back.

I, observing this scene, noted its oddity. They were reacting to this stress like people caught in a life or death crisis. They were acting a lot like Florine, the uppity daughter-in-law in the movie, *Driving Miss Daisy*. Remember the scene where Florine is putting on a Christmas reception? The house is decorated, most of the food has been prepared, but suddenly Florine can't find one necessary ingredient.

Florine lashes out at Katie Bell, the maid, blaming her and then lights into Boolie, her husband. "We're out of coconut, maybe *you* can figure out how to serve ambrosia to fifty people without coconut! I can't!" Long-suffering Boolie, used to such high drama, ignores Florine and comforts Katie Bell instead. "Don't worry," he says, "it isn't quite the end of the world."

Missed flights. Missing ingredients. FAX messages that go to the wrong places. Computers that go down during the height of a production deadline. Milk that curdles as you pour it into your morning coffee. A friend who always calls just as you're sitting down to dinner. A teenaged daughter who plays rock music loud and late.

Day in and day out, the price of being alive is dealing with stress. And when stress comes our way, it's annoying, it's infuriating, like a fly that keeps circling around our head, buzzing in the dark.

We swat at stress. We try to manage it. And we only have to browse in a bookstore to find shelves of books and tapes to help us. But stress, as aggravating as it is, is not the same as a life crisis.

A crisis is big. A crisis is truly painful. It rearranges our lives in huge and terrifying ways. It can sap our energy to such a degree that we have trouble functioning at all. When Kathy's fifteen-year-old son Mark attempted suicide by swallowing a bottle of sedatives, she remembers how she felt off and on during his three-month-long hospitalization. Somehow she and her husband Bob made it to work each morning and every single evening they visited Mark. But they felt exhausted, wiped out. "The most I could do was just survive the day. I couldn't help myself. I couldn't help my husband. I couldn't help our kid. I just had to hope that tomorrow I would have a little bit more energy and finally I did. And then I could begin to help us all get through it. Bob and I kept taking turns being `up' and `down.'"

Life's stresses nip at our heels. But life's crises have the potential to devour us if we don't turn our attention toward them.

A Flyswatter Won't Help

In a crisis we quickly discover that a flyswatter won't help. A crisis is like walking into a beehive and being stung all over. We hurt. Red welts swell up. We're shocked. We can't believe the ferocity of this angry swarm. We may think, if only someone had told us, we'd have taken some other path, we'd have avoided this encounter entirely.

Once we find ourselves in a real life crisis, we know in a flash the difference between mountains and molehills. We know we'd put up with a thousand day-to-day stresses, maybe even gain a sense of humor about life's little offenses, if only our pain would go away, if only we could rewind our life's tape to the day, hour or minute before this terrible thing happened. Once we find ourselves in a crisis, we know, or we have the potential to realize the vast difference between stress and crisis.

One woman, who refers to herself as a former "crisis junkie" said, "Everything used to be a big deal." But now, after almost losing her teenage son to a ruptured appendix, she says she sees life differently. "I rate things these days. When I start to get upset about anything, I ask myself—on a scale of one to ten, how serious is this? Half the things that bother me fall into the `one' slot: standing in the slowest line at the bank, getting stuck in five o'clock traffic. I face the little irritations now and put them in their place. I save my energy now for the big stuff. And I'm getting better at discerning which is which."

During the Gulf War, just before the ground-war segment of Operation Desert Storm commenced, on a two-hour flight I sat beside a woman whose twenty-eight-year-old son was a captain, a tank commander, on the front lines.

Before their son had left for Saudi Arabia, she told me, she and her husband, both newly retired, had been like kids in a candy store. They didn't have to set an alarm anymore and each morning they'd wake up with an array of choices. Which would it be? Would they hike, read, or play tennis? Gradually they were carefully selecting volunteer jobs that satisfied them.

But now, most mornings they found themselves wide awake, predawn, wondering where their son was and how he was doing. Now, all day they stayed glued to the TV news. Now, for them life was on hold.

"I can tell you one thing," she said as we were about to land, "a scratch on my car door is no big deal anymore. I just want my son back safe—alive."

I lost the scrap of paper with her name and phone

number on it. I pray her son survived, but I don't know. I do know, however, that the ways in which the differences between nagging stress and painful crisis become clearer are not necessarily ways by which we'd prefer to find out.

We learn, for instance, that stress is staying up all night with a sick, feverish toddler. A crisis is rushing our little one to the hospital, thinking he may die of meningitis, then finding out he'll live but will be totally deaf the rest of his life. Stress is being irritated with our husband because he refuses to unwind or take a day off to relax. A crisis is finding out this man we love has been in a terrible accident and will never walk or make love again.

Stress is when our daughter dyes her hair orange the day before her grandmother is flying in from Des Moines for a visit. A crisis is when that daughter admits cocaine has become her drug of choice. Stress is when we're bursting the seams of a cramped apartment, but can't move into our own home until our fifty-dollar-a-month savings deposits grow into a down payment. A crisis is losing our job, our life savings, and any hope of a stable financial future. Stress is suffering from PMS a few days each month and wishing our lover or husband would go away for a while. A crisis is being tired all the time, spending years going from doctor to doctor, and finally finding out that we have an incurable, debilitating disease.

Crises come in all shapes and forms—physical, psychological, spiritual, financial, and emotional. Any one can violently shatter a couple's life.

Honoring Our Own Realities

In making these distinctions between stress and crisis, we haven't meant to stand at a blackboard like an authoritative professor, chalk in hand, confidently writing *stress* on one side and *crisis* on the other, then neatly and without question listing the elements that fall under each heading.

For one thing, what one of us considers a crisis might simply be a stress, or no problem at all, to another. An example from my own life some twenty-three years ago comes to mind.

The first week after we adopted our first son, Matthew, I found myself in an intense crisis. I'd never imagined it would be this tough to be woken for 2 A.M. bottles. I wasn't prepared for all the effort it took even to go to the supermarket with a little one lying in the cart among the groceries.

My husband had left for a two-day trip after we'd had our son only a few days. When he returned I greeted him at the door, sobbing and saying I wasn't so sure I could make it as a mother. A few months later I was still tired. But I'd grown so attached to our beautiful brown-eyed baby that my fatigue was accepted as a tradeoff for the greater delight at having him in our lives. The acute crisis was over.

Several women I know shake their heads in amazement when I tell them how I reacted. They can't imagine viewing that period as a crisis. For them those early motherhood days were, though fatiguing, instantly satisfying.

What I tag "crisis" you may dub "stress." Our different reactions are healthy. We need to be who we are. We need to feel what we feel. We need to be wary of listening to others who discount our distress. In facing a crisis, we have a right to define it in any way we choose. Just because something worse is happening to someone else does not mean that we cannot and should not face and process our own feelings of loss or grief.

A woman suffering a miscarriage, for instance, may be told by well-meaning friends that she'll be able to have another baby. They may even tell her about a couple who just lost their three-month-old baby to crib death, implying that her loss is, after all, not that bad. But this couple knows that it is. They must put aside plans to turn the spare bedroom into a nursery, stop talking about what to name the baby, and mourn the loss of a never-to-be duplicated little one to whom they had already opened their hearts.

"You may have to give up the idea that you aren't entitled to mourn because others have greater sorrows," writes Ann Kaiser Stearns in *Living Through Personal Crisis*. Stearns recalls her visits to a professor's office when she was a young woman of twenty-three. She'd been pouring out her troubles to him, problems that seemed minor in comparison to his. He had young children and his wife was dying of cancer, yet he listened attentively to her. One day, feeling guilty that she'd voiced her own pain in the presence of his greater pain, she told him about her discomfort. "Don't let my suffering rob you of your own," he replied.

We can almost always cite the case of somebody else who is worse off than we are. But empathizing with their situation won't help us heal our own pain. The pain of a crisis will subside faster and heal more completely if we give it our focused attention. We all deserve to have our own reactions to whatever happens to us.

The Power of Crisis

Couples who find themselves facing harsh realities that involve outer losses or inner changes and couples caught in unexpected earth-shattering crises or entangled in lesser but nevertheless upsetting ones, are couples poised at a turning point. A crisis is, by definition, a crucial, decisive time.

Without a crisis, decisions, both mundane and major, can slide. But the presence of a crisis necessitates our intense effort and attention. We can, for example, spend years living in a house that needs a new coat of paint. Maybe the peeling, chipped surface bothers us a little, but not enough to spend a series of Saturdays perched on a ladder, scraping, applying primer, and brushing on fresh new paint. Or perhaps we deliberately let this improvement slide, choosing instead to spend money on a family vacation. Our delay, whatever our reasons, is not causing us any significant problems.

But if a fire were to break out in our house while we were sleeping, we'd dare not procrastinate. At the first scream of a smoke detector, we'd bolt out of bed, round up everybody, and beat it to the nearest exit.

In a crisis, we lose the luxury of lollygagging around. A crisis robs us of the status quo; the situation we've been existing in has somehow been altered. We can't go back home to a house that's smoldering rubble. We can't count on an income that disappeared when our company was swallowed up by a larger one and our job was erased along with the old logo. We can't make love when our mate is exhausted from battling a life-threatening illness. We can't turn the spare bedroom into a nursery when we're not expecting a baby.

A crisis demands action. Sometimes practical needs must be addressed quickly. We have to hire a carpenter to construct a wheelchair ramp. We must locate a regular babysitter so we can visit our wife in the hospital each evening. We need to list our house with a realtor because we can no longer afford the high monthly mortgage payments.

Psychological and spiritual needs may clamor for attention too. We may feel ourselves folding under the pressure and need to call a clergyperson to visit us, or ask a friend to recommend a therapist. We may need to search for a support group or ask the next-door neighbor over for coffee and conversation. We need to quiet our minds long enough to meditate or to pray for courage to go on.

These actions sound simple, but when we're immersed in a crisis they become more difficult. Besides the actual drama of the crisis itself, inside we are playing out a tragedy in our minds. The bad thing that has happened brings with it assorted feelings and responses ranging from self-pity and anger to guilt and blame. Who caused the crisis? Why did it happen? Wasn't it mostly my partner's fault? we may ask ourselves. Or phrases such as *I should have; he could have;* or *if only* are swirling in our minds.

You and your partner can survive this crisis, not by taking one giant leap into a new life, not by answering all the questions at once but by taking one step after another. Gradually, but surely, as you open yourself to the crisis process, healing will, in time, begin. Some days your will to go on may be minimal. On other days your mate may hit this low point. Some days you may be overwhelmed with longing to restore your life to what it was before the crisis.

Some days too, you may panic, wondering whether you have the energy to get through the crisis. It may then dawn on you that getting through it alone might be easier. There is some truth to this logic. Subtracting our relationship from our life would give us one less thing to do. We would at least reduce our emotional workload. A relationship is work. A crisis is too. Without our partner, we could put all our single-minded effort into getting through the crisis.

We would like to issue this caution. Often in the shock of a crisis our thinking is temporarily fuzzy. Especially at the beginning of a crisis, we usually feel the disorienting effects of anxiety.As a crisis dumps overwhelming new responsibilities on us, we can become so fatigued we lose our perspective. If you love your spouse, or if you think your love has a chance to be rekindled, hold on to your relationship until life settles down enough for you to thoughtfully and carefully sift and sort your priorities.

Anxiety is Normal

A crisis can, and almost always does, stir up our anxiety. It affects us like a special news announcement that interrupts our favorite TV program. Suddenly an announcer's voice is telling us, a camera is showing us, some very bad news. A city has been shaken by an earthquake. A president is announcing that a war is officially under way. A tornado has touched down in a populated area. An oil spill is spreading black death to the water, land, and ecosystem.

When the show we were watching resumes, we find we can't concentrate on it. It doesn't divert us anymore. Instead we focus on the number of casualties just announced or the fact that we don't yet know how many men and women or how many of earth's creatures have already perished or may yet die.

When we hear about disasters that are far away or potentially global, we feel anxious in much the same way that we do when a personally devastating crisis explodes into our lives. They shake the very foundations of our being. World disasters or personal crisis makes us anxious because they remind us of our own mortality.

It's not even death we fear so much as it is imagining our own "nonbeing," theologian Paul Tillich suggests in *The Courage To Be.* We may believe in eternal life or reincarnation; we may believe each of us has an appointed time to die--but temporarily, in our anxiety, it is the possibility of our nonbeing that haunts us.

None of us, Tillich points out, can "stand naked anxiety for more than a flash of time." And though we can't ever rid ourselves of such anxiety entirely, we can find courage in a crisis by establishing an object, a situation, to fear. "Fear," writes Tillich, "as opposed to anxiety, has a definite object, which can be faced, analyzed, attacked, endured . . . . Courage can meet every object of fear."

Beginning to locate where you are, taking a mental snapshot of your surroundings, looking at the size and shape of the crisis you're in, is to take a giant first step towards taming anxiety and turning it into a specific entity to fear and ultimately to confront.

When we're ready to identify a crisis, it's as though we've been awakened by a large crash. We could lie there, pulling the covers up higher, but we decide to open the blinds just enough to peer outside. We'd rather, we think, even as we're trembling, prefer to find out exactly what happened instead of tossing and turning with anxiety. Maybe a stray dog toppled over a trash can. Or maybe what we heard was a burgler slamming our back door as he ran out with his arms full of our belongings. We won't know unless we look and see. And though we may be frightened, we're ready.

Your partner may be ready to join you in acknowledging the presence of a crisis and identifying it. If so, you'll have two pictures of the same situation from different angles. You'll have an opportunity to communicate your view while listening to another perspective and comparing it with your own.

But many times the one we love isn't ready or able to go ahead. Though we may wake up one morning determined to confront a situation, we can't simply grab our partner and drag her or him unwillingly along with us. It may be that this crisis looms as a bigger threat to our spouse. Perhaps this crisis happened to our lover and is affecting our life only indirectly. When, for instance, our wife is facing major surgery that will mean six weeks off work, we feel bad for her but she feels even worse. Or when our mate's brother is killed in a random shooting, we are sad to lose a brother-in-law, but our mate is heartbroken, inconsolable.

Sometimes your example will give your mate courage to join you. Sometimes it won't and you'll need to exercise patience or eventually to confront him or her. For now, solo or together, identifying the crisis you're in is your best preparation for facing what lies ahead.

In the next chapter, we discuss four varieties of crises. Like criminals in a lineup, they're there all in one place, so you can point a finger at the one that knocked you down, drove you around, then left you by the side of the road wondering where you are and what happened.

Reflection Opportunities

1. Look through the list below of words that describe feelings. Which of these have you experienced in association with this crisis? Circle them. See if your partner would like to do the same thing. Think about how each of these feelings affects you. If you're doing this with your partner, share your lists and how experiencing these feelings is affecting each of you: accused, affectionate, afraid, alarmed, alert, alienated, angry, amazed, amused, annoyed, anxious, apathetic, appreciated, astonished, awkward, bad, bitter, blah, blamed, brave, brokenhearted, careless, cheated, confused, contagious, courageous, crippled, cross, curious, cynical, dejected, depressed, determined, discouraged, disgusted, don't care anymore, edgy, elated, embarrassed, empty, energetic, enraged, enthusiastic, envious, exhausted, frustrated, grateful, guilty, helpless, hopeful, horrified, hurt, ignored, ill, important, impotent, inadequate, infuriated, insecure, irritated, jealous, joyful, kind, listless, livid, lonely, loved, mad, meditative, messed up, miserable, my fault, neglected, nervous, numb, open to learning, optimistic, overwhelmed, peaceful, persecuted, picked on, pissed off, prayerful, puzzled, regretful, relieved, rejected, revengeful, singled out, sleepy, sorrowful, sorry, steady, stressed-out, strong, suicidal, tearful, tense, thankful, tranquil, unloved, unneeded, upset, uptight, vindictive, walked on, weak, weary, willing, wiped out, worthless.

2. Rate the intensity of this crisis on a scale of 1 to 10, with 1 meaning minor and 10 being major. Ask your partner how he or she rates this same crisis.

3. What do each of you consider to be the biggest crisis you've faced up until now? Share how you felt then. How did you make it through?

4. How could you utilize in this crisis the strategies you used successfully before?

5. How could this be a turning point for you? What is the worst that can happen? What is the best that can happen?

6. Each of you write down your definition of the crisis. What is the problem as you perceive it? See how your perceptions are alike. Look at how they differ.

Chapter 3

Where Are You Standing Right Now?

In dealing with fear, the way out is in.
Sheldon Kopp

As I was driving my mother to her chiropractor on a rainy afternoon last July, we got lost. Since her last appointment, a new highway had cut through the rural area on the southeastern outskirts of Atlanta, and we couldn't find one familiar landmark. Finally, after taking a misguided tour of the countryside for a half-hour, I gave up and pulled off the road, stopping at a weathered white-frame grocery store to ask for directions.

Inside, I found a sixtyish man with a kind expression, standing behind an old-fashioned cash register. "I'm lost," I said, probably sounding as frazzled as I felt.

"No you're not," he shot back. "You're standing right here."

Even before he pointed me another half-mile down the road to Dr. Burnett's office, I breathed a big sigh of relief. Fearing my mother would miss her appointment, I had, as an aunt used to say, "worked myself into a tizzy." I had actually begun to lose my orientation, not just toward the surroundings, but toward myself. But, as that philosopher-proprietor reminded me, no matter how lost I'd become, *I* was still there, wherever *there* was!

The crisis you're in may be causing you to feel lost, anxious, angry, upset, bewildered, and miles away from your partner. Something precious in your life has disappeared, forever or for a while. You may even have lost your bearings so completely that you feel estranged from yourself. But no matter what has happened, wherever you are standing, you are still there and your partner is still there. But where is "there"?

Crises generally fall into one of the following four categories. And sometimes they overlap. Which of these resemble the place where you're standing?

Four Common Varieties of Crisis

A Total Shock or Devastating Loss

Something you would never have willingly allowed into your lives arrives, rewriting your life's script significantly and sometimes permanently. Perhaps an accident disables you, your partner, or your child. An ongoing, incurable illness strikes. Your child dies or attempts suicide. You or your beloved is raped. You lose your home through a fire, earthquake, or other natural disaster. A close friend, parent, brother or sister dies.

A Detour

An uninvited circumstance keeps you from going straight ahead. Your goals are thwarted, routines are interrupted, lifestyles changed. Maybe you go through bankruptcy. You lose your job. You discover you can't ever, or at least easily, have children. An aging parent suddenly needs daily assistance. You are forced to pack up our belongings and move across town or halfway around the globe. You find out your child has a substance-abuse problem. Someone in your family faces an acute illness. An adult son or daughter moves back home.

A Shift in Values or Awareness

A transitional period comes along, one in which you or your partner reassess values or interests. When this happens, you look at your partner. You thought you knew him or her, but all of a sudden the one you love is someone you don't understand at all. Or you look at yourself and realize you're undergoing a major inner renovation. You finally find out how to nurture yourself after years of self-neglect and stop picking up your partner's and kids' clothes off the floor, and a whole bunch of other et ceteras you once attended to. One of you decides to stop working a sixty-hour work week and begins to enjoy vacations and days off. One or both of you changes careers. One of you wants to sell all your worldly possessions and join the Peace Corps while the other is just discovering the joys of collecting and refinishing antiques.

An Inevitable Rearrangement of a Life Pattern

Certain changes occur simply because it's time: birth of children, kids moving away from home, retirement. Sometimes these transitions or events take on crisis proportions before you adjust to their presence, especially if you haven't anticipated or prepared for them. Or their occurrence suddenly produces a shift in awareness and you begin to question everything in your life. Researchers have found that we all go through such passages. (For more detailed accounts you might want to read Gail Sheehy's *Passages* and Daniel J. Levinson's *The Seasons of a Man's Life*.)

What Have You Lost?

Throughout all four categories of crises, loss is the predominant theme. What have you lost in this crisis? Have you lost someone you love? A dream? Money? A career? Health? A home? Control over the way you spend your time? Freedom? Prestige or status? Peace of mind? A sense of integrity? Your image of yourself as a good parent? Your image of yourself as a careful or competent person? Be specific.

It helps when we can identify all the facets of our loss. Then we can see its magnitude. Some parts of our loss are glaringly evident. Other parts are subtle. For instance, when baseball's Dave Dravecky, the great pitcher for the San Francisco Giants, lost his arm to cancer, he not only became physically handicapped and lost his way to make a living, he also lost his star status, his prestige.

Judy had thought she might lose her son Michael to cocaine, but in his early twenties he quit touring with a drug-oriented heavy metal band and checked into a rehabilation facility. Four years later he was clean and sober and joyfully rebuilding his life. He and Judy got together at least once a week for pizza and conversation.

One day a friend invited Michael over to see his house that was under construction. Michael stepped into a hole on the second floor and fell to the basement, hitting his head on the concrete floor. He remained in a coma until he died a few days later. "I not only lost my son, but I lost my best friend," Judy says. Judy can never replace her beloved son, though with the passage of time she can someday find another best friend.

Only you can inventory your losses and identify them. It is well worth your time to record them on paper or tell

them to someone you trust. We can't grieve unacknow-
ledged losses. Our healing begins with our acknowledge-
ment: "this is what I lost . . ."

What Do You Fear?

In a crisis, our fears may be monumental or minute.
They all deserve our attention. Focusing on each one long
enough to identify it will help us evict them from permanent residency in our minds.

In the early 1980s when Marilyn needed extra time to
write her doctoral dissertation, she applied for a sabbatical
from her position as a psychologist at a high school. When
she was granted the leave however, she panicked and gave
it back. Her fears about having all that unstructured time
prevented her from going ahead. The following year she
reapplied. This time she took the sabbatical. But, to get to
the point where she could take the time off, she had to
catalogue her fears.

"I wrote out a list of all of them," Marilyn explains.
"They weren't huge fears; they were things like, Will I
wake up in the morning and not get out of bed when I don't
have to go to work? Will I sleep all day? Will I fall apart
without the structure of work? Will I get depressed with
nowhere to go? Will I raid the refrigerator instead of
writing my dissertation? These fears sound petty, but they
were very real and I had to face and confront each one."

Before our fears become specific they are free-floating
anxieties. They waft through our minds like sinister gray
ghosts. They're there, then they're gone, but their presence
makes us edgy and uncomfortable. We may even wake in
the middle of the night with a feeling of overwhelming
terror. It's as though something is going "BOO" in the

night, but what? One man whose teenaged daughter committed suicide said, "I'm afraid I'll go through my whole life blaming myself and there will never be an end to it."

Jenny, who is in a lifelong battle with lupus, had to give up her job as a school principal five years ago when she began to suffer longer and longer bouts of severe fatigue. After she resigned, she decided to breed canaries. Before long she had become an expert, and her birds were winning prizes in shows all over the country. Recently this also became too much effort. A bright, curious woman who has always thrived on setting goals and achieving them, she wonders if she'll ever find a new interest that she can pursue with her reduced energy. "I'm fearful that I won't find anything," she says.

Can you name the specific fear or fears that now haunt you? How do you feel now that each fear has a name? Or do your fears refuse to come forward and be recognized? If vague anxieties are causing you to feel panicky, perhaps you should consult a therapist who can help you identify the fears hidden in your mind.

Identifying Invisible Crises

But what about the situations we know are bona fide crises, but due to their spiritual or psychological nature are hard to pinpoint? Though not evident to other people, even friends, the presence of such crises is real enough in the lives of couples experiencing them.

For example, James and Ruth, married for thirty-five years, experienced a crisis when James, a Presbyterian minister, decided to enter therapy to try and heal some childhood memories which, though vague, kept passing through his mind like dark shadows.

At the time, in the mid-eighties, the phrase "reclaiming the inner child," was not widely understood. And so James went into therapy without the benefit of knowing that his was a common pain. He knew only that he felt very little, that he was, as he described it, "numb and lifeless." Though he is a powerful, eloquent presence in the pulpit and a dynamic force in the community, he described himself as "a hollow shell."

In therapy, James began to recall specific childhood instances in which he'd been abandoned several times and humiliated daily. He found some of the numbness subsiding, but felt like "a scared little boy who had no sense at all about how to become a being from within."

James had lost his inner core, his "self," growing up. As he struggled to resuscitate the long-lost child within, he sometimes felt like giving up. And he also wished that he could simply, by being near Ruth, borrow her "self."

"There was—and sometimes remains—a desperate struggle on my part to get Ruth to be the source of life and liveliness in me," he says. For instance, if something upsetting happened at church, James would tell Ruth about it in blow-by-blow detail, then expect her to become angry for both of them.

As James was facing issues like these, Ruth began to explore in separate therapy sessions how she had helped enable James to stay stuck in this pattern for so many years. By learning to better establish her own boundaries, Ruth feels she's strong enough now to resist James's attempts to get her to "feel for him." Now Ruth refuses to rescue him from the path of awakening he feared, but has courageously dedicated himself to.

The acute crisis for them came after James was intellectually committed to seeking a separate emotional self but before he could actually act on his new knowledge. Ruth liked the new direction he had bravely announced. For her there was now no turning back. She insisted on interdependence rather than enmeshment. Until James became consistently able to have feelings and act on them instead of trying to borrow Ruth's responses, their marriage was "in crisis."

Only their therapists and a handful of friends knew about the structural change in their marriage. Their lives on the surface appeared serene. Therefore it took a large dose of courage to face, then restructure, their separate emotional responses and their long-standing couple interaction. "As we remain separate from each other, we do indeed experience a common union and partnership for which all other earlier attempts were but false facades and teasing facsimiles," says James.

The resolution of their inner crisis has brought them a satisfaction such as a couple might experience after rebuilding a house ravaged by a tornado. The structure of their marriage is now a sturdy edifice for both of them. They are glad they took the time and effort to find out the source of their crisis. And that option is open to us all.

This is the Room I'm Standing In

How can we begin to acknowledge what has happened in our lives? How can we turn from anxiety to facing a fearful, painful situation? Here's the story of one woman's beginning.

One of Marilyn's clients, Lisa, had just made the honor roll her sophomore year at a local college; her parents Suzanne and Paul glowed with pride over their only child's achievements. They also supported Lisa's choice of seeing

Marilyn in weekly therapy sessions. In those meetings, Lisa emphasized to Marilyn that her goals were to learn to use her time more wisely and to get through exams without the excruciating migraine headaches she'd been experiencing. She seemed to be making progress. But after six months, Lisa broke into tears during one session, admitting she had a drinking problem and asking to be admitted to an inpatient treatment program.

When Lisa told her mom, Suzanne's pain was overwhelming. As she shared with Marilyn: "I filled out the papers to admit Lisa that first day, then hugged her and said goodbye. But the whole time—when I turned to leave her, when I pushed the elevator button to go back to the lobby, when I got into my car to drive back home--I felt as if I were in slow motion. I had to keep asking myself, is this really happening? When I got back home and Paul and I sat down for dinner, I couldn't taste the food, I couldn't even talk about where Lisa was.

"When Paul and I went to the first parents' support group last week, he seemed right at home, even glad to be there. That somehow made me angry. I looked around at a roomful of men and women who had kids with drug- or alcohol-abuse problems and I wondered, what am I doing here? I almost blurted out, `Your kids may have serious problems, but my daughter just joined a sorority and got into the habit of drinking a little too much.'

"There's another meeting tonight and somehow I'm in a different place. Tonight I'll be one of the group. I think I'll be able to say when it's my turn to share: `My daughter has a drinking problem.'"

For the next few months Suzanne distanced herself from Paul. Paul seemed more cheerful after Lisa's admission to rehab. This infuriated Suzanne. "Wouldn't a man who cared about his only child be sad like me instead of actually seeming happier?" She asked herself that and shared her anger with a close friend. Finally Suzanne confronted Paul with a hostile "How could you be acting like this?"

Paul's answer startled Suzanne. "I'd sensed something was wrong in Lisa's life though I couldn't pinpoint what it was," he explained. "Lisa had gotten moody and irritable for no apparent reason. She was sleeping an awful lot, too. Her addiction, once it was out in the open, made me feel relieved."

Once Suzanne heard Paul, she realized he was sharing the truth of his reality with her. However, once she stopped judging and diagnosing his responses she began to face an underlying guilt she had not yet confronted. Why hadn't she seen evidence of Lisa's drinking problem? With assistance from Marilyn, Suzanne was able to accept her own less-than-perfect parenting, to stop blaming herself, and to focus on giving Lisa ongoing support during her recovery.

Suzanne and Paul both loved Lisa a lot. They both loved each other a lot. But the initial shock of this crisis, the need to acknowledge its reality, plus their different timing and reactions to the crisis, disoriented them for a while. Their story is not atypical. Initial denial, anger at your spouse's reaction, guilt over your part in the problem—all these reactions are to be expected.

However, by acknowledging and identifying a crisis we have taken the first step toward coping. We have opened the door to let ourselves into a room, where, in reality, we were already standing. By facing a crisis and beginning to see it more clearly, we can now begin to grasp its impact on our life.

Misery Needs Good Company

As we close this chapter, we encourage you to seek help from friends, family, therapists, community, and groups of people in the same situations. Reach out and make a connection with someone or some group. Our feelings can be overwhelming. Even one other person or couple involved in a similar crisis can help you to feel less alone. Even one other person simply willing to listen or able to offer practical help can lighten your load.

While urging you to seek help we want to add a caution. It has been our experience as we've struggled through crises with our partners that people often offer advice that is sometimes off target and at other times downright destructive. Well-meaning friends may sympathize with you because your partner is not showing her or his grief as openly as you are, returned to work "too soon," or did something "wrong." They may encourage you to judge your mate instead of trying to understand your differences. You may be tempted to take the quick comfort of friends and to act on their advice rather than tackling the more difficult task of maintaining and renewing your couple relationship.

Few books or tapes explore the topic of surviving a crisis as a couple. Most of the solid ideas we found in print were directed to professionals and tucked away in journals or in books written specifically for psychotherapists.

Your best chance for survival comes when you courageously keep looking for support from individuals, professionals, and groups who are familiar with the nitty-gritty of the process and who can help you go through it together. Beware of professionals who take a dim view of negotiating this life situation together. Keep looking for appropriate, informed help—help from those who assure you it's possible and who validate your desire to make it a priority.

Reflection Opportunities

1. Take a mental snapshot of your surroundings, looking at the size and the shape of the crisis you're in. Begin by writing a letter to yourself, opening with: "You should see where I'm standing; it looks like this." Then detail the sounds, smells, textures, sights. Next add, "You should see how I'm reacting to all this." Again, add detail. Or, use this other method: turn your life into a comic strip; write and/or draw the strip seeing yourself and your partner as the main characters.

2. What type of crisis are you encountering? Do you and your partner agree about the category?

3. If you've been able to face what your specific losses and fears are, how do you feel now? Has naming them helped in any way? How?

4. How does your perception of reality compare with your partner's? How are the two pictures the same? How are they different? Do you share the same fears? Is asking your partner direct questions about how he or she is seeing the crisis possible right now? Are you assuming your partner feels a certain way, instead of asking?

Chapter 4

One by One, Two by Two: Embracing the Crisis Process

He who understands deeply the roots of suffer-
ing enjoys great peace.
                    from the Dhammapada

This morning I stumbled out of bed, entered the dim hall on the way to the kitchen, and glimpsed something small and light brown scooting along the edge of the carpet right next to the woodwork. Uniformed exterminators descend on our condominium regularly, so it couldn't be what it looked like—a Texas-sized cockroach in its pale molting stage. I grabbed my nearby walking shoe and whopped it. It still moved. Again, *wham*! I hit as hard as I could. It lay still.

Whew! On to the kitchen. As the coffee began to gurgle I went back to look and make sure I'd inflicted a lethal blow. And then, bending closer, I saw, oh no—it was a light brown lizard, a little gecko I'd killed. Its solemn dark brown eyes stared up at me. I had crushed a sweet little creature instead of a filthy despicable one.

After pouring a mug of coffee, I went back to the scene of my crime. A small miracle—the gecko was gone! I hadn't whacked it to death. It was making its way toward the front door.

I'm sharing this strange little story to illustrate this

point: Couples who find themselves in a crisis often behave like I did. In the early dawn of a crisis we decide that our task is to be an exterminator—we see our sadness, anger, fear, and anxiety as creepy things we'd better eradicate in a hurry. We panic, perceiving the emotions a crisis stirs and the chaos it creates as pests to be crushed absolutely—and as quickly as possible.

The problem with our response is this: What we are attempting to kill is the crisis process. By crisis process we mean a series of adjustments and feelings a crisis tailors for each of us and requires us to respond to in order to become transformed. Like the little gecko, this process (as opposed to the crisis itself) is a harmless friend to us. It is, in fact, the very process that eats the pests that haunt our psyches.

Therefore, rather than attempting to kill the crisis process, after identifying the crisis we're in, our next survival task is to yield to it, to feel our way through the range of emotions the process engenders. To do this, before a crisis loses its disruptive power and is integrated into our lives, each partner must expand or change his or her repertoire of coping skills in either slightly or vastly different ways. Then, for a couple to survive and grow together, both partners will need to fit the pieces of their individual growth into that relationship.

This is not an easy task. The crisis process packs a wallop. It has immense power, but this power can be harnessed and used to transform us as individuals and as a couple if we give it our attention and if we desire to be changed for the better. But if we attempt to ignore its power, if we run from it, if we pour, pop, or sniff temporary solace to anesthetize ourselves from it, the power of the process can undo us. Instead of growth, we'll experience bitterness, resentment, and strife within ourselves and our relationship. Instead of adjustment and transformation to a higher level of consciousness, we'll regress.

In order to grow and transform, you have to go through the feelings. While there is no avoiding this painful task, we'd like to offer you the solace of knowing what others have gone through so that you feel you're not alone and so the territory you traverse will not seem so alien. Part of the reason our thoughts and feelings overwhelm us is due to our unawareness. Knowing that you will feel anger, for example, will not keep you from being angry, but it might help you realize there's nothing wrong with you for feeling so.

As Marilyn surveyed her experiences counseling couples caught in life crises, and as I interviewed men and women, collecting their stories for this book, we put our findings together and cataloged the most common thoughts, feelings, and responses couples encounter during the crisis process. Some won't apply to your situation at all; others will be as instantly recognizable as a parking ticket stuck on your windshield. A few, like a soothing recording of ocean sounds, may calm you as they underscore the opportunities hiding in all crises.

Our findings are in no particular order because different people respond quite differently. We're listing them here without commenting on how to handle them; those tips will come in later chapters. Our purpose is to take the crisis process out of hiding—to show that it elicits somewhat predictable responses which, if not dealt with, can inflict great pain on us individually and can also lead us as a couple to quiet desperation, to a painful separation, or to a divorce court.

The rest of this book is devoted to facing, fixing, learning to live with, and learning to grow from whatever responses the crisis process elicits in us. But first, we need to turn and face the effects of crisis on our lives.

What's Happening to Us?

A Crisis Shocks Us

We deny what's happened. We can't, in fact, believe it. We may literally not acknowledge what's occurred. We find ourselves automatically driving to our little daughter's school to pick her up a month after she died. We pick up brochures for ski vacations, dreaming of carving two paths down steep, powdery slopes like we did last year, forgetting our mate will walk with a cane the rest of her life. We start to plan our son's high-school graduation party, not admitting to ourselves that his three-month stay in a drug rehabilitation facility will mean he won't be marching down the aisle with the rest of his class.

Most likely the time spent in this stage differs with each partner. When one of us becomes ready to face the situation and the other is still dazed, the wide-awake person may feel alone and judgmental, asking aloud or silently, "Why are you still avoiding reality?" If our partner continues not to confront the crisis, we may think about or find another person to comfort us. We're particularly susceptible now to having affairs.

A Crisis Depletes Our Energy

If we normally jog three miles each afternoon, we may now turn into a couch potato. We may muster enough energy to go to work and to attend to our most pressing needs, but we nevertheless feel wiped out. Laundry piles up. Bills go unpaid. Phone calls aren't returned. Appointments are forgotten. Making love is often viewed as a demand rather than a comfort. If our partner is coping better than we are, he or she may feel ignored or disgusted with our sluggishness.

Joan is a trim psychologist who usually rushes home to get out of her tailored suit and high heels and into athletic attire. But lately just the thought of what she used to do—running three miles, roller-blading in the park, working out at her athletic club, or riding her bicycle to train for the next biking event—makes her tired. Lately her husband, Troy, her partner in these after work activities, has been exercising alone.

Joan and Troy have been trying to start a family for a year and a half. So far medical tests haven't pinpointed what's causing their infertility. Now thirty-nine, Joan is facing her greatest fear—that she will miss out on the joy of giving birth to and raising her very own child. As she longs for new life to take hold in her body, the intensity of her yearning seems to be sapping all her energy. Her lethargy is now adding additional stress to their marriage as Troy feels he's losing both his dream of fatherhood and the company of his partner.

A Crisis Disorients Us

In addition to making us tired, the concrete demands of a crisis fill our days and rob us of the security of our comforting old routines. Filing for bankruptcy is a time-consuming procedure. Caring for a spouse with a disability means reordering our home and habits. Visiting a terminally ill child in the hospital means dropping out of extra activities. Caring for a frail elderly parent means spending all day Saturday cleaning his house, shopping for his groceries, and paying his bills in addition to taking care of our own chores.

Margo and Joe had been married only a year when she was diagnosed with bone marrow cancer. Her last and only hope for life is the experimental surgery she is currently undergoing. Joe is putting everything else on hold during Margo's six-week hospitalization. After work Joe used to play golf, serve dinner to homeless men at a shelter, and take long walks with Margo. Now he leaves his office early to go directly to the hospital, to spend the afternoon and evening with her. Around 9 P.M. he makes the one-hour drive home. From ten P.M. until midnight, he tackles mundane household duties before repeating the same process the next day. Joe's exhausted but he won't hear of skipping one day of his bedside vigil.

A Crisis Wounds Some of Our Belief Systems and Alters Our Identity

No matter what the crisis, some cherished belief is usually exposed and shattered. Beliefs such as: If I work hard and perform my job well I'll never be fired; Loving my children will keep them from succumbing to drugs or alcohol; Eating wisely and exercising often will insure good health. Without such beliefs and their accompanying behaviors we may ask, "Who am I? Who are we?"

When Marilyn's second daughter was diagnosed with diabetes at age six, she remembers, "I was sure I had had my share of chronic illness because my first daughter was born with congenital defects in her kidneys and urinary tract system. I had always believed that life was fair, and that I would be rewarded for my efforts to try to 'be good.' My truth blew up in my face when my second daughter's illness was exposed. If my belief system were true, then obviously I had failed miserably. If my belief system were false, then how could I make sense of the world? Did illness just randomly occur more than once without a rational basis? What was I to believe?

"The dilemma of trying to resolve this search for truth led me to more self-examination. What else had I believed in that would also prove not to stand the test of life's realities? Until I went through a sifting and sorting process, keeping some beliefs, discarding others, adding new ones, I experienced an internal civil war."

A crisis interrupts our orderly lives, leaving us with much the same feeling as a traveler on a precisely planned itinerary who somehow winds up lost. In a crisis we are suddenly disoriented, asking, Why me? Why now? Why this?

The crisis and its accompanying process create internal chaos that destroys some of our oldest and most cherished beliefs. These beliefs are like the old-growth trees in the Oregon forest. Before a crisis our beliefs stand tall and strong. We use them as markers to guide our lives. In the process of a crisis, however, our beliefs are uprooted when we find that many of them are baseless. Some of the beliefs a crisis uproots are deep, reaching back generations; sometimes they reflect themes many believe are buried in the subconscious, deep in the collective psyche of humankind.

This individual uprooting and examination of beliefs during the crisis process is so painful that often in therapy Marilyn hears clients describe it as ripping their insides out and being forced to examine them. During a crisis, most of us withdraw into ourselves for a period of time to reexamine our beliefs. It's as though we now need to look at the uprooted ones, survey those still standing, and finally decide which new ones to cultivate.

A Crisis Often Leads Us To Feel Guilty

Why did I do this? Why didn't we do that? What could

I have been thinking? How could I have been so blind? Why didn't we . . . ? If only . . . .

The reasons we feel guilty will vary but the agonizing underlying guilt gnaws at us. A man whose lover was attacked and raped while she was waiting for him to pick her up may torture himself: Why, was I five minutes late? I shouldn't have stopped to talk to my boss as I was leaving work . . . . A woman whose aunt died in a mental hospital still proclaiming on her deathbed that she was Madame Curie, may feel overwhelmingly responsible when her twenty-year-old daughter is diagnosed schizophrenic: Did I pass on the gene that predisposed her to this? Should I even have had children? she may wonder. A father who had a fight with his 16-year-old son just before he leaves for work may experience immense guilt after the son is involved in a serious car wreck on the way. Looking at him in his hospital bed, he may agonize: I never should have lost my temper like that. A husband who caresses his over-seven-months-pregnant wife, bringing her to a climax one morning may feel guilty and responsible when her water breaks later that day: I thought of our pleasure together more than our baby's welfare, he berates himself when labor has to be induced and their son begins life in an incubator.

Though the above examples illustrate exaggerated guilt, sometimes our guilt has an excruciatingly painful reality base. We *were* driving way too fast. We recklessly expanded our business. We were forty pounds overweight, out of shape, and smoking two packs of cigarettes a day when we had a massive heart attack.

Sometimes we aim intense blame directly at ourselves, deciding we are not worthy of our own self-love and that surely our partner could never love us either. Or we blame ourselves only a little, but it is still enough to cloud our ability to function in the here and now. "It's all my fault," we say; I'm the one who decided to do (or not do) this, we think. When we blame ourselves our positive traits fade into the background and we may generalize, concluding we're no good at all.

Whether exaggerated, real, or imagined, guilt and self-blame almost always accompany crises. We judge ourselves and sometimes our partner too as reckless, ruthless, careless, insensitive, stupid, mean, preoccupied--or something--that now makes us sick with regret, sadness, or anger. Our guilt can overwhelm us unless we go through the challenging process of self-forgiveness.

A Crisis May Lead Us To Blame Someone or Something

Who or what is to blame? That question can keep us from sleeping or eating or concentrating on the present. We may become obsessive as we replay the events leading up to the crisis, trying to pin the blame on a specific person or circumstance. A husband may blame his wife after their toddler wanders out of the backyard and drowns in a neighbor's swimming pool. "Why did you have to answer the telephone and leave him alone?" he may ask her again and again. A wife may blame her husband for insisting they move far from family and friends so he could advance his career, saying, "All because of you I can't find a job and the only people I can talk to are at the other end of a long-distance phone line."

When we blame our mate we usually pull out all the stops. Often we decide that our mate not only did something bad, but that he or she *is* bad: Only an insensitive jerk would have put himself first like this; or, I can't believe she'd invest all our money in such a scam. She's totally careless. When we blame our mate, it's as if we use white-out on our own faults while highlighting our mate's deficiencies with a fluorescent marker.

A Crisis Can Make Us Intensely Self-Centered

When we are sad, depressed, or angry about the arrival of some awful, uninvited crisis, we tend to focus on our pain. A woman may say to her husband, "You have no idea what it's like to lose a baby after carrying her for nine months." If we are fired for unfair reasons, though our mate is working overtime to help out, as she leaves for work we may remind her, "You can't begin to understand the humiliation." After our spouse breaks his hip, we may keep telling him how hard our life has become now that he's off his feet and we have to wait on him.

Despair, if we take up residency there, is the ultimate form of self-centeredness. In our preoccupation, we may ignore our partner's pain; we may imagine that no pain could equal ours and tend to minimize our partner's suffering.

A Crisis Can Cause Us To Act Like Super-Humans For Awhile

At first especially, we may be swept along by the adrenaline rush of a traumatic situation. We sift through the rubble after our house burns down finding a few treasured items left. We arrange for temporary housing, fill out insurance forms, and keep reassuring our wife and kids that being alive and together is all that matters. We're brave. Everything's under control. But like the filament in a light bulb, we burn the brightest just before we burn out. One day we awake angry or exhausted and in need of self-care.

During the 1990-91 school year, as the psychologist in an elementary school, one of Marilyn's jobs was to comfort and counsel the classmates of eleven-year-old Jerry after his death. Jerry had been riding his bike when he skidded on gravel and was thrown off into the path of an oncoming truck. "All week I calmly went into all the fifth-grade classes to announce the facts of the accident," she recalls. "I went to the three classrooms where Jerry had sisters and a brother, to explain how to help family members grieve. I explained the grieving process to a grieving faculty.

"I rode the school bus to the funeral with sixty-five of Jerry's closest little friends, explaining to them what to expect, and comforted them in their sobbing, after seeing him in the casket with his football uniform on.

"When I went home Friday afternoon I knew I had to do my own grieving. The tears streamed. The whole weekend was my own personal funeral for Jerry, remembering how his exuberance had touched my life and how sad I felt that he was dead. I had put all those feelings on hold for five days to be superwoman to the school, but now I had to pour out the unfairness of it all. Why at eleven? Why? I had to live the depth and expanse of my anguish that weekend and a little each of many weeks to follow."

A Crisis Exposes Our Strengths And Our Weaknesses

In a crisis much is learned. You find out that your lover is an attentive nurse who brings you breakfast in bed. You find out that your spouse faints at the sight of blood. You find out that although you and your mate enjoy attending plays and eating at posh restaurants, being broke leaves you wondering how to spend a succession of evenings at home together. In a crisis you see that you and your lover get an A+ in relating in bed, but that you're flunking out when it comes to sitting down and talking about what to do in the crisis.

One couple's startling discoveries about each other's strengths and weaknesses during a crisis began to unfold only six months into their marriage. Susan and Ron had both been married before. Susan had eight- and ten-year-old sons. Ron had two daughters, eleven and thirteen, and a seven-year-old son. Since Ron's children lived a thousand miles away, he only had them for one month during their summer vacation and before marrying Susan, he'd never indicated any wishes to alter these custody arrangements.

Susan felt sure that Ron would make a great dad for her sons. She had, in fact, been attracted to Ron because he seemed an ideal father. When they set their wedding date, Ron told Susan how happy he was that soon he'd be part of a family again. And he won the hearts of her sons by volunteering to coach their soccer team and by giving them his focused, firm, and kind attention.

After their marriage, however, being with Susan and her sons set into motion a crisis in Ron's life as he became intensely aware of his sense of loss that his own children didn't live with him. Instead of mourning that loss, he set out to change the situation by instigating what turned out to be a lengthy, costly custody battle.

When Ron lost, Susan breathed easier. It had not been in her agenda to emulate the Brady Bunch. What she had expected from Ron was not additional children to care for, but an opportunity to learn better parenting skills from him. Though she loved her children, she often felt inadequate and inept at handling the day-in, day-out responsibilities of parenthood.

This crisis did not end with the judge's ruling. At the news that his children would not be coming to live with him, Ron went into acute depression and was hospitalized for two months. He continues in outpatient therapy.

A Crisis Can Lead Us To Reevaluate Why We're Together

If we loved being parents, but a drunk driver kills our little son as he crosses the street, what binds us together now? If we organized our lives around athletics, what will we do together when one of us becomes physically disabled? A crisis always raises the issues: What attracted us to each other? What has kept us together? How or will we be able to come together in a new relationship?

Continuing Ron and Susan's story, here are some issues this crisis has raised in their relationship, questions that Susan is addressing in therapy. Ron's depression is forcing Susan to examine her own motives for getting married in the first place. Did she marry Ron only to provide herself and her sons with a parent figure—one she could emulate and one her sons could benefit from growing up with? If so, can he now become her "real life partner" instead of this other one-dimensional image? Did she idealize his parenting skills, but fail to view him as a husband? If her whole focus was on his parenting ability, would she want a continuing partnership with Ron when her sons were grown?

Such questions often expose faulty core reasons for forming a relationship but don't necessarily spell the end of it. Rather, it's possible to examine our motives, look at the real person we've aligned our lives with, and see if we can find a more solid base for our union. If wrong reasons for marrying precluded finding happiness together, many of us would have divorced long ago. (I married my husband because he was cute, friendly, and an exquisitely tender kisser. We've stayed together after discovering that fortunately we also share many similar underlying values.)

A Crisis Highlights Differences In Our Temperaments and Timing

One partner may face a crisis with a grin-and-bear-it philosophy, while the other feels intense angst and rails against the injustice and unfairness of it all. One of us may be certain that dwelling on a crisis only makes things worse, while our partner is immersed in analyzing each facet of the dreadful scenario. One of us may pray more during a crisis or turn to meditation, while the other makes a list of "to do" activities. Needless to say, we tend to want the other person to respond the way we do, and when, almost inevitably, our partner responds differently, great conflict can be generated.

Lynn and Christopher have five grown children who have recently been through three divorces, one bankruptcy, and the stillbirth of a daughter. Financially, emotionally, practically, their children's crises touch Lynn and Christopher too. Last year their twenty-nine year old daughter moved back home for a year. The year before that, they loaned their thirty-one-year-old son $10,000.

In each crisis Christopher liked to take action. He was ready at a moment's notice to help out by doing anything he could. Lynn views Christopher's instant action as irresponsible; she likes to mull things over. Instead of quickly drawing money out of savings to help out their son during his bankruptcy, as Christopher insisted, she favored spending time exploring other options. When a crisis of any sort arises, she likes to set an appointment with her therapist or schedule lunch with a close friend to talk it out. She spends an afternoon at a bookstore picking out self-help books or tapes.

Christopher thinks Lynn needlessly dilly dallies around and views all this nonaction as irresponsible and an excuse to procrastinate. In particular, when both are especially concerned about one of their children's problems, they tend to throw sarcastic barbs at each other, criticizing each other's manner of coping.

A Crisis Brings Any Nagging Doubts About Our Relationship To The Surface

We suspected before and now we really wonder: Would someone else be a better fit for me? Would someone else be there for me more fully than this person I'm with? If we married for frivolous, poorly thought out, or other less-than-wise reasons, we may wonder if our relationship was ever meant to be in the first place.

Melanie wanted to marry John because he was a bright, responsible achiever with a great sense of humor. In him she believed she had the best combination imaginable. He made her think. He made her laugh.

After John was accepted into a prestigious medical school, they got married. When Melanie seldom saw her husband because of his obsession with establishing a perfect academic record, she grew angry, resentful, and lonely. One evening, Melanie accompanied the wife of another medical student to a codependency twelve-step group (CoDA), and there she began to understand part of her attraction to John. He was, she decided, a workaholic. And she saw herself as his enabler, ready and willing to help him pursue his addiction by taking full responsibility for their household, working to put him through school, and being the manager of emotions in the relationship.

The crisis for Melanie was when she realized she was repeating her family-of-origin pattern. Her father, also a physician, was a workaholic. Her mother handled everything too. Seeing this scared Melanie. Did she want to be like her mother, who complained year in and year out about getting only leftover attention after hundreds of patients were served? Would stopping her enabling and confronting John force him to move to a better balance or would it upset him so much that he might leave her and seek out another woman willing to "do it all"?

Facing such questions is scary. Ignoring them, once they arise in our minds is difficult. Often we need expert help at this juncture.

A Crisis Can Cause Us Temporarily To Fall Out of Love

Author Anne Morrow Lindbergh compared marriage to "old twisted hemp ropes that hold the boats . . . not beautiful . . . but tough and holding." Love, she wrote, "is that serene spiral of seagulls above the lighthouse, untouchable, untouched, unhurried . . . ." Though a couple can choose to remain committed to each other during a crisis, often "in love-ness" exits temporarily. As one woman put it, when she and her husband were facing bankruptcy after his business failed, "What's a nice person like me doing in a place like this?" For a while she felt "out of love" and fantasized about making love with her sexy boss who still had a steady income.

Sometimes a crisis predisposes us to feel out of love with our partner for an hour. Sometimes for a month. Sometimes even years. Jane and Charles ran a small family lumber mill on the Oregon coast, a business Jane's great-grandfather had begun in 1912. Environmental concerns— outcries over the endangered spotted owl—plus a sluggish economy spelled the end for their operation. Charles found work at a hardware store in the nearest coastal town. Jane, however, was deeply depressed. She felt she didn't love Charles anymore. She wondered if some other partner might have better helped her keep the business afloat. She and Charles had been high school sweethearts, but she felt she had to leave both him and the scene of their pain and failure.

One day Jane tearfully announced she was on her way. For a year and a half, she roamed the West and Midwest, eking out an existence as a waitress, often living in her car, sending postcards home. Her heart, all her energy, was in the passion of despair. One day she noticed this saying by F. D. Mattieson above the desk of the owner of a small cafe: "He who has never failed somewhere, that man cannot be great. Failure is the true test of greatness."

Jane says that day she determined she'd stop blaming herself or Charles. It was, she decided, time to smell the salt air and get back into the arms of her husband. Her mourning process completed, there was room now for love to reenter the recesses of her heart. And so she went back home to a mate who'd been waiting for her.

A Crisis Can Alter Our Mental, Spiritual and Emotional Outlooks For Better or Worse

A crisis creates favorable conditions for a metamorphosis. We may stop crawling along and go from caterpillar to butterfly, gaining larger perspectives and greater capacities for loving and living. On the other hand, we may shrink, becoming shadows of ourselves. We may turn to alcohol, drugs, affairs, or bitterness. We may take on a permanent victim role, referencing everything else in our lives to the tragedy or loss we've suffered. Sometimes the changes we make are unacceptable to our partner; sometimes the changes cement our relationship. Always the changes require adjustments.

Diane and Patrick discovered that their youngest son, five-year-old Bobby, had a rare blood disorder that could be treated only by receiving a marrow transplant from a perfectly matched donor. The chances of finding a donor were one in twenty thousand, but the couple's church organized a donor drive. The local media supported the call for help and soon the search moved to a national level.

When a suitable donor was found, Patrick became convinced that the miracle was nothing short of God intervening to save Bobby's life. Patrick became an intensely devoted evangelist, at work, at home, and in the neighborhood. Meanwhile, Diane maintained her former "church-is-for-Sundays-only" attitude.

For this couple, the happy ending to a medical crisis contributed to a new relationship crisis. Would their differing views about the role of religion in their lives keep them apart? Could they be close as a couple, yet far apart in their interpretation of their son's recovery? Diane and Patrick have yet to settle these questions to their satisfaction.

A Crisis, if Ignored or Denied, Can Leave Us Exactly As We Were

If we do not deal with it, a crisis can leave us *inappropriately* the same. We can remain in a rigid state, untouched and unscathed; it's as though we become catatonic, frozen, out of touch with reality. Given what has occurred, we *should* be changed and moved in some way. When one of us opts not to learn from a crisis but rather remains trapped in sameness while the other person grows, the relationship is on the endangered list.

The Challenge of Crisis

The common crisis responses that we just shared illustrate how intricate the crisis process is. Our individual responses can take us to mountaintops of joy or to dark valleys of sadness. We can zigzag back and forth between hope and despair. Our mood, timing, and steps to resolution can all differ from our partner's and that disparity can create great stress unless we expect differences and allow them to occur. A crisis can spur us on to new growth together or it can create conditions for the death of our relationship.

Our greatest strengths and looming weaknesses emerge during a crisis. We may regress to the tantrum stage of the egocentric two-year-old, kicking our feet, banging our heads, and screaming "Why? Why? Why?" We may get stuck in the victim role, blaming everyone else. Or we may become the hero or heroine responding far above what we imagined humanly possible.

Out of our responses to a crisis and its inherent process we create for ourselves a new life philosophy. Perhaps we conclude: There's no sense trying, nothing will turn out right anyway. Or we now believe: Life isn't fair or unfair, it just is. Or now we see: Everything that happens has a purpose and I can learn from it. These kinds of statements reflect beliefs that help us reorganize our world into a sensible place. Some beliefs lead us to growth; some will make us slowly die. By examining our belief structure we can choose between life and death.

Thus a crisis forces us into a process that is an opportunity for change. A crisis creates stress and pain, a precursor to change. We can regress, grow, or die individually. However when we are in a partnership, such intense stress when it is doubled can cause our bonding to snap under the pressure.

Understanding the crisis process itself can create more realistic expectations, soothe the chafing, and assist in the rebonding process. When we know about the process, when we acknowledge it, we can anticipate what could happen. We can make the gradual changes necessary to preserve ourselves and our love for one another.

Equal and Separate Realities

In a crisis your first and most automatic response is often an overwhelming desire to be comforted by a like-minded partner—a partner who is at the same point in the crisis process and who is responding in exactly the same ways you are. We want that comfort desperately. We simply don't want to have to deal with confronting both a crisis and a clash of beliefs, coping styles, or timing. In fact, this is such a big deal for couples that we have devoted an entire chapter, "Chapter 8, You and Me Together, Separately," to helping you live with your differences.

Right now, however, it is important to simply recognize that you and your mate are probably in different phases of the process and you might be wishing that weren't true. Most likely you'd assumed that you and your partner would journey through the process taking the exact same itinerary. You'd imagined visiting sadness together, your tears mingling. You'd visualized stopping over at hope and joy together, sharing your relief and victories.

One reason people yearn for this kind of togetherness is that it seems to signify the validity of our perceptions. When our partner sees and handles a crisis the same way, we automatically gain confidence and can say to ourselves: See, my partner agrees, my ways of handling the crisis are correct.

We can get the validation of our reality that we long for from our partner, and we can give our partner that same gift. But not the way we may think. We can accomplish this goal only by switching from demanding sameness to desiring an understanding of each other. We can begin by acknowledging that we do indeed have two sets of perceptions and that our differing perceptions may have caused a breakdown in communication. Our partner is handling the crisis differently, is at a different point in the crisis process, or is experiencing different feelings.

Once we accept that reality, we can decide to leave our anger and disappointment about our differences behind long enough to try to understand how our mate views the crisis. We can ask, for instance: "Honey how do you feel about what's happened? What's going on with you right now? What's your worst fear? What's giving you hope? Now that I know where you are, would you listen to what's going on with me? I'm sorry I didn't understand and support you sooner. Can we start over?

When we approach our partner with respect and without any underlying agenda to manipulate or coerce, we can find out what our partner's reality is and validate it. Then we can share our own reality.

If we insist on forcing our partner to go through a crisis exactly as we are, we will create more conflict and alienation. A crisis is like a forest fire in our lives; parts of our lives are already scorched and burned. When we keep demanding our partner think the way we do and respond the way we are, it's as if we're lighting a match to our relationship too.

We can dramatically increase our chances of surviving a crisis together when we validate our two separate but equal realities.

Reflection Opportunities

1. Which of the adjustments and feelings that can occur during the crisis process are now happening to you? Which ones are having an impact on your relationship with your partner? List them. Now that you see them, what are you going to do with them? Ask yourself how seeing them might lead to individual and couple growth.

2. Is one of you still dazed by the shock? Are the two of you now experiencing different responses to the crisis? If so, how do you feel about the differences?

3. Do any of the adjustments and feelings you're experiencing seem totally unmanageable? If so, what options for help do you have? Have you considered therapy? A support group? Counseling with a clergyperson? Have you asked a trusted friend for specific help? Are loving relatives available? Is your partner available for more support if you communicate your needs directly?

4. Are you blaming each other, yourself, or someone else? Are you saying a lot of "if onlys"? Can you discuss them?

5. While you are aware of your own pain, is it possible to empathize with the feelings your partner is experiencing? Can you imagine his or her suffering? How might you convey your empathy to your mate in some small, but concrete way?

Chapter 5

_____

Making It Through
Just One Day, Hour, or Moment

> *Feelings cannot be "fixed," as if they were a torn patchwork quilt in need of a needle and thread. Like a musty blanket, feelings require sunlight, day after day, until the fresh air has finally cleared the cold dampness away.*
>
> *Ann Kaiser Stearns*

In a Ziggy cartoon, he, looking very small and worried, is staring up at tall bookshelf. Way up high are the "Self-Improvement Books"; below, within his reach, is a row of "Holding-Your-Own Books." This is a holding-your-own chapter.

As the opening quote says, our feelings can't be "fixed." They just are. And there are times during a crisis when we feel so sad, so angry, so depressed, so guilty, so *something*, that we wonder how we can face another day, hour, or even moment.

I remember one of those times. The ragged sounds of my sobbing, not just for a day, but for weeks, whenever I was alone, seemed to be coming from somebody else. They were cries rising out of a deep place of pain I'd never visited before. Though my husband could comfort me, though friends could help, I had to get to the bottom of my sorrow before I could crawl back up into the land of the fully functioning.

In other parts of this book we explore how we can learn and grow, even turn into stronger individuals and a more loving couple through it all. Here we throw out some lifelines; here we remind you that the way through a crisis is *through* it. You are not bad, weak, or lacking in character or courage because you are hurting. Courage, as many philosophers have observed, is not the lack of despair, but rather going through that despair.

Well-meaning friends may say, "Come on, it's not *that* bad"; or, "God must think you are strong to hand you such a heavy load." Forget them for now. Concentrate on caring for yourself, on feeling what you must feel, on grieving as you must grieve, one step at a time. And reach out to your partner when he or she is taking a turn down there in the depths.

You'll find two sections in this chapter. The first is for you as an individual in need of comfort. The second offers ideas to help you comfort a mate who's hit bottom.

Here then is an assortment of Band-Aids, remedies, and ideas. They're not in any order; skip around until you find ones that suit you. Some are rooted deeply in spiritual, psychological, or philosophical ideas. Others are as superficial as stick-on smiley faces. All are meant to help right this minute.

Remedies for You

Worry for Thirty Minutes

Time flies when we're worried about something. Before we know it, we've worried all day long and worry is keeping us awake all night. When worry is becoming a pervasive habit, try this experiment. Set aside a specific thirty minutes a day to worry. Spend this specific half-hour, no longer, facing each worry, one by one. Begin by making a "worry list." Write down everything you think of. Rate each worry. Which looms largest? Which belongs at the bottom?

Ask yourself what, if anything, you can do to change each situation. In areas over which you have no control or cannot come up with solutions, ask your Higher Power, whether that's God or some greater part of yourself, to help you release the worry. Even if you see some solutions, call on your Higher Power to give you wisdom. During this thirty-minute confrontation with worry, stop a few times simply to take a series of deep breaths.

When time is up, stop worrying, as best you can, until the scheduled time tomorrow. If a worry floats into your mind in between scheduled "worry periods," simply acknowledge it: there it is—I'm still thinking about how we're going to pay off our debts now that Eric has lost his job. If you like, add it to your worry list, knowing you'll be able to concentrate on it later.

If you feel it's appropriate, share your worry list with your partner. Ask if anything on your list is also worrying him or her. If your partner's open to it, find out what's on his or her list.

ABCs

Acronyms, letters of the alphabet that stand for longer words or phrases, can be comforting when a crisis is making it hard for us to think clearly. They are shortcuts for remembering principles that can cheer us up a little or remind us of strategies for getting through a tough period.

MADD is the acronym that stands for Mothers Against Drunk Driving. It makes us remember the organization instantly. Our goal is to do the same thing for ourselves.

For instance: a man who holds clinics for aspiring opera singers reminds them, "The difference between `scared' and `sacred' is getting the `a' before the `c.' When you're presented with a challenge before being aware of how to deal with it, you may be scared! But develop awareness first and the opportunity of challenge becomes sacred." He invites clinic participants to join him in changing from a scared devotee of opera to a sacred co-creator. Not a bad idea when we're in a crisis either, to become as aware as possible of the challenges of a crisis rather than running scared.

Acronyms don't have to spell anything so long as they become mnenonic devices to help us remember our intentions. In desperation during one crisis I invented this one, which I still use: FFRR—It reminds me to:

Face a situation.

Feel it.

Rate it.

Release it.

When I feel stressed or irritated, or when a crisis comes along, this shortcut helps me not to panic. It reminds me instead to focus, to allow and recognize my emotions, to give a problem a size, and finally to dispatch it from my mind. With all this processing out of the way, I can remain open to a solution or come to accept that a solution may not come soon or even ever.

If you like "Wheel of Fortune," Scrabble, or crossword puzzles, you're a natural to use acronyms. Don't try too hard, just plug in the idea, and one day, an acronym will flash its letters in your mind and you won't forget it!

Coping with Night Terror

There are some crises that frighten us so much that nights become black periods of sheer terror. When something awful has happened, we may, during the day, be able to pull off some semblance of normalcy. Distractions and duties can temporarily take our minds off the situation.

But nights are different. We can't sleep. We are wide awake, unable to focus on anything but our anxiety, fear, rage, or sadness. As one woman expresses it, drawing on the imagery of Psalm 23 in the Bible, "It's going through the valley of the shadow. It's feeling overwhelmed with helplessness and hopelessness and feeling as if the dark is going to swallow you up."

We may feel like this when our health has been taken away. Or we have lost a child. Or we have been raped. Or we've just been fired. Or our mate has undergone some tragedy. Or we are waiting for a diagnosis or a report to find out just how serious our situation is.

Here are a few suggestions to hang onto during the night.

Listen to a relaxation tape or watch a relaxation videotape. Many bookstores now carry them and mental health professionals are familiar with them. Even if you still can't sleep, these aids can help quiet fear and anxiety by calming your mind.

Watch something inane or silly on TV. CNN Headline News or documentaries on the shrinking rain forests won't help, but a stand-up comedian or a re-run of "Leave it to Beaver" might. Go ahead and distract yourself with a laugh.

Find someone you can call any time of the night. One woman with an incurable on-going disease has a friend with the same illness. They have agreed to call each other *anytime* night terror strikes. The person who's scared simply pours out her fears while the other listens and consoles. There's a deep security in knowing someone will answer and listen. Sometimes our mate can be that person, but a backup outside of our immediate crisis can help too.

Sit down on the sofa or at the kitchen table with a soothing drink such as herb tea or hot cocoa. Take slow sips, then put your cup down and focus on breathing out and breathing in. Concentrate on pushing the fear from your mind long enough to find a word or phrase that might comfort you. Say this over and over.

During a recent health crisis, I had to wait several weeks for a diagnosis and the waiting was excruciatingly difficult. "Wait" became my nighttime word of comfort. I told myself I might as well wait to let panic and fear totally take over. I couldn't banish them altogether, but this tactic helped them subside a little.

What else may help? Share your terror with those you can trust. Though during the night we may imagine no one else could have ever been quite this shaken and scared, there are many of us who have suffered like this.

Finally, as we have said before, get help. Marilyn and I know from our own experiences and from those others have shared with us, night terror is hard to handle alone. Call a physician, therapist, spiritual advisor, crisis hotline or friend.

Tell Me, How Did You Survive?

I once saw a touching scene in an old late-night movie. Two soldiers were standing in the trenches somewhere.

One complained, "I'm having terrible nightmares." The other answered wearily, "I wish I could have nightmares; I can't fall asleep."

Not always, but usually, someone somewhere is in a situation worse than ours. Conventional advice is to think of that poor soul and realize we don't have it so bad. Following such advice leads us to minimize our problems and away from processing what's happening to us in a way that can be transformative.

What may help, however, is to talk to someone else who has been through a tough situation similar to ours and who has begun to climb out of the depths of despair. Ask them how they survived. Ask them if they too hit bottom and had trouble making it through the day. Ask them what their turning point was.

Marilyn has a friend who just found out that her cancer of four years ago has reappeared and spread through her body. She finds comfort in volunteering in a hospital's spinal injury unit. Being with patients who have obvious and serious injuries helps keep her from obsessing about her illness. The courage they display and the coping strategies they invent give her new ideas for dealing with her own engulfing fears.

Take a Break to Create

"IF BEETHOVEN HAD FOUND A GOOD THERA-PIST, WE MIGHT NOT BE HAVING THIS CONCERT." The Houston Symphony ran this catchy newspaper ad, pointing out that when Beethoven was losing his hearing, while the woman of his dreams was not available, the great composer dealt with his depression not by delving into his psyche, but by plunging into his work. Among many masterpieces produced during this low point in Beethoven's life was his Piano Concerto No. 4., the music that filled Jones Hall in Houston on a spring weekend.

We don't have to be genius composers to renew ourselves through creative work. Some of us are musicians, composers, painters, or sculptors. Others crochet, sew, quilt, or knit. Some of us are photographers or writers; others restore or craft furniture. Some of us are carpenters; others concoct creations in the kitchen.

Take a break to focus only on the joy of creating. Set aside an hour or a day during which you temporarily give yourself permission to stop trying to figure out yourself, your relationship, or the crisis you're in. Try out a new creative outlet or renew an old interest. Write a poem. Build a birdhouse. Bake a loaf of bread. Interpret a sonata on the piano. Photograph your neighborhood. Discover something new.

Hug Somebody

I once bought *The Angry Book* by Theodore Isaac Rubin, M.D., at a used bookstore. Tucked inside the pages were a Narcotics Anonymous meeting schedule and a free-hug coupon that said, "Good for one hug, redeemable from any participating human being." I've often wondered what else besides anger, besides an addiction to drugs, the previous owner of this little book was dealing with. Whatever his or her needs, whatever our needs, a hug does help.

In a crisis we may sometimes distance ourselves from our partner, our friends, our relatives. Who could you hug today? Might your partner welcome you into her arms? (Making love might take too much energy today, but what about a hug?)

When we're down especially, we may forget it's okay to voice our needs. It's not just okay, it's crucial! So go ahead and say, "I need a hug." An arms-around-each-other embrace feels so good and makes our sadness, anger, or frustration subside a little. We are, all of us, just trying to get through the night. Somehow a hug reminds us of our common human lot that includes both suffering and joy.

The Love Yourself List

When my son Timothy was five years old he plopped down beside me one day. "Mommy I love you," he said spontaneously. "I love you too," I answered right back. Looking up at me with solemn denim-blue eyes he added seriously, "I love you more than *you* love you."

During a crisis we may love ourselves hardly at all. We may blame ourselves, berate ourselves, feel sorry for ourselves—but love ourselves? It's easy to lose track of. But no matter what our mistakes or lapses in judgment, no matter what blow life has inflicted, we are worthy of self-love and it is important to be reminded of that.

List some of your positive traits, some of the things you love about yourself. "I keep on trying," wrote one man who was devastated over his sixteen-year-old daughter's drug addiction. That was all he could think of at first, but then his list grew. "I'm open to learning. I listen well. I keep on loving my daughter, no matter what." He went on, adding more.

You can make your own list, leaving space to add on as you keep focusing on the lovable parts of yourself that a crisis may have made you forget. Then start a second love list. Jot down the specific things you love about your partner, then share them with him or her.

Cry Now—Explain Later

"I decide I'll wait until I know what my tears were for before I burden him with them," said Grace Dowben, a

Jewish housewife in Joanne Greenberg's novel, *A Season of Delight.* She's letting us in on her decision not to tell her husband Saul what had happened earlier in the day. While she was out grocery shopping, a young man, a member of the Unification Church, asked her for a donation. Much to her surprise, she started bawling about her son Joshua who'd turned away from Judaism, joined the Unification Church, and now was somewhere in Illinois "dressed in yellow" and "chanting someone else's ancestral language." Grace had already grieved that, and now exactly what the tears were about and why they erupted so suddenly was a mystery to her. Therefore, she kept her emotions from her husband.

When we mimic Grace, when we decide to let our partner in on our grief, anger, or sadness only after we understand it, many days and nights may slip past in which we feel utterly alone.

While we're puzzling about the source of our pain we have at least two options: (1) We can struggle to figure out our feelings, and then, only then, tell our partner about them; or (2) we can share our feelings as they arise, saying "Darling I don't know where these tears, this anger is coming from, but this is how I'm feeling right now. I don't expect you to do anything—I'm not asking you to *do* anything, but to be close by. I can't tell you what's going on because I don't yet understand it myself."

When we ask our partner simply to be with us in our crisis process, when we approach our beloved confused about the source of our pain but clear and direct about our need for comfort, we extend trust to the one we love. We extend trust to ourselves.

We don't have to figure it all out instantly or possibly ever. We can allow ourselves untidy, hard-to-put-into-a-box feelings and we can share them with our partner without wrapping them up into a neat package.

Let Motion Come Before Emotion

I've lost the source of that sentence from a short story I read a long time ago, but I've never forgotten its wisdom. However, on occasion, I have disregarded it. When a crisis first presents itself, I have a tendency to become catatonic for a while. Late in the afternoon, I get out a bag of anything crunchy, salty, fattening. I turn on the television and watch anything, anything at all. I leave the empty bag of munchies on the floor. I go to bed early. I sleep in as late as possible, start work disheveled, and drink lots of coffee to keep working. I quit work and do a rerun of the day before. I usually act like this when I'm coming out of denial but still a long way from acceptance.

Some "vegging out" is okay. If we allow ourselves this crutch we may not need a stronger one such as depending on drugs or alcohol. Or getting an ulcer. So we need to honor our lethargy, at least for a while. But there will come a moment or a day when we need to get moving whether we feel like it or not.

I approach that moment of truth cautiously, like a woman I once saw in a comic strip. She is in the kitchen bending over the sink. Notes are posted around the kitchen:"Take dishes to kitchen"; "Fill dishwasher"; "Turn on." The caption reads: "Susan's days are built upon a series of short-term goals."

In the chaos of a crisis, short-term goals are attainable. Get up and do one thing. Wash a load of clothes. Change the oil in the car. Mow the lawn. Make a phone call. Pay one bill.

Let motion come before emotion and one day you'll

unite the two. Meanwhile think small. Do a little something.

Laugh

When things aren't going well, when my heart is weighted down, I only have to walk out my front door and take a walk up and down the sidewalk along the seawall in Galveston to lighten up a little. It's the parade of statements people make with their T-shirts that makes me laugh. I have seen, for instance: a woman about eight months pregnant with a "Just Do it" T-shirt stretched tightly across her stomach; a guy with a belly shaped like an ice cream scoop wearing a shirt picturing a big bowl of Blue Bell Ice Cream; and a long-haired thirtyish man with a shirt that says "Yuppies suck." An older couple in a heated argument walk past, her shirt's message: "Carpe Diem, Seize the Day!" An immaculately groomed Texas beauty wears the ultimate statement of truth during a crisis: "HAWG'S BREATH IS BETTER THAN NO BREATH AT ALL."

What's there to laugh about in your world even on the grayest days? Without denying our pain or sadness, sometimes we can stop dwelling on it long enough to laugh. If we lost someone dear, our only source of laughter for a long time may be the memory of a fun time together or of something funny the one we loved said or did. If we lost possessions, health, or a job—or if we've had to add more duties to our lives than we can imagine handling—a little laughter can lighten our burdens.

Allow Bewilderment

In the 1990 season playoff game against the New York Giants, the San Francisco 49ers lost in the last six seconds. Forty-niner fans were stunned! The Giants never even scored a touchdown—they won with field goals! Previously planned Superbowl parties were suddenly called off all around San Francisco.

Sometimes a crisis has that same aura of unreality, only much, much worse. Everyone said our business would be a success. Everyone believed our daughter would lick her illness. Everyone thought the hurricane would rage offshore, miles away. But everyone was mistaken and we are shaken to the core.

At the beginning of a crisis we may feel like asking for an instant replay. Did it really happen? Did we really lose someone or something so precious? The crisis process begins with such agonizing questions. Much more important than any football game lost is this unexpected cruel loss in our lives.

"We feel as if we are on the outside looking at the normal, happy world through some sort of glass wall," wrote Dick Maxwell, a father grieving the death of his six-year-old daughter Cathy, who "found herself in the path of a drunk driver going twice the speed limit. The world seems to make no sense, so don't expect us to make sense," he added in an essay in the *Denver Post's* "On My Mind" column.

This plea that he made to family and friends is one we need lovingly to direct to ourselves too. When a crisis we never anticipated turns our world into a senseless place, to act sane, to function like a well-oiled machine, is not a realistic or even desirable goal.

In one way or another, we'll never be our old selves again. And for a while we are in a never-never land. We are not who we used to be. We don't know who we'll become. And we may act a little lost and that's okay. Give yourself permission to feel dazed and confused. Your bewilderment is part of the healing process.

Reach Across

It seems exceptionally cruel. A crisis not only upsets our lives but at times it also illuminates some of our previously hidden character defects. It's enough to make us feel like shouting "HOLD THE LESSONS—DON'T SHOW ME ONE MORE THING!"

If a crisis is showing you a previously unseen not-so-nice side of yourself, hold on to this thought rather than attempting to retreat into the bliss of ignorance: "We are not worse than we were; on the contrary, we are better. But while our faults diminish, the light we see them by waxes brighter, and we are filled with horror," said Fenelon, in Aldous Huxley's *The Perennial Philosophy.*

Here's what happened in Kathy's life. One scary night five years ago she almost lost her only son to a suicide attempt. Before that crisis, Kathy had always showered love and attention on family and friends. But underneath her geniality, Kathy says she was also a stern judge. Her kindness, her generosity were handed out the way a queen might dispense gifts to her subjects. She gave of herself from an exalted position of never having experienced a serious crisis in her life. (And silently she congratulated herself on being so wise, so smart.)

Today Kathy is still the caring person she always was. But now when she reaches out to others, instead of looking down on them, she reaches *across.* "I'm not so quick to judge anymore," she says. "I feel a tremendous empathy now—I've run across a lot of good people who have had some heartbreaking times."

After we've been humbled by some new bit of self-awareness, we can, like Kathy, connect with others in down-to-earth, truly helpful ways—ways we might never have even imagined before.

Put Your "If Onlys" Down in Black and White.

In order to heal, we need to take our regrets, those whispering, nagging "if only" voices out of our heads, and make them concrete. We need to process them one by one and then release them. That way regrets can be turned loose to free our minds and energy for other activities.

Here's one way to begin. Make a regret list. Fold a piece of paper into two vertically divided sections. Make two headings. Label the top-left half, *MY REGRETS*. On the top-right side write, *ACTION/AMENDS*. Under the first column write down every single regret you have, from those that loom large and black to those small "I should haves": "I shouldn't have let John skip a grade and then he might not have felt so pressured; I should have known better than to expand the company so quickly; I wish I'd made her go to the doctor sooner; I wish I hadn't been speeding that day. After listing every regret, think about each one and ask yourself: What can I do about it now? Is there anything I can do to make it right? Do I need to ask someone to forgive me? If I can't take action or make amends, what do I need to do to let it go? Jot down your preliminary answers across from each regret.

Take a few moments for quiet contemplation. Empty your mind. In the stillness be open to ways to process your regrets. If you believe in a Higher Power, pray for forgiveness and for wisdom about how to lay these regrets to rest.

Answers about how to release your regrets may not come instantly or easily but, one by one, you can decide either to take action, make an amend, or accept that nothing can be done. As you process each regret as best you can, do something symbolic, specific, and memorable to get rid of every single one. Cut up your list and light a match to each regret. Take a hike, carrying along your written regrets and something to dig with; find a spot and bury them, then hold a short funeral service for your regrets, returning home with a lighter backpack and lighter spirits.

Turn off the Flood of Thoughts

Are you thinking too much? In *Reconciliations,* Dr. Theodore Isaac Rubin examines a seldom discussed mental malady he calls "overthink." Excessive thinking is a common response to crisis.

Do you go over and over the events preceding the crisis and think about what you wish you could change? Do you dwell on how things used to be? Do you keep thinking about what you might do, drawing up mental plans but not implementing them?

When most of our energy is channeled toward thinking, it never gets to our feelings or actions. Our thoughts are master con artists. They pass themselves off as us; but they are only ideas passing through our heads. When we find ourselves letting our thinking substitute for feelings or actions, we can get out of our head and into our gut by consistently asking ourselves: How do I feel about this? Though our thoughts ramble on, inventing countless complicated scenarios, our feelings deliver more-to-the-point messages: I'm exhausted; I hurt so much; I'm petrified; I've never known such fear.

By staying in our heads, preoccupied with myriad thoughts, we tend to stay stuck. We cover miles and miles of territory, but we haven't actually gone anyplace. By identifying our emotions and feeling them, we can become energy in motion. Consciously turning off our flood of thoughts in order to allow and honor our feelings creates energy.

Here's one suggestion to help banish negative thoughts. Set aside a half hour and find a quiet place. Visualize your thoughts as guests milling around in your mind at a big party. Hear their noise and chatter, then imagine yourself walking out of that room into a quiet place, perhaps an empty church or deserted beach.

Alone now, close the door on the noisy thoughts and *be* in this tranquil place. Take several deep breaths, then invite your feelings to sit down beside you. Allow each feeling without judging it. Simply note what it is.

Climb into Your Tree House

Many of us had a special childhood retreat—a tree house, a fort, a tent pitched in the far corner of the backyard. We all need what Joseph Campbell called "a sacred place."

Claire had no sacred place in the whole house. She had five small children in a small three-bedroom home and almost no time alone. Finally, in desperation, she found her sacred place in the bathroom! For five minutes every day Claire locks herself in and mentally conjures up this scene: She is on vacation in Maui, sitting on the beach at the Sheraton Hotel, watching a diver make his long slow ascent up a black rock. He stands poised at the edge, then makes a breathtaking, slow-motion dive into the aquamarine water below. While the diver is in flight, Claire dives deep within herself to check out her innermost feelings, needs, and desires.

Her self exploration is short but effective. It gives her back a sense of herself.

In the chaos of a crisis it's easy to rationalize that we have no time or even no right to renew ourselves. Especially during a crisis, however, we need one nourishing ritual to look forward to.

Where is your sacred place? When can you make an appointment with yourself to go there? Keep this important date with yourself.

Get Informed

Your initial response to a crisis may be to want to run as fast as you can from any more knowledge of it. But no matter what the shape and size of the crisis, whether its impact will be permanent or will pass with time, becoming informed will increase your ability to cope. Information helps ease fear and uncertainty. What you find out can empower you to go on.

"I never knew anything about drug abuse," says one woman whose son is recovering from an addiction to cocaine. "Now I'm an encyclopedia. Did you know that by age thirteen, 12 percent of our kids have tried marijuana and 8 percent have tried cocaine?" Besides information she uncovered in books, she also found out about support groups for parents and attends one weekly. She leaves each meeting with new awareness and practical information from other mothers and fathers.

Each day an estimated 1,300 new stepfamilies are formed. In 1989, 800,000 people filed for bankruptcy. Every year 5,000 to 7,000 adolescents in this country kill themselves. We mention these statistics to point out that because lots of people are undergoing crises related to these situations, information abounds on these and many other topics.

Under "Hospitals" in the yellow pages in the Galveston

phone book, there is a comforting list of helpful numbers for: crisis helpline, senior health network, women's health services, mental health services, special services and programs, plus more. A therapist, physician, or clergyperson can usually direct you to sources of information. Neighbors and friends can also sometimes help. Visit a library and enlist the aid of a librarian. Browse through a bookstore.

We know you know this! We offer this suggestion in case a crisis is temporarily clouding your thinking as to where to find help and information. It's there for you. Good luck as you begin your search.

Ideas for Helping Your Mate

Empathize Often

To empathize is to understand another's feelings and to reveal that understanding to the afflicted person, while still maintaining some objectivity. When we empathize with our partner we're literally *in pathos,* that is, *in suffering* with them. We don't, however, *become* them. If, for example, we feel so sorry for our depressed mate that we wind up being depressed too, we've dropped our own boundary and become engulfed in his or her emotion.

Keeping in mind the need to remain separate, empathize often with your partner. Ask, "How are you feeling today?" Then listen. If you don't understand, ask questions to clarify. Share some evidence that you understand what your partner said. Sometimes it helps simply to paraphrase your mate's words in your own: "Honey, if I understand you, you're saying you don't see a way out of this and don't know where to turn." Or if you've had a common experience, relate it: "I understand how bad you must feel; I remember feeling terrible when . . . "

When we empathize, we seek to understand our partner's internal experience. We don't give advice, judge, or criticize. We listen and assist our partner in identifying and understanding his or her feelings. When we empathize, we are there for our partner. We walk with him or her through the pain without rescuing or taking on his or her feelings as our own. Our separate strength and compassion can help the one we love to go on.

Forcing empathetic sharing won't work, however; so respect a partner's "I just can't talk about it now." But if your spouse stays locked into his or her solitary suffering for a long period of time, get outside help, preferably for both of you.

Treat Your Partner Like a Stranger

It's easy to make pleasant, polite conversation with a brand-new person. We have no history of hurt with strangers so we can focus on what they're saying and act charming and polite. In a crisis it helps if we can give our partner that same treatment. To do this lovingly and sincerely, we need the right frame of mind.

First, try and distance yourself from old relationship wounds or fresh ones suffered during this crisis, so that you can view your mate as another human being who needs polite gestures and kind, appropriate words. This putting aside of hurts and misunderstandings does not mean that you won't need to confront them eventually. But for now, deliberately set them aside. (The bonus: once you habitually treat your partner with respect and politeness, your chances of finding resolution improve.)

Start treating your partner as though you just met. Say "thank you" for chores done. Say "hello" when he or she walks into the room. Listen attentively. Don't interrupt. As you would with a new acquaintance, ask your loved one a personal question—something you somehow have never found out about. For instance: What books did you read when you were a kid? Who was your hero? What were you afraid of back then? How about now—what's your greatest fear? Do you have a fantasy about escaping all this?

When your beloved is weighted down by a crisis, simple words and attitudes that convey your love and interest take little time or energy, but help renew your relationship. Your kindnesses can soften a cruel or unfair blow from life at least a little. Such attentiveness can't help but lessen the distance between you.

Whose Problem Is This?

During a crisis, you need to give your partner an opportunity to solve problems that are primarily his or hers. If, for instance, your mate must now be confined to a wheelchair, encourage her to master its operation, rather than always offering instant help. If your partner is confronting an addiction, resist attempts to rescue him from the ups and downs of the recovery process. If your spouse finds retirement stifling and boring, offer sympathy without grudgingly abandoning all your own activities to fill the void.

Allowing your mate to function allows him or her to hold on to dignity and self-worth. If you prematurely rescue and try to help too much, the message conveyed is: You're helpless and you can't handle it. Your well-intentioned assistance can actually contribute to your partner's helplessness and depression.

When a problem is your partner's, the best you can do is to empathize and support his or her actions.

Compliment Your Partner

When you first fell in love, what qualities in your beloved did you admire and cherish? What qualities have you since grown to love? Make a mental list of her most shining qualities. On a daily basis, tell him exactly what you appreciate. Do you feel awe over his ability to adjust to a disability? Do you wonder how she can still work so hard even though her grief is overwhelming? Do you see kindness in your spouse even after life has been exceptionally cruel to her? Let your mate know you still see his or her goodness even during a difficult life passage.

Besides such noble traits, what else about your partner appeals to you? Pick some specific things. His hairy chest. The way she looks in jeans. His deep voice and the sexy way he says "hello" on the phone. Her special warm smile. As some wise person once said, we cannot compliment our mate too much or too often.

Help Your Partner Reframe the Picture

"I'm no good or I would never have been fired"; "My body is disgusting after this operation"; "I should never have moved us to this lousy town." When your partner feels responsible for a crisis or when a crisis has impacted his life directly and yours only indirectly, for a while your mate may see a distorted reality, but one which, to him, is vivid and real.

If you are a little more objective about the crisis than your partner, you can gently help her reframe her picture of reality: "Honey, you weren't fired because you were no good. You have great qualities, but that job was just not right for you"; "Sweetheart I know you're grieving losing your breast, but you're the most appealing woman I know";

"We both agreed to come here. I hate this place too, but you're not to blame. Let's try to figure a way to move since we're both unhappy." Sometimes input from the outside can get us to look at the tragedy in a new light.

Forget the Golden Rule

In comforting someone else, "don't follow the Golden Rule," says psychologist Kathleen White. "Never assume your spouse wants what you do, or that a different emotional style means he or she is unloving." We are all different. We shouldn't simply do for our partner what we'd like done for ourselves. And while you're at it, don't assume you know what he or she wants. Our comfort needs vary as much as our choice of clothes. We don't dress like identical twins! We don't need identical comfort.

When your partner is down in the dumps, what will help him or her the most? Your answer may only be a question or two away. "Darling what can I do? Is there something that might make you feel better?"

Often our partner's reply is a surprise. We like to talk out our distress. Our partner says she's "talked out," but would appreciate it if we'd fix the disposal. We assume our partner needs more holding and cuddling, but when we ask, she says she's been wondering if we could take care of the kids so she can just get in the car and drive a hundred miles to spend the night with her best friend.

Sometimes our partner's comfort needs clash with our own. Then it becomes a matter of balancing needs—to oblige our mate's needs within the parameters of comfort we can offer comfortably. For instance, if our partner wants to make love, but in our grief or distress, we feel unable to respond, instead of moving to the edge of the bed, back turned, perhaps there is a loving compromise such as just holding each other. If our partner can't bear to be in our arms without making love, we may have to accept the disparity of needs as a temporary consequence of the crisis.

Forgetting the Golden Rule also means that we can talk over our differences instead of pretending they don't exist. We can restrain ourselves from harshly judging our partner for differing needs and energy levels. Honoring each other's individuality, tailoring our comfort to fit one another—these attitudes and actions make our mate want to do the same thing back to us.

Surprise!

Usually we stage a surprise party or give a surprise present when things are going well or we reach a milestone. It's our tenth anniversary. It's his fortieth birthday. She's just been given tenure. We finally move into our own house.

A crisis is just as fine a time to surprise our partner with unexpected attention. Our surprise can become a gesture of celebration, not of good times, but of weathering a "for worse" season together.

Especially when your partner is down, take the lead. Prepare and serve breakfast in bed. Hand your partner two tickets to a play with a note that you've already lined up a babysitter. Put a "Personals" notice in the newspaper declaring your love, then figure out some way to stumble across it together. Take over one or two chores your partner is normally responsible for, giving your mate formal notice that you will be cooking, doing the laundry, or mowing the lawn for the next two weeks. Go by the library and check out a couple of books you think your partner might enjoy. Take care of the children, answer the phone, take care of anything that comes up, while he has an uninterrupted four or five hours locked in the bedroom curled up with some good reading.

Pick up your partner from work and whisk her off to a hotel and room service for one carefree night. Mike, when he did this, packed Pam's cosmetic kit and toothbrush, a swimsuit, gown, plus work clothes for the next day so she couldn't protest, "But what will I wear tomorrow and what about my makeup?"

Celebrate the toughness of your love. Let your partner know you love and value him even in the worst of times. Surprising your partner with loving attention may not solve anything, but it's likely to raise the corners of his or her mouth into a smile.

Reflection Opportunities

1. What else might help you cope with the crisis you are in? Brainstorm on paper using this heading: This Might Help. Write down anything and everything you can think of from the absurd to the easily attainable. Consider everything from a change in your habits or attitudes to securing more outside help. (A sample list: talking regularly with one person in a similar situation; meditating fifteen minutes a day; getting a second medical opinion; spending one night a week out with my wife away from the kids; winning the lottery; walking every morning; entering therapy; limiting time with friends and relatives who are negative; taking up kayaking; forgiving the person who caused my accident; volunteering at a hospital.)

2. Can you identify any new coping skills or areas of self-knowledge you're gaining through the pain of this crisis? If so, how is your new awareness changing you? Your relationship? If you see no new growth as yet or if the

crisis' lessons are still unclear, try and remain open. If you will, growth is a certainty.

3. After hitting bottom, do you have more empathy for your mate and others in pain? How might you show your partner you care today? How might you show another family member, friend, or stranger? Implement one act of caring toward someone today.

Chapter 6

Why Me? Why Us?

Why do bad things happen to good people?
Rabbi Harold S. Kushner

A few weeks ago my husband and I took a walk along the seawall in Galveston. The sky was swirled with pewter-colored clouds. Some billowed into puffy balls. Others were elongated funnels, not dipping all the way to earth to become tornadoes, but stretching horizontally across the sky like thick gray cables. Because the sky promised rain, we stayed near home, walking one direction for fifteen minutes, then turning around. That way, if we got caught in the rain, we wouldn't get soaked.

My husband is good at calculating when the rain will actually fall. "Do you feel how dry the air is?" Jack asked. "That means a cold front's on its way." Ten minutes later the temperature had dropped from seventy-five degrees to sixty-five, and the air smelled strange. "It's ozone," Jack explained when I asked. "It accompanies static discharges, thunder, and lightning."

Meanwhile the waves had flattened out. The great mass of Gulf water was now glassy and as gray as the sky. The air was still. "This is the proverbial calm before the storm," Jack said.

Determined to beat the rain, we picked up our speed and opened our front door just as the first raindrops fell.

Soon sheets of water were coming down and the winds grew so fierce that a huge piece of plastic floated by, riding the air currents like a magic carpet.

Upstairs in our apartment, we sipped herb tea and felt smug. We were dry and safe because my husband could judge the evidence around us and calculate almost to the minute when we should go inside. We'd avoided getting drenched by being smart, by planning, by using good judgment. But it isn't always like this. At other times, the torrential downpour of a crisis has swept into our lives uninvited and unfairly despite all our attempts at controlling our destiny.

"Why *do* bad things happen to good people?" Rabbi Harold S. Kushner explores this question in his compassionate and comforting book, *When Bad Things Happen to Good People*. When his son Aaron died two days after his fourteenth birthday from a condition called progeria or rapid aging, Kushner, rabbi of a large congregation, knew he and his wife were not alone in their suffering. Again and again, he wrote, he had "seen the wrong people get sick, the wrong people be hurt, the wrong people die young."

Kushner came to believe that though we can't always make sense of, or pin the blame on, someone or something—we can always ask our Higher Power, however we define him/her/it, to give us the courage to make it through some tough, undeserved crisis.

Still, most of us feel compelled to ask questions. Is there any way to make sense out of a senseless tragedy? Did fate single us out thinking that we, in particular, deserved cancer or financial ruin? Or that we needed the experience of seeing a parent slip away to Alzheimer's disease? Or that we or our child deserved a blood transfusion tainted with AIDS? Did God position our daughter, when she walked across the street, in the path of a drunk driver? Is God doling out punishment for some previous wrongdoing when a crisis sweeps into our lives?

In our desire to link cause and effect, we search for reasons when a sudden tragedy or ongoing crisis visits us. And once upon a time science backed us. When seventeenth-century physicist, Isaac Newton named and explained gravity, many scientists believed Newton had unlocked a door behind which lay the laws that governed everything, even human behavior. Just over the threshold, it seemed, was a set of laws that would enable us to predict all that would occur in the universe, once we could measure it all simultaneously.

At the beginning of the twentieth century, however, scientific determinism—the belief that everything is a result of a sequence of causes—was exposed as wishful thinking. Today, physicists studying atoms work with a twentieth-century theory called quantum mechanics, based on the Uncertainty Principle. That principle, in the words of theoretical physicist Stephen W. Hawking as recorded in *A Brief History of Time*, is this: "One can never be exactly sure of both the position and the velocity of a particle; the more accurately one knows the one, the less accurately one can know the other."

Equations that lead us to exact calculations fail us in our own little worlds as well as in the world of the atom. And this ambiguity may seem threatening. After all, it's not the way many of us were taught. Sometimes parents instilled in us and some of our religions led us to believe, that if we are good enough, if we try hard enough, if we sin hardly at all—all would be well with us and the ones we love.

If we button up our overcoats, if we put enough

money in the bank, if we leave early, if we tell our child, "remember to drive carefully," we'll be okay, won't we? Unfortunately, these "ifs" don't always protect us. And sometimes despite all our trying to understand. we will never know exactly why a crisis has landed in our lives.

After a DC-10 crash in 1989 in which a close friend of my husband's was killed, a survivor of that fiery tragedy was interviewed on television. Miraculously, many passengers survived, and this woman's story was especially touching. Not just she, but her entire family—her husband, her young son, and her baby daughter—had emerged from the crash with only minor injuries. With great emotion she told a reporter, "My sister says, `Now do you believe in God?'"

Her spontaneous words of gratitude at being alive and having her family intact obviously weren't intended to hurt those who had lost loved ones in the same crash. But what line of reasoning would comfort them? Could those who were burying family or friends now assume that God was *not* on their side? Would they lose faith in a Higher Power who protected some but not others?

Philosophers and theologians have always debated such issues. In November 1755, a devastating earthquake shook Lisbon, Portugal, killing thirty thousand people. On that particular day, All Saints' Day, churches were packed with worshipers. Trying to make sense of the tragedy, the French clergy called the disaster punishment for the sins of the people of that city. Hearing this enraged the French philosopher Voltaire and he penned a poem denouncing that view and intimating that the vastest mind could not figure out why something like this happened. "Silence: the book of fate is closed to us," he wrote.

Reading Voltaire's poem and not liking the philosophy that denied the possibility of explaining such events, another French philosopher, Jean Jacques Rousseau, responded in public, saying that men were to blame for the disaster; after all, if they had chosen not to live in towns, but rather out in the country, they would have been spared. And if they lived under the sky instead of in houses, those buildings would not have fallen upon them.

When a crisis finds its way into our lives something impels us to seek reasons. And in asking we join a great company of sufferers from all time. Why am I—why are we—in this crisis? Do we deserve it? Did I or my partner actually cause it? Could we have avoided it? Why did God or fate allow this to happen?

Whenever a crisis takes something important from us forever or even temporarily, we may begin to query ourselves and our Higher Power. And we may begin to question our beliefs and assumptions about life in general. To quiet these questions we have to face them. Otherwise they will keep waking us up at 2 A.M. Otherwise they will be like tapes on a loop, continually playing in our minds forever.

Once these questions enter our consciousness, they dog us until we approach them head-on. Our questioning may lead to only partial answers or to none at all, but the process of facing them and wrestling with them ultimately frees us to get on with our life and to resume a satisfying relationship with our partner, if that's what we choose.

When others suffer misfortune or loss, we may reach for platitudes or proverbs to make some sense of their situations. When others hurt, we may play the part of grown-up philosopher, pulling at our beard and intellectualizing. When others hurt, we may admire their courage as they walk across a bed of red-hot coals. But when suddenly we're no longer observers, but are forced to take that walk ourselves, we feel the heat. And sometimes, instead of striding across the smoldering embers unscathed, our flesh is scorched and burned. And we are left to wonder, why me? Why us?

Ideally, we and our partners would at least be able to agonize together leisurely, without interruption, say at a luxury hotel for a couple of days, with our meals served in an elegant dining room at a table spread with a white linen tablecloth.

There, a single long-stemmed red rose in a crystal vase would be the only object between the two of us. There, with soft piano music filling the background, we'd start to talk about our pain, our guilt, our disappointment. There we'd listen attentively to our mate pouring out his or her heart and then we'd share our own feelings. Later, back in the room, after eating the imported chocolates the maid left on our pillows, we'd make warm, passionate love, knowing that no lingering anger, guilt, or blame obstructed our union.

If you can, make a reservation right now.

Most of us, however, don't have that option. Depending on what happened, either our energy, our budget, or both, are low. Depending on what happened, our routines have been interrupted; either our responsibilities have multiplied or, if we're sick or disabled, we're hardly able to take care of ourselves at all.

In a crisis, most of us are trying to face and answer the questions the crisis raises while in front of a sink full of dirty dishes, during a one-hour lunch break at our company cafeteria, in a sterile hospital room, or just before we fall into the bed we didn't have time to make.

Besides less-than-ideal outer circumstances, our inner space is in shambles as well. At first, when a crisis enters our lives, we may be as brave as superheroes and as efficient as robots. At first we may be too numb and too supercharged to stop and ask about anything. But when the initial anesthetic wears off, when the adrenaline starts to ebb, we begin asking questions.

A Lonely Search

As I finish this chapter I sit at the computer wearing a T-shirt with red block letters that spell out "SHIT HAP-PENS." There is no cosmic connection between this chapter's subject and the fact that I chose to put this particular shirt on this morning. I'm wearing it because sitting at my computer has taken precedence over laundry for so long that this shirt is the last one in the drawer.

I know my shirt offends some, but its crude message comforts me. Several times when I've tried to understand why a particularly painful crisis happened, I've given up on cataloging the reasons. While I have determined to change any patterns of mine that may have invited these crises, still, even in retrospect, I cannot find a single clearcut reason as to why they occurred.

Ultimately all of us must make a lonely search to find answers to "why me?—why us?" issues when we've been visited with a crisis that seems cruel or unfair.

Did the belief I just stated above, that some things just happen, offend you? If it did, you might, if we were friends, allow me that belief even if it differed radically from your own. But when our mate disagrees with us, sometimes a holy war begins in which we pit our own religious or philosophical views against our partner's. In a crisis we may become less tolerant than usual. And when we're already hurting because of a crisis, we may want at least the comfort of having a unanimous vote on why something terrible happened. If the two of us happen to agree, it's reassuring; but when we don't, we at least have an opportunity to grow closer by examining our differences.

In her book, *The Bereaved Parent*, Harriet Sarnoff Schiff tells the story of a couple whose young daughter had died. The mother found solace in saying things like, "Now that Pammy is with God how can I be sad? It is the most glorious thing that can happen. I only thank Him for taking her so young, before she came to know the pain of this world."

"Damn it," her husband finally yelled in response one day. "I am getting sick and tired of hearing how great it is that she is dead. It is not great. It stinks. She was beautiful. She was smart. She was my daughter and I will never be thankful she is dead. What is wrong with you?"

Eventually, through the counsel of their parish priest, these two came to understand and accept their different views of one tragic reality. The wife became more sensitive to her husband's viewpoint and he no longer tried to undermine her main source of comfort.

When we are in conflict about our beliefs, sometimes, like the couple above, we can simply learn to accept the other's point of view. And sometimes, when we're disagreeing, we may find ourselves moving to the middle, to new beliefs that suit both of us better than our old ones.

Whether we revise our beliefs or keep the old ones, we must respect each other's opinions. For that to happen, we need to dig deep to discover our own beliefs and then express them to our partner as clearly as possible.

Understanding that our underlying beliefs are motivators of behavior builds trust and mutual respect. In short, though we may not understand why we are in a crisis, we can begin to understand why our partner is reacting as he or she is.

Couples frequently have beliefs that are in conflict. If our beliefs are at opposite ends of the continuum, there is a good chance both are irrational. Irrational beliefs create painful feelings, so both of us can be hurting for opposite reasons. One reason we find ourselves in pain is that we may be acting on beliefs that we haven't yet articulated clearly to ourselves. And so we know only, for instance, that we are angry and that we feel as though we're being punished. But we don't know why we believe that.

At this point we can quiz ourselves. Why are we angry? Why do we believe we're being punished? One woman reasoned: "God brought this crisis to teach me a lesson." Once a specific belief like this is uncovered, we can investigate it to see if it is rational, if it works for us, or if there is a better belief we might replace it with.

We can change beliefs that add to our pain, and our partner can too. Once we make our beliefs concrete—once we can state to ourselves and to our partner exactly what they are—we can be more respectful of our differing views. It's when our beliefs are ambiguous assumptions that they are difficult to accept.

Reflection Opportunities

1. Why do you believe this crisis happened? List all the reasons that come to mind—practical or philosophical, mundane or major.

2. Why does your partner believe this crisis occurred? As in the question above, pinpoint beliefs as specifically as possible.

3. Can each of you respect each other's beliefs and ways of coping? If not, why?

4. If differing beliefs are separating you, schedule a time to sit down with an unbiased third party—a therapist, clergyperson, or trusted friend who won't take sides—to air your beliefs.

5. What do you now *not* believe that you did believe before the crisis? Without censoring your thoughts write down your beliefs that have been crushed by this crisis.

6. Have any new beliefs started to take hold? Write them down. They may be unclear as they emerge; go ahead and record them anyway. (They may be as negative as "People will cheat you every chance they get," or as positive as "Life itself is a gift even on the darkest days.") Emerging beliefs are much like the first draft of a book. Some ideas will stay in our new belief system as they are, others will need clarifying, and some will be discarded. Recording them helps us go through this editing process.

Chapter 7

The Commitment
Question

*All relationships go through trying times—
economic or psychological crises, illnesses,
disappointments,betrayals. Expressing your
love may mean self-sacrificing devotion and
loyalty and unrequited caring during those
acute periods. That is the nature of ethical
love; it is a promise made and kept.*
      Judy Sellner, Ph.D. & Jim Sellner, Ph.D.

I n Latin the verb *committo* means to cause to go together. Like hot-fudge syrup on vanilla ice cream, like
a football game on a brisk fall day, like quiet in a
library, when we make a commitment to our partner something happens as close to magic as we'll find in this real
world. We are more natural, more right together.

When a crisis is driving you crazy, when your world is
turned upside down, there's no better time to go ahead and
deeply commit yourself to your partner. Right now. No
matter *how* you feel.

When we read about couples who've been married for
fifty years and whose commitment has knit them together
as closely as two different-colored strands of thread in a
durable garment, we may get tears in our eyes. Or when we
think of making a commitment to our partner, we may feel
a warm glow, just from letting the thought drift through

our minds. But admiring someone else's commitment or contemplating our own are sentimental substitutes for going ahead and putting our energy into a real, here-and-now commitment to our partner.

Maybe your commitment won't be forever. But if you want to try to make it through a crisis together, making a commitment for the next few months or for the next year will give you time to consider forever later.

To commit you do not have to be doubt free. As Rollo May points out in *The Courage to Create*, "Commitment is healthiest when it is not *without* doubt, but *in spite of doubt* ... To believe fully and at the same moment to have doubts is not at all a contradiction: it presupposes a greater respect for truth, an awareness that truth always goes beyond anything that can be said or done at any given moment." In essence, you're not committing to a certain outcome, but recognizing a risk and saying to yourself and the other person, "I'll give my partner and this relationship my full attention and effort."

When you make a commitment you are defining your relationship not just as a love affair, but as a marriage. A love affair, according to scholar Joseph Campbell in *The Power of Myth*, is "a relationship for pleasure." With that in mind, he concludes that when it is no longer pleasurable, "it's off."

In contrast, Campbell pronounced marriage "a life commitment" and believed that if a marriage is to survive, there must be loyalty. "Not cheating, not defecting—through whatever trials or suffering, you remain true." Some of us have relationships that, though not official marriages, fit that description. We never said our vows before a justice of the peace, minister, rabbi, or priest. We have no certificate. But we are married in the sense that we're together in an ongoing "for better or worse" partnership.

Some of us entered our relationship for pleasure only, and now we find we don't "do pain" with our partner very well. A crisis has a way of forcing us into finding out what our relationship is all about. We can't comfortably sit on the fence.

Are you in a love affair or in a marriage as defined above? Be aware that often a crisis leads someplace—toward a firmer commitment, a breakup, or at least an acute awareness of doubts and uncertainty that before could be ignored.

Our intention is not to stand on a soapbox waving a banner extolling the virtues of a committed marriage while calling love affairs bad. We're just noting their differences.

A love affair is like a beautiful satin evening dress; a marriage is like a sturdy raincoat with a zip-in liner. The flowing gown is fine for dancing cheek to cheek but it won't help much in a torrential downpour; we'd end up shivering and drenched.

If we value our relationship, if we want it to continue, when the puzzling questions a crisis stirs flood our minds, and when we feel guilty or are blaming our partner for the crisis we're in: it is precisely this period that is the best time to sit down with our mate and let him or her know of our commitment.

"I'd like to stay with you through all this"; "I care even if I can't show you so well right now"; "We'll make it together." Direct statements like these reassure the one we love and give us a safe setting in which to process the troubling questions a crisis has raised.

A Dangerous Stretch

Somewhere after the initial shock of a crisis and before we look to our partner for comfort, there is a dangerous stretch in which we may distance ourselves from each other and be tempted to seek sympathy, and sometimes sex, elsewhere.

In the moving novel, *At Risk,* Polly and Ivan's eleven-year-old daughter Amanda has contracted AIDS from a blood transfusion given five years before during an appendectomy. For months these two distance themselves from each other. Each seems to find just enough strength to make it through the day. But they are too drained, too stressed, and too wrapped in their separate griefs to reach out to each other.

Finally, one day when Amanda's condition worsens and she has to be admitted to the hospital, we see Polly and Ed Reardon, Amanda's pediatrician, sitting in his Volvo station wagon outside the hospital. Ed chooses this time to tell Polly that he's been leading her to believe there is hope for Amanda, when in fact, there is none. Polly reaches for Ed and the two of them hold each other for a long time.

Then we read, "When Ed Reardon strokes her hair, Polly feels safe. Their breath, which is fogging up the windows, is creating its own cocoon . . . . What they're doing is more intimate than making love; they don't exist without each other. Polly can no longer tell where Ed Reardon's heat leaves off and hers begins. The way she feels makes Polly believe that things can be alive. She's desperate to believe something."

In the disruption of a crisis, we may become desperate to believe in something, to feel something besides our pain. When Polly and her husband, Ivan, were together, their pain seemed to double. Making love offered little comfort. After all, it was their lovemaking that produced Amanda. Just being together reminded them of the impending loss of the child they created. But in Ed's arms, for a little while, Polly could forget the specter of death hovering over their lives. And she could feel a rush of sexual pleasure she'd denied herself from feeling with Ivan.

When our partner represents a not-so-pleasant reality, we may seek out someone who is totally outside the crisis, someone who can bring some joy or laughter into our days. Or we may seek an understanding soul who is a part of our crisis, but not inside it as we and our partner are: our child's pediatrician or the lawyer who helps us through bankruptcy proceedings. We might fantasize about making love with our therapist or a sympathetic co-worker.

In a crisis we don't usually stop to think about why we're feeling alienated from our mate. Often we blame her or attribute our feelings to his failings, not realizing how the crisis is coloring our outlook. Without knowing why we may think: I just don't love her anymore. I know I could talk to someone, almost anyone else, more easily.

Mike Reagan, M.S.W., a veteran therapist who for years worked with adolescents and their parents at a drug and alcohol rehabilitation facility in Denver, points out that feeling negatively about a spouse, and fantasizing about or finding empathy or sex elsewhere, is a predictable but potentially serious scenario.

"Anyone with any sense at all would not want to go through a crisis like the ones I've seen couples facing. If you simply followed your feelings, you'd run as fast as you could. But emotions are transitory. Feelings are like temperature, pulse, or respiration—they're indicators of how you're thinking and what's going on."

Rather than going with the flow of these feelings, what most often helps to preserve a couple's relationship is a decision not to *react* to passing emotions, says Reagan, but to stop and *act* on their value systems.

What do you value most in life? What value do you place on your relationship? Are you committed to an ongoing relationship?

Fictional Polly and Ivan made it through their period of estrangement the same way real couples do--with one powerful resource: a commitment to each other which ended up defeating their short-term desires to find pleasure, or something--anything--except pain, outside their relationship. And when they finally found their way back to each other, pain had sculpted their love into something stronger and sturdier than before.

Most of us won't resemble the soap opera pairs who instantly melt into each other's arms every time some difficulty arises. Many of us may need time to huddle alone in our own dark corner for a while, grappling individually with grief, anger, and disappointment. But with a sturdy commitment in place, at least we know we can struggle through the crisis without anxiety over the status of our relationship. When we choose to stick by each other, for better or worse, in sickness or in health, we can feel secure during even the longest, coldest nights.

Reflection Opportunities

1. How are you feeling toward your mate right now? Do you feel alienated and estranged? Do you find yourself attracted to others, seeking to share your hurt with someone else? Do you experience a mixture of feelings depending upon the time, circumstances, and emotions prevailing?

2. What do you truly value most in life? Where do you spend your time, money, effort, energy, and talents? Go through your appointment book and ascertain if what you say you value most gets most of your time. Go through your checkbook and determine what it reveals about your values. Go to your heart and be as honest as you can: what comes first, second, and third in your life? Where does your relationship rank? Is it in the position you want it to be in?

3. How committed are you to this relationship? Is your relationship a "love affair" or a "marriage"? What would it take to make you leave or would you ever leave? What must happen for you to stay? What must occur for the relationship to be at the intimacy level you desire? What is pleasurable in the relationship? Is your relationship just tolerable but not growing? What steps might you take to make your relationship grow? How is the pain of the crisis affecting the quality of caring between the two of you right now?

4. If you have convinced yourself that it is time to make a commitment, write out a few short, direct statements to share with your partner. "I know we'll make it through this terrible crisis, and we'll be stronger for going through it. We can survive this together"; "I know my mind is on this crisis all the time, but I still love you even though I'm not saying it often." Such thoughts are helpful to the other person, but are often difficult to say spontaneously. Our minds often feel short circuited in a crisis, and we think of what we wanted to say only after the fact. Consider practicing your reassurances so that they are available when you—and your partner—need them.

Chapter 8

You and Me Together, Separately

When you accept the limited nature of your own perceptions and become more receptive to the truth of your partner's perceptions, a whole new world opens up to you . . . . Marriage gives you the opportunity to be continually schooled in your own reality and in the reality of another person.
Harville Hendrix, Ph.D.

As a teenager, when life dealt me a big blow, I'd meet my best friend at a little diner after school. We'd both order cherry Cokes, cheeseburgers, and fries, and we'd sit for a couple of hours at a red Formica table in a booth way back in the corner.

Sometimes both of us were hurting, so we'd commiserate in ladylike, Southern drawls. We'd hurl insults at football players who broke up with us and at the little hussies who lured them away. We'd stay in "ain't it awful" mode until finally we'd complained and comforted each other enough. And then we'd pay our checks and leave to walk our separate ways back home, feeling lighter, better. We may want our partner to be that kind of friend. But what if our partner is not like that? Often we make friends with people who are very similar to ourselves, but choose a romantic alliance—a marriage or a committed relationship—with a person who is in many ways our opposite.

Often a more introspective person is paired with one who emphasizes action and minimizes contemplation. Perhaps your partner feels this way: "Things that are done, it is needless to speak about . . . things that are past, it is needless to blame." Confucius said that.

His modern-day counterpart, a man who retired early to care for his wife who has an ongoing, incurable disease put it this way, "Life is full of crises. You handle them."

A partner with this approach to life can still come along with those of us who must find verbal expression for our angst. When we don't ask our partner to be *like* us, but simply request that he or she be there *with* us as we process our thoughts, we can still be together, each of us respecting the other's way of coping. But it's not easy.

Ten years ago my husband Jack handed me a big glossy Valentine card with two cartoon dinosaurs, one pink, the other yellow, standing facing each other. One's about to tear into a hunk of meat; the other's nibbling on a bowl of leafy green salad. One has four toothpick legs; the other only two gigantic tree-trunk-sized ones. Different or not, they're deeply attached: "I'm glad we're not two of a KIND," one grins, adding, ". . . it's much more fun being ONE OF EACH!"

This card conveys the essence of why we're still a twosome after thirty-some-odd years. Not easily, but gradually, we've given up on the goal of making each other over into like-minded clones. Over the years, we've come to enjoy many of our differences, tolerate some, and confront each other about the ones that are unacceptable.

Even now, however, when I know better, a crisis can still trigger a regression in which I attempt to make my husband think exactly like I do. I say "I" because in our marriage, I'm the ring leader in this scenario. When I'm hurting, when I'm attempting to understand and adjust to something painful—something beyond ordinary daily stress—my first impulses embarrassingly resemble a two-year-old's frantic insistence on getting her own way. I want Jack to cry with me *now*, not later. I want him to talk about the crisis using the same words that I do. And once he begins resisting my efforts, as he surely will and always has, I become distrustful. If he really loved me, I reason, he'd agree with me, that is, he'd view the crisis *exactly* the same way as I do.

When I fall into these ways of acting and thinking, I'm ignoring the truth of that card. Jack and I are of two different "orders." I'll always be pink. He'll remain yellow.

It takes me a while to see the good in a bad situation. I take my time trying to figure out the lessons of a crisis, by reading books that instruct or inspire, by meditating and praying, or by ranting and raving to close friends. Jack, more optimistic and active, usually sees the opportunity hiding in a crisis sooner than I do. And often he makes that breakthrough riding his bicycle or developing a roll of film in his darkroom.

When I can remember all this during a crisis, I save my energy for *communicating* with Jack, not trying to convert him to my way of thinking. That is, I resist such reproaches as: How could you be smiling right now? or I don't understand why you're not more upset; after all this *is* an upsetting situation. When I don't remember, we take a one-way path leading straight to misunderstanding and alienation.

How can couples avoid the cloning battle, and how can we get back on track when we find ourselves getting into it? This is possible when we adhere to the following three beliefs. First, when two people respond to a crisis, each person's view of reality is always slightly, and sometimes vastly, different. The saying, "Reality is nothing, perception is everything," is usually at the core of the conflict between partners during a crisis.

Second, relationships crumble during a crisis when partners insist on attempting to convince a partner he or she is wrong for feeling or acting a certain way. And finally, in a committed relationship, two entirely different people can comfort each other if they allow and respect their differences and focus on understanding each other rather than changing each other.

Though these beliefs may sound logical, implementing them is difficult. Not trying to change our partner is not easy! The seduction of trying to change the one we love beckons us. And knowing it's not good for our relationship may not stop us any more than knowing that eating half a box of chocolate-covered nuts is not good. We pop one into our mouth, then another, and we feel better instantly.

Changing our partner offers instant gratification during a time when we're grasping for any comfort we can find. For when we focus on changing our partner, we divert ourselves from the pain of the crisis. When we focus on changing our partner, we can ignore taking responsibility for our own actions and attitudes. And if we can convert our partner, we can still "win" even when life has temporarily defeated us with a crisis.

The problem is, refusing to understand our partner and trying to change him or her doesn't work.

Conversion Attempts

Often our attempts to convert our partner to our way of thinking or reacting to a crisis stem from fear. When we're scared, we like to draw our partner close to us. We like to snuggle with one who soothes us with, "Yes darling, I know," not with someone who stirs our insecurity by asserting, "I don't feel that way."

When our partner perceives or handles a crisis differently than we do, we may feel alone, angry, resentful, or sad--or all those emotions and more. After all, we welcomed our partner into our life for support. When everything is going along fine, we may view our differences philosophically. We may even discover that our partner's different approach enriches our life. It's fun to be different when we're not hurting.

In the pain and anxiety of a crisis, however, we may revert to a belief system that states that our truths are the real truths and that the way we deal with a crisis is the correct way. If, however, we keep fighting and insisting that our views are the only correct ones, we rule out the possibility of comforting each other or of solving the challenges a crisis has dumped into our laps. Our conversion attempts, in fact, shut down the very process that is necessary to survive the crisis together: intimate communication. They don't work because they involve judging and declaring our partner's beliefs as lacking in integrity and truth. And when our partner feels judged, he or she quits communicating, stops being open and vulnerable, and digs in his or her heels, refusing to change.

When we continue trying to create a clone, we risk alienating our best potential support system. Still, we may persist anyway. If, for example, your wife thinks a crisis has left her cup "half empty," you may insist she share your optimistic view, saying, "Come on honey, look at all we've still got." If your husband is moping around, you may urge him to start smiling again with the reminder, "After all, life goes on." Or, if your grief is still raw and painful, you may tell your partner his banter about everyday topics is insensitive and cruel. But each person is entitled to his or her own reaction and response. Period.

So how can we put a halt to our conversion attempts and start communicating? How can we come to understand our spouse and respect his or her point of view, even if we don't agree?

First, A Caution

We should allow only those differences that don't hurt us. If a crisis pushes our partner to the edge, we need to draw certain boundaries of safety around us. Marilyn and I do not intend to encourage anyone to stick around while his or her partner turns physically or emotionally abusive. No partner has that right. The human psyche cannot and should not tolerate emotional abuse of a consistent or severe nature. If your partner is constantly downgrading or blaming you, this behavior is unacceptable. Your partner is being emotionally abusive when he or she repeatedly says things such as "Only an idiot would have gotten us into this situation," or "It's all your fault," or "I should have listened to my best friend's advice and never married you." Crises bring out the angry irrational child in us and it's not unusual to see some regression on both sides, but if and when verbal bashing is frequent or severe, the partner under attack may need to seek a physical separation.

Physical or sexual abuse is cause for immediate separation. Marilyn urges clients never to return before their partner has undergone intense therapy, and then to resume their relationship only after a consultation with the therapist. Be sure to seek out a therapist or clergyperson or talk with a trusted friend if you're wondering whether your relationship has crossed the line into emotional, physical, or sexual abuse.

Vive la Difference!

For those of us not trapped in an abusive relationship, but temporarily estranged from our partner because of our different ways of reacting to a crisis, we offer the following suggestions. None of them points out a way to become more alike. All of them invite you to understand and respect your differences and to stick together as a cohesive pair—even when you can't always arrive at a consensus.

Make Allowances for Different Timetables

Not only when someone we love dies, but in many crises, we move through a somewhat predictable process of grieving a loss, and often partners move at different paces. The possibilities for misunderstanding each other are as varied as each relationship. For example, Susie is sipping her morning coffee, guffawing over Garfield's antics. Brad stumbles in, no coffee yet, feeling forlorn, devastated, and light years away from recovering from the rotten blow fate has dealt him. Instead of being glad she's cheerful, he jumps straight to the conclusion that she's a cold-blooded monster, not a fellow human being occupying a different emotional space. Brad would like to get a hold of the SOB who fired him and punch him out. But Susie smiles sweetly saying, "I've forgiven him." Out loud or to ourselves in such situations, we judge the one we love as utterly lacking in judgment.

Jenny shared her insights about how easy it is for couples to misunderstand each other. A decade ago, this mother of five and former grammar school principal, now in her mid-fifties, found out she had lupus, an incurable disease that affects the immune system. Sometimes the disease goes into remission and she feels almost normal; other times flare-ups put her to bed for weeks. Jenny is certain she had lupus for at least fifteen years before it was diagnosed, and therefore, for much of her thirty-five year marriage to Merv, she's been ill.

To deal with her disease and to encourage others with the illness, Jenny takes an active part in a lupus support group and draws her observations from her involvement there. Since the majority of lupus sufferers are women, what she relates reflects that fact.

"When you find you have a chronic illness, when you know it's not going to go away, it's like dealing with death--you go through the grief process. The divorce rate for a couple when one has a chronic illness is about 80 to 90 percent. The husband and wife aren't working at the same rate. Many of the marriages in our group have broken up over this illness.

"At every support group meeting there are people who are at all different levels of dealing with the disease. When they're first diagnosed, they go through denial. They'll come and say, 'This isn't going to change my life at all. It's not going to change any of my relationships.'

"Then they go on to the next stage—they get really angry. Often they strike out at their partner—at everybody. They see it is affecting their life. They see the disease does make a difference. Some storm out of a meeting, slamming the door.

"Then depression sets in. There's nobody they can hold accountable. They're left with a sense of hopelessness. Then, hopefully, they finally come to acceptance.

"When a marriage breaks up, it's not just the well

spouse who walks out on the sick one. Sometimes when a husband stays in denial, when he won't admit his wife is sick, she decides that since she's dealing with the disease `alone' anyway, she may as well divorce. Often women I've known have remarried a man who's more understanding than their first husbands and already knows she has the illness and accepts her. Many have been happy in these second marriages."

Jenny believes her marriage to Merv has survived because he's faced her illness head on. "I've dragged Merv to all the meetings. He understands this illness as well as I do. He's even served on the board of our support group."

Are you and your partner at a different stage in the grief process? Where would you place yourself right now— in denial, anger, depression, acceptance? How about your partner? Observe your partner and ask how he or she is feeling. Just knowing it's likely that the two of you will be in two different emotional places during a crisis can help us better understand one another.

Remember too, we often backtrack, revisiting phases we'd thought we had finished. With that in mind, check in daily with yourself and your partner—that is, take time to ask yourself "where" you both are emotionally. Try to judge yourself and your partner less harshly as you zigzag toward acceptance.

Take into Consideration That You and Your Partner Have Different Support Systems and That a Crisis Has a Different Impact on Each of You

In a crisis, we receive varying degrees of support from society, friends, family, and our workplace. For example in a paper entitled "The Impact of Illness on Late-Life Marriages," published in the *Journal of Marriage and the Family*

(February 1985), researcher Colleen Leahy Johnson studied a group of married couples over age sixty-five. The common factor among the couples was that one spouse had just returned from the hospital and was recuperating from an illness or accident. She found that the well spouse generally offered the other a high level of support, but that the husbands who were helping take care of sick wives reported less stress than wives caring for ailing husbands. Healthy husbands, it turned out, used more formal community supports and had more relatives to help out, while the wives were more likely to function alone.

Though the author didn't cite specific cases, I can imagine a scenario like this: Henry, who's never been in the kitchen except to raid the refrigerator or pour a cup of coffee, is perceived by relatives and neighbors as being in dire need of help while his wife, Mary Ellen, has to be off her feet for a few weeks. And so the casseroles arrive at the door, along with notes of encouragement and offers to sit with Mary Ellen while "you get out and play a round of golf." But if Mary Ellen were nursing Henry? She might get sympathetic phone calls, but it's likely she'd be cooking Henry's food.

This blatantly sexist example is not intended to categorize males as inept in the kitchen—my husband and sons range from good to great in the culinary arts, while I trail with a fair—but to point out that in various crisis situations, each partner is apt to have a different set of support systems readily available. That reality influences how each of us react to a crisis.

Think about you and your partner. What kinds of support are you receiving during this crisis? Is someone cheering you up? Helping you out? Listening to you? Giving you time off? How are your partner's sources of support different from yours? If one of you is lacking in support, how might either of you go about changing that?

It seemed as though the women in the above study automatically fended for themselves. I wonder if they thought of support options? Often we don't. My friend Trish told me recently she was upset about the amount of time her seventy-five-year-old mother was demanding she spend with her. Though still physically and mentally well and able, her mother seemed depressed and expected Trish to come by each evening after work, eat dinner, and stay with her until bedtime. In addition, she asked Trish to spend all day Saturday with her.

Trish's mother, widowed ten years earlier, had out-lived two other children—Trish's two brothers had died in their forties. Now she seemed mired in a deep self-pity and was saying such things to Trish as, "You have so much and I have so little. I know you don't mind sharing time with me. And I'm certain Richard understands."

Trish's husband Richard had been understanding at first, but as her mother's requests increased, he was growing alarmed. Most recently Trish's mother had begun hinting that Trish should stop working full-time so they could spend more time together. Trish was considering that possibility even though she liked her job managing a floral department in a supermarket. Although she and her husband would have trouble making ends meet without her salary, she wondered, Don't I owe my mother that much?

Meanwhile, Richard tried gently to ask Trish if she might not be overreacting. He asked Trish if she was forgetting about spending time together as a couple in her single-minded quest to be "a good daughter," and if she were ignoring how much she loved her job and how her salary made their lives more comfortable. Their three daughters were all grown and finally there could be some time for the two of them; plus, he reminded Trish, she'd always wanted a career and finally had one.

Trish called me recently, sounding relieved. She had, she said, "decided not to be the perfect daughter." She'd also realized she had a right to take care of herself. Then she began to round up support for her mother from other sources. She called the minister of her mother's church, asking him if church members might schedule regular visits with her mother. He, in turn, called an active church member, an older widow who still was able to drive, who said she'd love to stop by "just to chat" once a week. Trish also gave her mother some information about a nearby senior recreation center that had van pickup service and classes of all descriptions. Her mother wasn't too enthusiastic, but was mulling over the possibility.

Trish had, in addition, contacted a nursing service, which, for a reasonable fee, would now be stopping by to check on her mother for a half-hour every morning. Trish and her husband were paying for that service as a Christmas gift. With her full-time work, Trish could afford this generosity. Trish would, she said, also be visiting her mother twice a week, after work. Trish had consulted her mother before making each of these decisions, telling her she knew she was lonely and asking, "What would you think about this?"

The particulars of Trish's situation are not so important as her change in attitude. She turned from despair to hope after she established her boundaries and allowed herself to seek support beyond herself. For women, in particular, in our society, taking this route away from "doing it all" is difficult. In Trish's case, guilt still tugged at her in the form of her own inner voice—she'd always been the "good daughter who never caused any problems and was always there to help," and now she knew she was abandoning that old role. And guilt was still activated by her mother who, though grudgingly happy about the changes, still intimated to Trish that "nobody else loves me and cheers me up like you do." By and large, however, Trish felt that by preserving some time for herself and Richard, by continuing to work, and by not abandoning her mother, but setting loving limits, she had made decisions she could live with.

It's not just our support systems that vary; each crisis also hands different consequences to us and our partner. During a bankruptcy, one partner may be crushed over the loss of a fulfilling career, while the other is distressed about the "For Sale" sign on the lawn and the necessity of moving into a smaller, cheaper home. When a child is chronically ill, one partner may do more caregiving, while the other partner works longer hours to pay medical expenses.

Even the death of a child holds different degrees of pain and loss for each parent. After the tragic 1932 kidnapping and murder of her eighteen-month-old son, Charles Lindbergh, Jr., Anne Morrow Lindbergh poignantly noted how her grief differed from that of her famous aviator husband. She desperately missed playing with her toddler—touching him, seeing him. Charles focused more on never having the satisfaction and pleasure of one day standing eye-to-eye with an adult son. In *Hour of Gold, Hour of Lead*, she wrote, "There is something very deep in a man's feeling for his son, it reaches further into the future. My grief is for the small intimate everyday person."

Take a Look at Your Own and Your Partner's Belief Systems

Even if this is the first full-fledged crisis you've been through, your already established belief system is present. If we asked four people, "What's the best way to get through a crisis?" we'd most likely hear four different suggestions. Some examples: "This too will pass if I'm patient"; "I'd better *do* something right now because it never works to sit around and wait for things to get better"; "Don't waste time feeling sorry for yourself, after all there's always somebody else who's worse off"; "I'll never get over this—there's no use trying."

Two people both questioning the validity of their previously held belief systems equal a perfect environment for misunderstanding fueled by inner chaos. When I'm feeling foolish or doubtful about some of the beliefs I based my life on, and when my husband is struggling with similar issues, what we all often do is attack each other's beliefs rather than rethink our own. Pinpointing someone else's faulty assumption is, after all, less painful and involves less work than focusing on our own.

What works best, however, is when each of us focuses on examining our own beliefs when they are uncomfortable or unworkable, and stops trying to edit or rewrite one another's beliefs. The wording in this suggestion *to take a look at* is deliberate. It's an invitation to stop judging and simply to see. Understanding why we act as we do, and pinpointing our beliefs, are tasks that require patience. We won't suddenly understand ourselves or our spouse in a great flash of insight. It takes time and repetition. This suggestion is simply a reminder that we can dedicate ourselves to that process by beginning to observe ourselves.

To begin observing your different frameworks of be-liefs, ask yourself this: if you videotaped your lives right now, from morning until night, what scenes would you capture? Now color in more detail. What is a day in the life of the two of you like? How does each of you act? What do you say? How do you two spend your time? Is there a marked contrast between your two sets of behaviors and attitudes? How do you differ? What is similar? What differences hurt a lot? Which ones don't matter? Are any differences helpful? Can you discuss these points?

Here's how one couple came to focus on and then deal with their different reactions to a crisis. For Lisa, a psychia-trist, and Scott, a psychiatric social worker, Lisa's mastec-tomy had been tough. Now, as she was undergoing chemo-therapy, they hoped and prayed that any remaining cancer cells would be killed.

Though this couple felt intensely close to each through-out the ordeal and though they were consciously going out of their ways to express their love to each other, they found themselves really getting on each other's nerves right after Lisa's chemotherapy treatments. As Scott describes it, "When Lisa returned from a treatment, which would prompt most people to take a long nap, she would begin to clean the entire house, and then call up her friends."

Scott, who got off work early to drive Lisa to her afternoon treatments, said he came home feeling drained. While Lisa was getting out the vacuum cleaner and furni-ture polish, he would make himself a cup of tea, plop down in his favorite armchair, and read a page from a comforting book of meditations.

Last week while he was unwinding, Lisa stormed into the living room, yelling, "Didn't you see that trash can in our bedroom? It's full?"

"Yeah, I saw it," Scott countered, "It was full." (Thinking, so what?)

Then Lisa yelled angrily, "Why didn't you empty it?"

After one such scene, they were finally able to step out of their situation long enough to figure out what was going on. As Marilyn describes it, Lisa, feeling threatened and frightened by her illness, was compulsively trying to order her world in areas she could still control. Even though she was sick, she could still vacuum, dust, and straighten. She could still pick up the phone. And, as an extrovert, she found it natural to turn to a friend's comforting voice on the other end of the line. She gained energy from other people.

On the other hand, Scott, worried that he may lose the wife he loves so much, was more laid-back and was isolating himself, drawing on the inner resources of his introverted temperament. He gained strength and energy from his internal world of ideas. Scott and Lisa simply respond differently to the same stress! And knowing that has made all the difference.

After making concerted efforts to keep communication open, Lisa has begun to relax her demands on Scott and has realized that his resistance to joining her in her flurry of activity does not mean he's being unloving. Scott, though he still needs some time alone for reflection, has started asking Lisa which chores she'd like help with after he finishes his break—and then he does them.

Sometimes we find that observing ourselves like this is not possible. Sometimes we're submerged in the crisis so fully that this suggestion is as realistic as asking a drowning person to stop and analyze the temperature of the water he or she is flailing around in. If and when our situation is blurred or confusing, we need someone else to help us make some sense out of it. Enlist the help of a therapist or clergyperson or seek out a support group if you need an outside perspective.

Understanding each of our belief systems and coping mechanisms, though sometimes painstakingly difficult, can be a crucial step toward establishing a more intimate relationship with our partner. We can love ourselves and our partner better, it turns out, when we know what's motivating our actions and attitudes.

Give Up Your Belief That Your Reaction to The Crisis is The Only Correct One

This suggestion is not easy for many of us. We seldom land in a crisis exclaiming, "Wow, now I have a chance to see how differently my husband responds. And maybe I'll even come to learn something from my significant other. And if I'm really lucky, I'll be psychologically and spiritually stretched when the one I love reacts in ways I don't understand." Instead, we typically see our partner's differences as threats to our security and we quickly instigate a power struggle. Rather than trying to understand, we try to convert him or her to our way of thinking.

Without trying to figure out who's right and who's wrong—who's getting an A+ and who's flunking out of Crisis 101—a simple acknowledgment that our own reaction is not the only appropriate one will open the door to resuming communication with our partner. Maybe your way is better; maybe your partner's is. Maybe both are fine. Maybe one legacy of this crisis will be that each of you revises certain beliefs that prove to be ineffective or irrational.

Forget these "maybes." Acknowledge that your ways of coping, though they may be your only means of staying afloat right now, your cherished life raft, are not necessarily the best means of survival for your partner.

When we're in the middle of an ongoing crisis, when we're exhausted, when we're expending huge amounts of energy just making it through each day, it's easy to get locked into polarized positions. The only way out of this lonely configuration is to take the crucial first step of giving up believing our own way is the only right way.

John and Mary, married over thirty years, have learned how to do this beautifully. They have been through the crisis of one teenaged daughter's pregnancy and giving up the baby girl for adoption, and another daughter's drug abuse. Mary explains, "I no longer try to get John to rail against the injustices of life when they happen. He processes his losses in fewer words and with less inner searching. But he does, in some way I can't fully understand, go on.

"I do see serenity in John's life. He admits mistakes. He gets on with life . . . . For a while I was not so serene in dealing with him because I kept on trying to make him cry as much as I do when something bad happens.

"I've been a slow learner, but finally I'm approaching him differently. Now when I'm upset I just ask him to listen to me. I tell him I don't want him to `fix' anything, or to see things the way I do, but that I simply need to tell him how I feel. Now that he knows I'm not trying to make him over, he's `with' me in his quiet, steady way."

Mary has found a way to be herself and to allow her husband to be himself. As for John, he's relieved: "I used to spend a lot of time trying to explain myself to Mary. She seemed determined to cast me as an insensitive male. I felt I had to defend myself. Some of the things we've been through, especially the crises with our daughters, hurt like hell. I looked at the kind of father I'd been and how I might have contributed to their problems. I did this quickly. This doesn't mean I feel it any less, but for me, there's nothing to be gained by dwelling on things. If I did, I'd start to lose sight of current problems. I respect Mary's way, but I need to *go on* not *talk on*."

Open Up And Continue a Dialogue with Your Partner

Most of us know how to disagree with our partner and present our own point of view. Few of us, however, know how to listen to our partner and how to be listened to without attempting to settle anything. Settle differences we must; however, our chances of resolving them increase greatly when we employ a seldom-used tool—dialogue.

The late psychologist Sydney Jourard, quoted in *How to Have a Perfect Marriage—With Your Present Mate* by Jess Lair, Ph.D., offers the clearest definition of dialogue we've found: "... dialogue is to speak your truth in response to the other person's truth, with no effort in a concealed way to lie or to con or to manipulate the other person to be in some way what he is not. It's speaking your truth and then waiting to hear the other person's truth, which you can never predict or control."

When we stop insisting our way of dealing with a crisis is the only way, we open our previously closed hearts and minds. We become ready to see our partner's reality. But after focusing entirely on our own perceptions, we won't suddenly awaken, automatically "knowing" what our partner is thinking and feeling. When we begin a dialogue, we stop guessing what he is thinking; we stop diagnosing her words or actions. We stop being know-it-alls and instead approach our partner wanting to hear his or her truth. In that loving climate, we also share our own truth.

Thus, in a dialogue we question only from a heartfelt desire to get to know our mate's point of view better. For our questioning to lead us to a deeper understanding of our partner, we need to be able to validate his reality. Validation does not mean that we agree. It does not mean that either of us is right or wrong. "Validation means that you communicate to your spouse that, if you were seeing things his or her way, standing on his or her platform, with his or her assumptions about things, then it would make sense and be reasonable to feel that way," as Dr. John Gottman and his co-authors explain in *A Couple's Guide to Communication*.

A couple in a crisis entering into a dialogue might sound like this:

She: I wish we had never had children. Losing Johnny was like losing a part of myself. I never want another child; I'm not sure when I'll feel like making love again even.

He: I'm longing for another child. I know we can't replace our son, but I want so much to have another baby together. And I'm scared right now that I'm losing you. I don't think I could bear that.

She: I hear you. I have no answers now. Hold me.

He: I love you.

In a dialogue we seek understanding, not harmony. Encased in our separate realities, we listen to, respect, validate, and care about each other. Our dialogue is frank, but not cruel. Such meaningful dialogue is hard to schedule when our spirits and energy are low, but it is worth finding the time for. Such dialogue has the power to diffuse even potentially explosive and terribly hurtful differences. In a crisis, dialogue is possible only when we're willing to set aside our notion that to be intimate we have to agree or at least pretend to agree.

Dialogue is defined as "interchange and discussion of ideas, especially when open and frank, as in seeking mutual understanding or harmony." That dictionary definition can come alive for us when we regularly decide to: (1) listen to our partner's viewpoint; (2) state our separate reality; and (3) validate our partner's right to his or her way of seeing things.

We enter into a dialogue to gather information and insight. What we do with our findings will vary. Sometimes our differences are intolerable. Sometimes they are inconsequential. Sometimes we need to address them. Sometimes they can be ignored. Our dialogue is a necessary first step toward helping us decide how best to handle them. The following story illustrates how dialogue can work.

We Talk and Talk—About Everything

Peggy and Stan have been married for thirty-three years. Peggy attributes the intimacy they share, in large part, to their commitment to each other, which they nurture by engaging in ongoing dialogue. Finding time and energy for such communication hasn't always been easy.

Peggy and Stan's five children range in age from eighteen to thirty-two. Their oldest son suffered near-fatal injuries in a motorcycle accident five years ago. They took care of him during the year he was going through physical rehabilitation. Their twenty-eight-year-old daughter, Deborah, recently divorced an abusive husband after a six-year marriage, during which Peggy and Stan periodically took her and her young son into their home when she'd flee his abuse. Six months ago, Terri, their youngest daughter, now eighteen, went through a rehabilitation program for drug and alcohol abuse.

In addition, last year, Stan, a high-level executive with an oil company, was laid off. Since then he's been working part-time as a consultant. Peggy, a talented potter, used to sell her unique, prize-winning bowls, mugs, and other pieces, bringing in sporadic pay which they used for luxuries or put into savings. Since Stan lost his job, she's had to quit doing pottery and has gone to work as a real estate agent. Still, their income has dropped substantially and they fear they may lose the rambling split-level contemporary house they helped construct when their children were small.

On the evening I spoke with Peggy (Stan was to be there too, but was out of town interviewing for a job), she related how she and Stan make it a priority to keep a dialogue going.

"Twenty years ago, when we were building this house ourselves and only had one part of it finished, we were all living in eight hundred square feet. That's when we started taking walks. We'd just walk away from the kids' commotion. Now, even with all of them away, we still take walks together. It seems to be the ideal time for us to talk.

"We talk and talk—about anything. Even though we know we might get angry and we might not be saying it in the right way, we still talk things out. We present what's real to each of us. But this isn't easy.

"When our children were growing up and we had some tough decisions to make that involved them, I learned to tell them, `Dad and I don't always agree—this is what we both think.' Then Stan and I would work out a compromise or decide on one way of handling a situation or the other. We wouldn't put each other down, but we'd be up-front about our differences. If we'd tried to put on a united front, one of us would have ended up seething underneath.

"I think we've been able to keep talking largely because we don't have to agree. We tried in our early years to change each other, but through therapy, Marriage Encounter, and Lifespring (a seminar that grew out of EST) and through a whole series of crises we've been through—I haven't mentioned nearly all of them—we've learned to be two independent people.

"Stan tried to share that concept with our daughter Deborah just before she got married. He took her aside and drew three circles to illustrate how a marriage works. `One represents you,' he told her. `One represents your husband-to-be. And the last one is your life together. That third circle can never be complete unless the first two are.'"

The latest crisis to test their ability to keep a dialogue going had just happened. Terri, the "baby" in the family, was in a recovery program, attending AA meetings and finishing her last month of high school, sober and making all A's and B's. Stan and Peggy felt immensely relieved. It looked as if their daughter had a good chance to make up for the year she'd fought drugs and alcohol.

Two weeks ago, however, Terri had moved out of the house and into her twenty-two year old boyfriend's apartment. Though Peggy viewed her decision as "dumb," she was trying to be philosophical about it. At least, she thought, her boyfriend was clean and sober. In fact she liked the boy since he had been supportive to Terri during her rehabilitation. However, Stan didn't see it this way—he was devastated.

"It's broken her father's heart," Peggy went on. "Stan said to me, `At this point I don't think I have a daughter.' I know how he feels—we're both Catholics. We don't approve and she is too young. But I had to speak to what Stan was expressing. In times past I would have let it go. But when he seemed to be disowning Terri, I told him how I'd felt rejected by my father when he let me know he would rather have had a son and how that rejection has stayed with me all my life.

"Last week, I told Stan, `You're doing something to Terri like my father did to me. You can't do that to Terri.' But he went ahead and told her anyway.

"A couple of days later we talked again. I told Stan that it's one thing not to like a person's actions but it's another to reject the person. I reminded him of the fair treatment he'd always shown his employees when one of them used bad judgment. I tried to point out that he could be in agony about what Terri was doing, that he could let her know he disapproved, but that he could not just disown this daughter he's crazy about. This time he listened.

"He and Terri went out for breakfast this morning and he told her he loved her, but not what she was doing.

"You have to present what's real," Peggy continued. "You have to say it and not fear it will damage your relationship. Stan does the same thing for me."

Peggy and Stan have learned that their intimacy depends on their right to have and to express different points of view. Their intimacy flourishes in an atmosphere in which they speak up when they see each other stepping out of the boundaries of acceptable, healthy behavior. When Peggy pointed out to Stan that he was, in effect, rejecting Terri, she was acting as a mirror for him, holding up unacceptable behavior saying, "I don't think you see this. Would you take a look at this behavior that seems to be hidden from your view?"

A key point not to be overlooked in their interaction is that Peggy did not insist Stan *had* to change. She did not threaten him or tell him how terrible he was. She simply told him what she saw and let him do what he thought was best.

If Stan had remained closed to Peggy's suggestion that he rethink his stance that he "no longer had a daughter"; if he had persisted in rejecting or even disowning Terri, how would Peggy have reacted? There are many negative options. She could have told Stan he was an unloving person no longer worthy of her love. She could have started throwing subtle or sarcastic barbs into their conversation, letting him know she was more spiritually evolved than he. She could have distanced herself from him, remaining silent yet projecting a stern disapproval of his faulty judgment.

Peggy says she and Stan resist such tactics, although they had done such things earlier in their marriage. Now they use dialogue. Even so, dialogue won't always save a relationship. In a worst-case scenario, if Stan had permanently written off their daughter and had shamed Terri or treated her cruelly for months or years, Peggy would have had to face that reality. She would have had to evaluate whether she wanted to remain married to someone whose behavior had gone beyond the limits of what she felt was acceptable.

As it turned out, the risk of a gentle confrontation, without insisting that Stan change, worked. Both still see Terri's live-in situation with her boyfriend differently. Stan is still angry, sad, and disappointed that Terri made this decision. But both are in touch with themselves and with the daughter they love.

"Stan and I allow each other to *be* what we are," Peggy concluded. "And," she laughs, "we've learned long ago we can't control each other or *anything*! You just *think* you can . . . . I don't think we ever get to nirvana in a marriage. It's just a day-by-day thing."

Telling our partner truthfully and lovingly how we feel, not what we think he or she wants to hear, is critical in a dialogue. We must be honest for this to work. Out of such dialogue trust is built and differences that must be settled can be approached as lovers and friends instead of strangers or enemies on opposing sides.

Not By Words Alone

Not long ago, on a three-hour flight, a forty-two-year-old aerospace engineer who sat next to me shared an obviously painful slice of his life. He cared for his wife deeply, he explained. She was experiencing a lot of pain over the death of her grown son from her previous marriage, a twenty-two-year-old, who six months earlier had been killed instantly in a car wreck after being hit head-on by a drunk driver.

"I've told her I'm right beside her. I've told her how much I care, but damn it, she puts me down because I don't know how to talk the way she wants me to—I'm sensitive, but I'm not the Phil Donahue-type articulate male she seems to expect. When I don't sound like a self-help book, a psychiatrist, or a talk show host, she doesn't seem to hear me."

This man was perplexed. He sounded puzzled and hurt. His story, like many Marilyn hears from clients, points out a flaw in some of our expectations. In order to open up and continue a dialogue with our partner, we need to respect our partner's uniqueness. Some men and women with a great capacity to be loving partners will never become highly articulate or comfortable with the vocabulary for expressing feelings. If we listen, these same partners often offer a solid comfort; their caring and insights

into love simply aren't conveyed with silver-tongued elo-
quence. But if we put down our partner because he or she
is not as verbally skilled as we are, or does not relish heart-
to-heart talks as much as we do, we may never move into
an intimate partnership.

The actions of a loving partner can speak as eloquently
as words. And there can be communication, even dialogue,
in silence once we've stopped trying to control our partner.
Poet Kahlil Gibran wrote:

> There are so many things
> in my heart that I want
> to say to you.
> I cannot say them.
> There is something cold in words while there is
> nothing cold in me.
> But you understand.
> You see me as no one
> else sees me.
> We both trust silence.

Back to the Dinosaurs

Remember the two dinosaurs on the Valentine card
discussed at the beginning of this chapter? When we give
up on trying to change a pink partner into a yellow one, the
prognosis for our relationship improves greatly. The good
news is that many of us will see our love grow and our level
of intimacy deepen if we acknowledge and allow our
differences.

Here we need to read the realistic fine print, too: *even
positive change is stressful.* If your partner had grown used to
your nagging and attempts to control, he or she may be
suspicious or puzzled if, during this crisis, you begin

showing respect for and interest in his or her separate reality. You may begin hearing things such as, "Why are you acting so understanding?"; "I thought you didn't want to make love for a while"; or, "I'd given up on you ever forgiving me."

Our partner's reactions may hurt as they serve as vivid reminders of how we were acting. And when our changes are still new and not yet habitual, our partner's resistance may tempt us to fall back into familiar bad patterns of relating. When we regress, as we all will, we can forgive ourselves. Our progress can be measured, not by our perfection, but by our ongoing dedication to allowing our partner's differences and respecting him or her as a separate entity.

"We select with astonishing precision the other person who can teach us what we need to know to be a more whole human being," write Drs. Thomas P. Malone and Patrick T. Malone in *The Art of Intimacy*. In a crisis, many of us are forced into learning new perspectives from our partner. Sometimes in the process, we begin to learn the art of intimacy as we discover how to honor not only our own perceptions but also those of our partner. And sometimes the synergy of our two separate views lovingly allowed and communicated ends up making us stronger both together and separately. For two people who nurture each other's uniqueness can better face what happens next.

Reflection Opportunities

1. Have you accepted your partner for who he or she is or do you still want a like-minded clone? Imagine for a moment that changing your partner was possible. How would life be better? (One woman answered, "If Wayne

were still grieving as much as I am, I'd have someone to cry with and I wouldn't feel so alone in my sadness.") Since we can't ever succeed in forcing change in a partner, erase that scene. Now picture some words you could use simply to convey your reality to your mate, demanding no altering of his or her reality. ("I feel as though I'm dragging my feet. You're getting on with life, but I can't just yet. Can you understand?")

2. Are you endeavoring to comfort your partner and respect that he or she is different? If you're having trouble, what's stopping you? Are friends or relatives judging your partner and influencing your attitudes? Did your parents put down each other's realities?

3. Are you prepared for the hard work of breaking old patterns of relating? How might your relationship improve if you persist in pursuing this higher level of loving? Keep in mind some possible rewards to help you persevere. Might your lovemaking warm up? Would you get your best friend back? Would your partner start listening attentively again? Would you feel better about yourself?

Chapter 9

Facing Guilt,
Finding Self-Forgiveness

To err is human, to forgive divine.
Alexander Pope

A favorite bumper sticker of mine says simply, "FIRST THINGS FIRST."
When we believe that something we did or failed to do helped cause the crisis we're in, one of the first things we need to do is to begin forgiving ourselves. Yet many of us procrastinate, putting forgiveness at the bottom of our "to do" list. We may reason that to take time out to process our guilt would make us feel even guiltier. After all, if we helped cause a crisis, shouldn't we focus exclusively on repairing the damage, rather than on forgiving ourselves?

The problem with pushing aside our guilt is that it stays inside us, growing instead of shrinking. So long as we carry it around, it weighs on our hearts and souls. It wears us out. Even before we get out of bed in the morning, we're exhausted. So long as we hold on to our guilt, we have an excuse for not functioning fully, for putting our lives and our relationships on hold. So long as we feel guilty, we may feel unworthy of our partner's love and respect, or of our own love and respect.

Until we enter into the process of unloading our guilt and forgiving ourselves, we're not very good company. We're apt to make ourselves and our partner miserable. To extricate ourselves from guilt, we have to make a clean break, choosing forgiveness.

In this chapter we'll look first at some barriers to self-forgiveness and then at the process of forgiveness. What do you wish you could go back and undo? In what way do you suspect you failed, messed up, or made a mistake that has contributed to this crisis?

Until you ask yourself this directly, your guilt may be a vague ghostly presence roaming somewhere just beneath your consciousness. Now by identifying it more specifically, it may flash in your mind like a neon marquee, announcing your star status in a role you wished you'd never played: I drank too much; I was a workaholic who neglected my family; I was careless even when I knew better; I used credit cards like I was made of money; I was preoccupied and didn't see what was going on until it was too late; I wouldn't quit smoking even when my husband kept begging me to stop.

The pain we feel when we first pinpoint our guilt may be so sharp that we're tempted to stop the forgiveness process even before we plunge in. But the apparent never-ending quality of the pain we feel when we start to forgive ourselves is not real. What is real, many of us have discovered, is that once we go through the forgiveness process we feel like a prisoner finally released from a dark cell. Maybe we'll never totally forget what we did, especially if we hurt someone very badly, but, forgiven by ourselves, we can go on living and loving ourselves, our partner, and others. The pain subsides as we run toward our guilt, not away from it.

As you begin to turn and face your guilt, remember to go easy on yourself. This is difficult and is not something you should rush into the day after the tragedy has occurred. You'll know when the time is right. If the time has come, let's begin by taking a look at some barriers that may, if not understood, block your way.

Regret

Regret is either a barrier in the way of self-forgiveness, or a bridge over to it, depending on your view. Buddhist teachings shed gentle light on regret, pointing out that all wrongdoings originate in the mind and occur because of our lack of "mindfulness." In other words, at some point we were not all there; we were not fully living in the present in a healthy, enlightened way. We made a mistake in the past because for an instant or for years, our attention wandered or our judgment was faulty, and now, we are filled with regret.

However, regret can compound our error if we let it rob us of living in the here and now. As we face our error, we can learn to take our regret and use it in a constructive way.

Buddhist monk Thich Nhat Hanh, explains it this way in *Our Appointment with Life: The Buddha's Teaching on Living in the Present*: "When we know that something we have said or done has caused harm, we may give rise to a mind of repentance, vowing that in the future we will not repeat the same mistake. In this case, our feeling of regret has a wholesome effect. If on the other hand, the feeling of regret continues to disturb us, making it impossible for us to concentrate on anything else, taking all the peace and joy out of our lives, then that feeling of regret has an unwholesome effect."

Buddhist teachings remind us that our minds can transform the present, no matter what our past mistake was. What are you learning as you look back at your error? How will you live differently in light of it? How will your regret make you more the person you want to be now?

Regret can make us stronger, better able to love ourselves, our friends, our mate, our world at large. It becomes constructive when we allow it to be our teacher instead of our tormentor. When regret begins to pull us into a black hole, we can fight back, refusing to obsess on our error, focusing instead on learning its lessons.

Tom and Cynthia's story is illustrative. In trying to finish an apartment building exactly on schedule, Tom had worked for twenty consecutive twelve-hour days and on the last day had a horrible accident that left him paralyzed from the waist down. If only she'd insisted he get some rest, Cynthia reasoned, he would never have been in the awful accident. She couldn't stop thinking that if only she had nagged him more to take a day off, he would not have been hurt. Needless to say, her regrets did neither of them any good. One lesson she learned from her regret is to be sure to take care of herself despite all the care she must give Tom. Another is that she can't control the choices her husband makes. It was Tom's responsibility to decide when to work and when to rest, not Cynthia's.

Judging Ourselves "Unforgivable"

In its classified ads, the *Galveston Daily News* features a section called "In Memoriam." There, relatives of a loved one who has died publish a photograph of the one they miss and remember him or her with little poems and words of affection. On the second anniversary of her son's death, one mother wrote, "I'm sorry for what I could not do, things that you had asked me to, but life's weaknesses are so strong . . . "

I do not know what this mother is so sorry about or how the handsome twenty-year-old with the mustache and piercing dark eyes died, but her words, in their regret, haunt me. Many of us, at one time or another, did or did not do something that leads us now to agonize about our mistake. And sometimes we pronounce ourselves unforgivable.

When we hurt someone because we were negligent or preoccupied; when our carelessness, greed, anger, or impaired thinking due to drugs or alcohol caused pain, even death, we may not see how we could ever be worthy of forgiveness.

Helga had to make a quick dash to the supermarket for butter and parsley, the two ingredients she needed to finish preparing a gourmet dinner for guests who were due to arrive in less than two hours. The store was just three blocks from her house. Just this once, when Helga put two-year-old Tracy in the car, she didn't fasten her own seat belt or Tracy's car seat. When a fast-moving pickup truck ran a red light, impacting Helga's van on the side where Tracy sat, Tracy was thrown onto the pavement and killed instantly. Helga suffered massive cuts and bruises and a broken leg, but is recovering and wondering how she could have been so negligent. How will she ever go on living with her guilt and without her precious daughter?

In situations like this, regret never completely subsides. It stays forever in a corner of our hearts. We cannot recall that moment. We cannot go back and rewrite our life script. But we can forgive ourselves and go on with loving ourselves and our partners as best we can.

Christian theologian and author Dr. Lewis B. Smedes

offers this compassionate comfort in *Forgive & Forget: Healing the Hurts We Don't Deserve*: "We do not have to be bad persons to do bad things. If only bad people did bad things to other people we would live in a pretty good world. We hurt people by our bungling as much as we do by our vices.

"And the more decent we are the more acutely we feel our pain for the unfair hurts we caused. Our pain becomes our hate. *The pain we cause other people becomes the hate we feel for ourselves. For having done them wrong.* We judge, we convict, and we sentence ourselves. Mostly in secret."

If you are judging yourself so harshly that you feel unworthy of forgiveness, count the cost of your verdict. The past can't be changed, but you can go on in the present, sadder, wiser, and more sensitive to other people. We can have a life even after we did or failed to do something that caused another great pain, injury, even death. We find the day-by-day courage to keep on living by entering into the process of forgiving ourselves.

Exaggerating Our Faults

Sometimes we exaggerate the role we played in causing a crisis in order to lessen our feelings of helplessness. Marge wishes she hadn't been such a permissive parent and that she hadn't taken over most of the parenting while her husband Peter sat passively on the sidelines. She is sure her laid-back style, coupled with Peter's detachment damaged their daughter Eileen's self esteem and pushed her into using drugs.

We have heard others express sentiments such as: "I should have left for work a half-hour earlier and then the accident wouldn't have happened"; "God is punishing me now, keeping me and my wife from having a baby because years ago I encouraged my girlfriend to get an abortion";

"If I had chosen that other location for my business we'd never have gone bankrupt"; or, "If I hadn't taken that promotion and made my son move away from his friends, he'd never have turned to alcohol."

Often we try to trace the cause of a crisis directly to something we did or did not do. For many of us, the anxiety of guilt is easier to live with than the anxiety of not knowing. At least, when we blame ourselves, we can preserve our belief that the world is an orderly place. We can think, my action (or inaction) made this happen.

In truth, it's often impossible to assess whether or not our behaving differently would have resulted in a happier outcome; sometimes we simply can't know. However, cause and effect comforts us. We'd rather feel guilty than not in control.

When we do this, our faults take on a magnitude they don't deserve. When we are sorry about some past action or attitude, when we wish we'd acted differently, we need forgiveness, but at the same time, we need a sense of realism about the size of our roles. If we played a bit part in causing a crisis, we can own that part. If we starred in the drama solo, causing almost all the problems we now face, we should acknowledge our larger role.

The point is, the more realistically we face our large or small mistakes the easier it is to forgive ourselves. One way to check our reality base is to ask ourselves: if a friend of mine made the same error, how would I "see" that mistake? How might I offer comfort, yet not excuse or minimize what my friend did? What would I say to that person I love? Using that same friendly yardstick, we can put our own faults into better perspective.

The Forgiveness Process

The theme of how to crawl out from under guilt and back into the sunshine of living in the present, cleansed and forgiven is explored in the Vedic Scriptures of Hinduism, in the Eightfold Path of Buddhism, in the philosophy of the Tao, and in both the Old and New Testaments of the Bible. Many of us are acquainted with these spiritual principles. Some of us have rediscovered them in twelve-step programs.

But what if "spirituality" is not a part of your life? A woman who was on TV promoting a book she'd just written told Phil Donahue that she'd been clean for eight years after battling a cocaine addiction. But, she explained, she could not enter a twelve-step program, which emphasizes turning over problems to a Higher Power, because she has always been and will always be a confirmed atheist.

Even if we feel the same way, even if not believing in a Higher Power is at the core of our belief system, we can make use of the forgiveness process. Though the forgiveness process includes calling on a Higher Power in Alcoholics Anonymous and other twelve-step programs, it's often noted that those who don't believe in a Higher Power in a religious sense can think of *God* as *Good Orderly Direction*. In other words, you can call on the deepest, most loving, sensible parts of yourself. Because forgiveness asks so much of us, we need all the help we can get, if not from a Higher Power then from the highest part of ourselves.

The forgiveness process is simple yet not easy. We step into it by acknowledging that we are not perfect and that we are powerless to go back and relive the moment or years that contributed to the crisis.

Since we cannot by our own control erase our mistakes, we must stop trying to and instead focus on forgiving ourselves. The process involves four steps: (1) confess our wrongdoing to ourself; (2) confess it to our Higher Power, however we define it; (3) confess it to another person; and (4) make amends whenever possible. (These are adaptations of step 5 and 9 in the twelve-step process of AA.)

In the first step—confessing our wrongdoing to ourself—we need to get very specific. Instead of diverting our eyes from our error, we need to look directly at it, seeing it clearly and precisely. Instead of saying, "I was a bad parent," we need to specify: "I didn't take time to listen to her"; "I ignored all the symptoms of drug abuse when they were right there under my nose"; "I was more interested in his grades than in him."

At this point when we actually see our mistakes, our remorse may be overpowering. How could we have been so blind? How could we have been so careless? Why did we allow a destructive pattern to build over the years?

As we make our confession to ourselves, it helps to say "I did this and I'm sorry" instead of slipping into "I did this and I'm bad." Old scripts from childhood—experiences with stern parents who tagged us "bad" every time we made a mistake, or hellfire-and-brimstone sermons we heard growing up—may predispose us to pronounce ourselves all bad because we did something wrong.

When we feel the guilt of our mistake without shaming ourselves for being bad people, our self esteem grows through confession. It takes courage to forgive ourselves. It requires loving the people around us more than we love our guilt. By forgiving ourselves, we begin to take the spotlight off ourselves. We get ready to resume our lives without the self-centered preoccupation of guilt. By facing our mistake, we consider ourselves worthy of love.

In the second step, we confess the error to our Higher Power. Some of us believe God resides within us. Others simply try to tap into the deepest, strongest part of ourselves. Some see God through the writings and traditions of a particular religion. Others commune with a Higher Power not defined by a specific creed.

Sometimes, when we're in need of forgiveness, even if we've never had a spiritual hunger before, a desire for help from some source beyond our individual strength arises. We can follow that desire without interrupting the forgiveness process. As one woman who needed forgiveness, yet found herself wondering if she should wait until she was "more religious," said, "It worked for me to go ahead and seek my God, then choose a religion."

To insist we need to choose a church or decide on a framework of religious belief before we forgive ourselves is counterproductive and distracts us from the process. We don't need a Ph.D. in religion to utilize the forgiveness process. Later there will be time to sort out our beliefs. Later we can process some of the hurts we may have incurred growing up in a rigid religious atmosphere. Later we can grieve our lack of spiritual training. But during a crisis, when we're weighted down with guilt, we're fooling ourselves if we delay forgiving ourselves until we fully understand our Higher Power.

We don't have to memorize a passage of scripture to turn to our Higher Power in confession. We don't have to be Orthodox Jews. We don't have to be enlightened Buddhists. We don't have to attend Catholic Mass. We don't have to *do* anything. Any way we phrase it is fine; we simply state what we did and then say, "I'm sorry."

We can make our confession to our Higher Power anyplace. Some people prefer the formality of a church setting. Some make their confession snuggled under the covers in bed. Others hike into the woods and sit beside a serene blue lake. Whatever works for you is fine.

In the third step, you confess your wrong to another human being. Look for someone you trust, someone who will not repeat your story, but will hold it in deepest confidence. Look for a person who will listen without judging, without minimizing your mistake, without preaching or offering an abundance of advice. That person may be a therapist, a minister, rabbi, priest, or other spiritual adviser; a sponsor in a twelve-step program, a friend, a relative, or your partner. Should you pick someone who seemed trustworthy but was not, someone you're not comfortable with, if something isn't quite right—even if you can't put your finger on what it is—search for someone else.

Going ahead with this step is crucial. It's tempting to procrastinate before taking it because it's an exercise in true humility. But when we keep silent, our soul yearns for closure; when we disclose some dark secret or some act we deeply regret, we feel our sense of self worth grow.

As in the second step, you don't need to worry about being eloquent; you don't have to make a "perfect" confession. You simply tell another person what you're feeling so bad about.

Confession to another is for our own benefit. We find, in this person-to-person revelation, a serenity. After dropping our masks, after admitting we have a shadowy side, we feel whole. When we let someone else know what we're sorry about—what we did—we're smashing any remaining walls of denial.

In the fourth step we make amends for our mistake if possible. Who was hurt by our action or inaction? Are they available to talk with? Will we make amends by saying something to them or by simply behaving in a loving way toward them now? Don't overlook yourself as you ask these questions. Do you need to make amends for not loving or taking care of yourself?

In making amends, you are the one who decides what is appropriate. If you have hurt someone, you may at first think you need to spell out, blow by blow, exactly what you did. I once alienated someone very close to me by doing this. This loved one was not ready to hear my confession. My attempt to make amends by disclosing a violation of privacy caused a rift instead of healing. Healing is taking place only now, as I keep treating this individual with respect.

Sometimes a direct apology or making payment or restitution, is appropriate. If we put off something we promised, we can do it now and apologize for our delay. If we owe money, we can set up a payment schedule. If we neglected or abused ourselves physically we can begin to adopt a healthier lifestyle. If we let our own needs slide in favor of taking care of everybody else, we can determine to strike a better balance.

Several years ago, weighted down with a heavy personal crisis, I let some professional obligations slide. Last year I decided to write a letter to a publisher apologizing for not responding to a request I'd ignored during the crisis. In my letter I didn't make excuses for myself. I told them the nature of my crisis and let them know I'd "fallen apart," not keeping up with my responsibilities during this period. I asked if I could do anything, at this late date, to fulfill their request.

Their letter back to me was so kind, so loving that I cried reading it. The person responding had just gone through a similar crisis. She understood. She forgave me. Their request that I revise a booklet I'd written some years before was no longer relevant now. But they were happy to be back in touch. Since I had moved several times, they had lost track of me and now could send along a royalty check they'd been holding.

Making amends is not always magic. But when we carefully consider our options and follow through with a phone call, letter, conversation, repayment, or an improved way of behaving, we can close that part of our life. Like clearing a file on a computer disk, the data is no longer cluttering our minds and keeping us from functioning fully in the present.

When we helped cause a crisis, when we treat the ones we love poorly during one, when we practice self-neglect, or any time we've made a mistake serious enough that it's filling us with guilt, we need to forgive ourselves and take this last difficult step.

Facing Guilt, Finding Forgiveness Together

Facing guilt and forgiving ourselves can lead to renewed intimacy and a new lease on life, even when all hell has broken loose. Here's a story that demonstrates this.

Back in the mid-1980s, things were going well for Deborah and Jeff, an energetic couple in their early thirties. By working together, they'd built a profitable aluminum-siding business. Deborah was general office manager and bookkeeper. Jeff supervised and scheduled jobs and sometimes worked on projects himself. By the end of their second year, their teamwork and hard work had paid off. The company earnings were a half-million dollars a year with a comfortable margin of profit. As their good reputation grew and the economy flourished, their continued success seemed certain, which led them to start thinking that they could afford a nicer house.

Six months later, they'd moved out of their cramped 1,000-square-foot home and into a sprawling 3,500-square-foot, two-story, brick "mini-mansion" as Deborah described it. Their eight- and ten-year-old sons now had separate rooms, and Deborah and Jeff had a lovely master bedroom suite in an opposite wing of the house, all to themselves. But one thing was missing.

Set beside a large lake, their home had a boat slip. Deborah and Jeff decided they wanted a boat, one they could fish from and take the kids waterskiing in. They started collecting brochures from local boat dealers and before long had decided on a $20,000, twenty-four-foot cabin cruiser with twin V-8 engines.

Deborah tells the rest of their story. "Jeff said this boat was the one he'd been wanting all his life. And I wanted it too. But the way we figured our budget, we'd have to lay off an employee to afford it. We decided to fire a man we'd lured away from another company. He was a great foreman, but we were paying him a large salary and we figured that, by working harder ourselves, we could get by without him.

"We gave him notice and bought the boat. And our business began to go downhill. Finally, the company went under.

"We knew that a recent slump in the economy had contributed, but we didn't analyze much beyond that at first. We were busy closing down the business and filing for bankruptcy.

"We had to walk away from our beautiful home. We moved to the country into a pathetic little house. We had been on our way to the top, we thought, but we ended up in a place where the plumbing didn't even work. I had to pour a bucket of water into the toilet to make it flush. And we were afraid to tell our landlord because we had gotten a month behind, even on our $300-a-month rent.

"Jeff and I worked at various jobs just to stay alive. I raised chickens. He fished. Finally, we found work together in another state, running an aluminum-siding business, not ours, but at least we were back into something we both were familiar with.

"I don't remember exactly when during that miserable period I admitted to myself that my greed had played a part in our failure. By the time I brought this up to Jeff, he was already struggling with the same guilt. We could deal with the bad-luck part—the hard economic times—more easily than the part we both had played in contributing to our situation. We felt bad about our greed. The man we fired was the only person we'd ever walked on to get ahead.

"As we talked this over, I can't begin to describe the anger we felt, the fact that *we* did this. Nobody did it to us. But once we admitted our mistakes we went on from there. It took time to think this through and see where we went wrong. Our spiritual error was the one we had to face. That's what we felt guilty about."

A couple of years after their business folded, Deborah and Jeff decided to write the employee they fired and ask his forgiveness. "That was a tough one," Deborah remembers. "I couldn't believe it, but he called us up and told us he forgave us. He had never even known we'd let him go for the reasons we did and he forgave us anyway.

"It had been easy for us to know we should get in touch with him, but actually doing it—finally taking action—was hard. But when we did, we felt so relieved. It was as if a weight had been taken off our chests."

Recently, Deborah and Jeff have had to face another crisis. Two months ago they found out that their older son, Chris, now sixteen, has Hodgkins disease. The prognosis for his recovery is good, but his chemotherapy and the interruption of his junior year, plus massive medical bills, have put a strain on their time, emotions, and budget. And in addition, their son, in denial about his illness, is lashing out at Deborah and Jeff. They're looking around for a therapist to treat Chris or the entire family. At this writing, Chris is refusing any help and blaming his parents for his pain.

Though upset, Deborah nevertheless feels sure she and Jeff would not be getting through this crisis as well as they are without the lessons from that earlier crisis. "We became stronger people through acknowledging our weakness," she reflects.

"Our trust grew a lot when we admitted our mistakes to each other. I could never replace this trust we have. I couldn't go into the store and buy it. It's rare. You can start over with physical objects. You can't keep starting over with people."

"A deep love held us together during that financial disaster," said Jeff. "We have a `marriage' not an `arrangement.' A lot of couples we know think they might be in love but when things get bad they're not so sure. A marriage bonds two people together to become one. You don't split that oneness. Things are pretty tough now. But there's no question that we'll get through this together."

After saying that we need to be realistic about our guilt and see it clearly, we'll amend that slightly. When we forgive ourselves, even if in our shortsightedness we picked out the "wrong" mistake, even if we see later that our mistake was something entirely different, the forgiveness process works anyway.

Attitude seems to count even more than accuracy. By honestly facing ourselves, as best we can at the time, we often peel away another layer, getting deeper into the truth of who we are. One woman's story illustrates how this works.

Maureen, age fifty and a member of the so-called "sandwich generation," remembers a crisis time in which she became responsible for putting her father in a nursing home. Her eighty-year-old mother had been caring for him at home for years. But eventually, as Parkinson's disease made him progressively weaker, he became totally bedridden. Late one night her mother had been rushed to the hospital in a state of "acute exhaustion."

It fell to Maureen, during a two-week annual vacation her company let her take during this emergency, to do the persuading, to make the arrangements, in short, "to push my mother into going ahead with making the change so at least her health would not fail."

Maureen found a suitable nursing home for her father and helped him get situated, but months later, after she'd driven six hundred miles back home to her husband, two teenaged daughters, and job, she felt guilty. She admitted she might have made a mistake. Maybe in-home nurses would have worked; maybe something else would have worked, she kept thinking.

Finally after agonizing over all this she forgave herself for "rushing my parents into this decision" and was ready to help move her father back home if that proved to be best. As it turned out, both her father and mother adjusted relatively well to the new situation. "It seems to be the only workable thing at this point in our lives," her mother assured Maureen over the phone.

Maureen processed her feelings about all this with her husband—first the guilt, then the admission to herself that perhaps she'd pushed her mother into making a wrong decision, then the relief that everything turned out better than she'd imagined.

The surprise in the process—the bonus—for Maureen was that she discovered some deeper truths about herself. "I see now that often I have trouble making decisions. And that almost every time I make a major one, I go back and second-guess what I do. And often I feel guilty about any decision I make! It's as if decision making itself is evil.

"Somehow all this came to light after this particular crisis. I had to become a `general,' so to speak. I *had* to take command of the situation because no one else was available. At first I thought this was wrong, but later I learned that the biggest mistake can be *not* making a decision.

"The payoff for my marriage is that now I see that I often asked my husband to make decisions, then would blame him when things went wrong. Now I'm facing my indecisiveness and deciding to do something about it. My family is full of `I wonder if I should have' and `maybe it would have been better if we had' members. I just let my membership in that club lapse, for good!"

"The Holy Spirit comes to set the whole house of our soul in order," wrote Thomas Merton in *The New Man.* When we face our mistakes, we see not just imaginary "sins" or the surface mistakes we obsess on and feel guilty about; sometimes we're given a guided tour of the musty basements and cobwebbed attics, out-of-the-way parts of ourselves we haven't seen before.

The freedom and self-knowledge gained by facing our mistakes and submitting to the rigorous process of self-forgiveness are expressed in these lines of a Buddhist gatha:

After repentance, my heart is light
like the cloud floating free in the sky.

Reflection Opportunities

1. Write out all the reasons why you feel guilty, listing every minor and major criticism that you berate yourself with, making each as concrete and specific as possible. Our "should've, must've, wished-I-would've" statements range in intensity, but it is important to articulate them and see them written out in front of us. It helps to give these dreaded thoughts form and substance so we can begin to take hold of them, not vice versa. What is the most painful thought that you face? What does the pain feel like? Can you describe it to a trusted friend?

2. What are some barriers that block your way to forgiving yourself? Does regret block your progress? Do you over exaggerate your faults? Do you overblame yourself for every aspect of the crisis? Do you judge yourself completely and attach a negative label to yourself? Do you overgeneralize and believe you are bad at the very core of your being?

3. Have you made a decision to forgive yourself? At what stage are you in the forgiveness process? Have you confessed your wrongdoings to yourself? To your Higher Power? To a trusted other person? Have you made amends when possible?

4. What rewards do you anticipate could come out of the forgiveness process? How could the outcome be worth all the pain? What's in it for you? That is, how can self-forgiveness benefit you? Benefit your partner?

Chapter 10

From "How Could You?" to "I Love You Anyway"

Do you want to learn forgiveness? Then whom can you forgive more completely than your partner?
  Gayle and Hugh Prather

How many couples can you think of who cherish and respect each other and who forgive each other when necessary? Those who have been together less than six months don't count. Their adoration is new passion, not ongoing I-know-you-and-I'm-still-sticking-around love.

Besides those shiny new relationships, who comes to mind? Perhaps an aunt and uncle, who wrote love letters to each other during World War II and who today, in retirement, hold hands and hold each other dear after decades of ups and downs, inspire you. Perhaps a friend of yours is in a relationship in which the two of them respect each other's realities and forgive each other's mistakes from time to time. Perhaps you and your mate desire and often succeed in making yours that solid rock of a relationship.

Most of us, when asked that question, don't find dozens of examples flooding our minds. When we're blaming our partner and we want to forgive and get back to the business of loving him or her, we have only a handful of role models.

The most common attitude Marilyn sees when couples initially enter therapy is "two people coming in with one person to blame—the other one. Often both are eloquent and articulate about each other's faults. Their communication skills shine in this area. Most likely they've practiced their complaints about their partners so many times to themselves and to their friends that they've got them down pat. Seeing ourselves and owning our own responsibility—that comes harder to most of us." Atlanta psychiatrist and author Patrick T. Malone, M.D., adds, "Most people live with each other in a marriage with these attitudes—It's your fault and I blame you. I accuse you. I judge you."

Since therapists usually see couples whose relationships are causing some degree of pain, their professional opinions may not reflect the way things are for couples in general. But we suspect these observations, in varying degrees, hold true for the majority of ongoing couple relationships. Even when our relationship is a loving one, especially in a crisis, the temptation to blame the most significant person in our life—our partner—is great.

In this chapter we won't be examining the problem of habitually blaming a partner, of reaching for blame as easily as we might reach for aspirin. If you find that in general you or your partner rely on blame too much and too often, therapy can help you learn how to break this destructive habit. And simply admitting it is a crucial first step.

Here, however, we focus on the tendency many of us have to blame our partner *in the wake of a crisis*. This blame is often based on reality. Our partner really did do something to hurt us or change our lives in some negative way.

Through a mistake or error, deliberate or unintentional, our partner helped bring on the crisis we're in.

What if our wife were going thirty miles per hour over the speed limit when she lost control of the car, hit a tree, and injured us so badly we'll be hobbling around with a cane the rest of our life? What if our husband smoked three packs of cigarettes a day and now has lung cancer and emphysema and we must care for him because he wouldn't care for himself enough to stop? What if our mate signed a two-year lease on an office before she knew her new business would succeed and now that it's folded, we're stuck with one more year of high monthly payments? What if our spouse left a loaded gun in a drawer and our five-year-old son found it and shot himself to death?

These "what ifs" could go on and on. In many crises, our partner made a big or little mistake and now the error is affecting our lives and threatening our relationship. If you think your partner did or failed to do something that contributed to your current crisis, the first thing to do is be specific. What, exactly, happened?

While there is usually truth in our perceptions—our partner made a serious error, or at the least one significant enough to change our lives for the worse—often we focus exclusively on that one error. We see only that mistake, forgetting temporarily that our partner is as complex a human being as we are, full of both strengths and weaknesses. Our partner instead becomes the dummy who took away our financial security, the reckless driver who caused our disability, or the careless monster who killed our son. We may obsessively replay what our partner did or did not do over and over in our minds, and so long as blame is blaring in our consciousness, it drowns out the deeper pain of a crisis.

By blaming we numb the deep pain of a loss. By blaming we don't get around to making the tremendous or troubling adjustments a crisis calls for. In using blame to mask our feelings, blaming our partner can become our drug of choice.

It's a tempting drug. So long as we blame our partner, we're "one up." We can, godlike, look down on our lover, asserting subtly or adamantly that *we* would never, could never, have been so stupid, careless, insensitive, or something equally horrible, as he or she was.

As we acquire a taste for this position of superiority, we imagine that we can manipulate our partner from our morally superior position. As we feel holier, our partner appears more evil. We're wearing the white hat and he or she's got the black one on. The only problem with this tactic is that it never works, at least not for long.

Even if we truly believe our partner is unforgivable; even if we decide not to invite him or her back into our lives, we only make ourselves suffer by focusing on our resentment. Holding on to it causes us anxiety, stress, and feelings of anger that can swell into uncontrollable rage. If resentment remains unresolved, if we continue blaming our partner, we may suffer serious physical and emotional consequences. Prolonged resentment can even create life-threatening depression.

Blaming our partner may give us temporary relief. Blaming our partner may seem to put us in a loftier position. But we solve nothing by persisting in blame. And we risk a lot—our health, and of course, any possibility of intimacy.

If you find yourself continuing to blame your partner, it may help to ask yourself, Couldn't I have made an equally stupid mistake? Haven't I had lapses in judgment or sensitivity? Haven't I been careless at times, but perhaps lucky enough to escape serious consequences? Most of us can think of near misses or almosts that happened to us and could have had devastating results. We left the gas on but the house didn't burn down. We were speeding but all we got was a ticket. We worked too hard and too long but we ended up with the flu instead of a lifelong disability.

Such self-questioning reminds us of our own humanity and makes it easier to stop our incessant judging. And once we stop judging and blaming, we can start to hold our partner accountable. We can ask our partner questions, discuss the crisis and his part in it, and express our feelings about that participation.

When our partner sees that we're attempting to let go of blame, often he will begin to trust us enough to talk about his mistake, to open up about the anguish and shame she's feeling. If you want to try to forgive your partner, if you're going to stay in this relationship, hearing your partner's regrets and listening to his or her reality is a crucial step toward restoring intimacy.

What if Your Partner Denies Responsibility?

We may find it harder to forgive our partner if he or she is not fully aware of a mistake. When our partner denies responsibility for something that clearly caused us pain, that denial can take many forms. Sometimes she may pretend the crisis isn't happening. Sometimes he may admit he had a part in causing a crisis, but may minimize his action or be unwilling to acknowledge its severity. Other times she may blame somebody else entirely. Sometimes he may attack us, becoming angry and irritable, projecting the blame on us, thus avoiding dealing with the real issue. Sometimes she changes the subject when we attempt to discuss the crisis and thus avoids dealing directly with it altogether.

Sometimes the two of us simply see an event differently when there is no clear-cut way to interpret it. For instance, when a business fails, one person may have seen the other's spending habits as too lavish while the "big spender" insists the business would have gone under anyway due to a sluggish economy.

Can we forgive a partner mired in denial? Can we forgive a partner who sees a situation in a different light than we do? Do we have to wait until he or she owns responsibility for a mistake?

Each of us will have to weigh those questions carefully. Forgiving someone who has not admitted his or her real part in a crisis is loving above and beyond most of our natural capabilities. Theoretically, however, it doesn't matter whether our partner realizes what he or she has done. As Dr. Lewis Smedes writes in *Forgive & Forget*, "If the people you forgive want to stay where they are, let them. You can make a solo flight to freedom."

Most of us would prefer taking that flight together. Yet, we forgive our mate as much for ourselves as for him or her. For to forgive our partner, even if he or she is not yet aware of the error or sees it differently, is to be able to go on with our own life, out from under the bitterness of blame. We simply cannot live happily and healthily with a person we cannot forgive.

One woman, an artist, related how her husband had chosen to take an exciting career promotion, which kept him away Monday through Friday every week for two years, during a time when their children were small. Looking back, she's sorry she encouraged him to take the position and she felt it necessary to forgive him for "his selfishness; neither of us were thinking of our children." She thinks their middle son felt neglected during that period and that he turned rebellious later in part because his father saw so little of him for several crucial preteen years.

Her husband disagrees, refusing to see his decision as "bad." Who's right? Who's wrong? Both their views no doubt have some validity. But this woman found peace with herself and left behind some bitter feelings about that period by forgiving her husband for an error he doesn't believe he made.

"He's a loving person with the same framework of values I have. And he was a pretty good parent, but in my opinion he was just blind in this area," she says. "If he *never* admitted a mistake, I'd see this differently. But by and large he's realistic about himself. This time and on a few other occasions, we just did not interpret the ramifications of a choice anywhere close to the same way."

The Need to Express Anger

Part of the difficulty in forgiving our spouse is that we may be angry about his or her role and afraid of expressing that emotion. But we do need to express our anger as part of the forgiveness process.

When we're angry about a crisis, expressing that anger is threatening. We're already in a vulnerable state due to the crisis and to risk anger is very scary. Many of us believe that anger is wrong or bad and if we express it our loved ones will abandon us.

Maybe our parents implied that anger was one of the seven deadly sins by banishing us to our room or abandoning us emotionally when we got angry. "I know you don't really feel like that!"; "Don't ever talk like that to me again";

"How dare you raise your voice"; "Nice girls don't get angry." Sentences like these, uttered by parents and other authority figures when we were growing up, taught us to suppress our anger.

Most of us have never seen the healthy expression of anger modeled. As one woman explained, "In my family we had dreadful silences for weeks, but no one ever shouted. In my husband's home they screamed, yelled, carried on, and the next day all the knives were hidden for fear they'd be used in one of his dad's alcoholic rages. We haven't seen people talk out angry feelings to resolution. If I'd had lots of practice at showing healthy anger, I might, just might, be able to do it now in this crisis."

Practice might have helped her. But even if we grew up in settings in which anger was expressed in a healthy way, when in the stressful situation of a crisis, we regress to some very primitive beliefs and we act on them. Regression is why we sometimes resemble two-year-old kids when in a crisis. We pout, we pitch tantrums, we lash out, we blame—most of which is counterproductive.

Perhaps we believe the people we love will leave if we get angry or that we will lose control and hurt someone beyond repair. It takes a rational belief system to be able to say: "It is healthy to reveal how I feel—to myself and then to others."

A crisis may reveal to us that we don't have such a belief or that we don't know how to put it to use. A crisis affords us the opportunity to practice.

As we seek to stop blaming our partner and forgive him or her, we'll reach our goal more quickly if we can tell the one we love how we feel. This does *not* mean bashing the other person over the head, literally or figuratively, with our rage. But it does mean in a conscious, clear, way to say how we feel.

Even those of us who are beginners at expressing our emotions, can begin to do this by utilizing simple "I" messages that draw word pictures. For example, "I feel like an explosion about to happen when you won't talk about this crisis"; "I feel as cold and poor as a ragged streetperson since we lost our house and I'm storing up a lot of rage about it. I want to go on together, but I've got to process this out loud. I need you to help"; "I feel as vicious and angry as a mad dog since our son died. I love you so much, but I want to tear into you for your carelessness. I need to talk about our loss and exactly how it came about."

How do you feel about the crisis you're in and, in particular, about the part of it you feel your partner caused? Talk over your feelings with your mate. After you've expressed your anger in a straightforward and non-hysterical manner (and most likely received an "I'm sorry"), you will be more ready to stop blaming and start forgiving. The process of forgiving your partner, a simple yet demanding set of steps, will take you to that moment.

Forgiving Our Partner

What follows are the four steps we can take to stop blaming and start forgiving our partner. They are very similar to the steps we took in Chapter 9 to forgive ourselves.

These steps may seem impossible to do when we're hurt or angry, yet without forgiveness, it will be impossible to restore our relationship. Therefore, many of us have found it helps to approach this process with an attitude that says taking these steps seems beyond our power. In doing this, we stop relying on our power to forgive and simply submit to the process:

(1) We acknowledge to ourselves exactly what our

partner did that needs forgiveness and look at it directly.

(2) We feel the emotions this error is stirring in us.

(3) We ask our Higher Power, however we define Him/Her/It, to assist us in forgiving our partner.

(4) We tell our partner when appropriate, or simply show him or her through our attitudes and actions, that all is forgiven and we'd like to start rebuilding our relationship.

In the first step we take a mental snapshot of our partner's wrong. When we view it, we don't retouch it in our minds or deliberately blur its details. We look at what our partner did as objectively as we can and resist any impulses to minimize or soften the error.

Once the image is clear, we go on to the second step: we feel the emotions this error is stirring in us. We feel the hurt and anger, the disappointment, the sadness, the rage— all the emotions our partner's mistake evokes.

Sometimes this second step makes us feel guilty. Maybe our partner never meant to do the thing that led to the crisis. So when we take this step, we may ask ourself, How can I be angry about this? If I were a more decent person, I'd be feeling sympathetic, not madder than hell; She never intended to slip on the ice and break her hip; He didn't mean to leave the iron on and burn the house down; I shouldn't be angry.

Feelings are not bad, they just *are*. Even if our partner's mistake was entirely accidental or unintentional, even if this crisis is also causing him or her great pain, if we acknowledge and allow our feelings, we'll be able to forgive our partner more easily and more completely.

We return to Tom and Cynthia's story from Chapter 9 to illustrate how this can work. Cynthia at first felt guilty when her husband Tom was in the terrible accident in which a beam fell down on him from the open rafters during the construction of a high-rise apartment building. Cynthia had known Tom was working too hard and she wished she'd been more forceful in her objections. At first she kept thinking if only she'd insisted he take a few days off, maybe he would never have been in this accident.

After the accident, Tom had to undergo nine hours of surgery. Before the operation began, Cynthia knew Tom was paralyzed. She sat in the waiting room, hoping and praying it was temporary. The look on the surgeon's face as he walked toward her told her the news was not good. "I asked the doctor if Tom would ever walk again," she recalls. "He said `no.' I asked, `Will he have bowel or bladder control?' He said `no.' I asked `Will we have sex again?' Again, `no.'"

For weeks, Cynthia kept hoping the doctor was wrong. She kept thinking that the swelling might be causing a temporary paralysis. When finally Cynthia admitted to herself that Tom's disability was real and permanent, that he would remain paraplegic, the feelings that welled up inside shocked her.

Any guilt Cynthia had felt earlier was replaced with a deep and terrible rage, a rage she directed toward Tom. Though she never voiced these thoughts to him, she kept thinking to herself, How dare you do this to me? How dare you get yourself all screwed up, so now I have to wait on you hand and foot.

Over a period of months, Cynthia began to lay her blame to rest, but not before she examined these painful feelings. "Tom's accident happened at 5:30 on a Saturday afternoon. Why was he still working? The accident was traced to the carelessness of one carpenter who was exhausted after a twelve-hour day. Why did Tom allow the crew to keep on working? He was a workaholic. I'd been on his case. I feared the stress would make him sick, but I never could have imagined this."

Three years later, Cynthia and Tom are still together, rebuilding their lives. By expressing her anger, Cynthia was able to go on and to accept the drastic, heartbreaking changes. She was able to forgive Tom, who worked too much and who, one terrible day, was standing in the wrong place at the wrong time.

Feeling these emotions, going through them, is hard but not impossible. Arriving at the point of forgiveness is seldom one glowing moment. More often it's a process of taking a few steps forward only to move back again. Our *willingness* to forgive, not our ability to forgive perfectly or quickly, will eventually prevail. Even if you can't yet forgive, you can keep holding on to the attitude that you'd like to.

In the third step, we ask our Higher Power to assist us in forgiving our partner. In partnership with God, or the highest part of ourself, it occurs to us that we too are not perfect, that in different ways we have also caused pain to those we love. Though the spotlight is on our partner right now, we realize that by being human and less than perfect, we too will take our turn.

"If you live in the real world, you *will* be hurt. You will also hurt others," write Drs. Thomas P. Malone and Patrick T. Malone. When we view our partner as a fellow human being subject to stress and fatigue, to distraction and greed, to poor judgment and callousness—just as we are—we stop looking down on our lover and instead look across.

We can come to this attitude through a love Christians call *agape,* or divine, Godlike love. This love requires that we will ourselves to love even when we don't feel like it.

We find the need for this extraordinary love when we're blaming our partner because if we waited to "feel like" loving a mate who has done something serious enough that we're needing to forgive him or her, we'd be waiting forever. *Agape* goes beyond that natural human response towards helping us restore our feelings of love.

Agape has gotten a bad rap through sermons and essays that have insisted it has other dimensions as well, such as self-sacrifice (your welfare is more important than mine), obedience (I love another because I feel I should), and benevolence, (I love another who is less worthy).

In his book *Caring Enough To Forgive*, Dr. David Augsburger concludes that this high-level love does not include any of these attitudes that tend to make us seem better than the one we love. Rather, he defines *agape* as "equal regard." In other words, we value our partner equally with ourself; we are concerned for his or her welfare; and we're ready to confront together any issues needed to restore our relationship.

After reaching for this high-level love, we come to the fourth and last step: We tell our partner when appropriate, or simply show him or her through our attitudes and actions, that all is forgiven and we'd like to start rebuilding our relationship.

One caution: make sure you really are ready to forgive your partner before telling him or her all is forgiven. Ed remembers how his wife, Anne, said she forgave him for starting to form a romantic attachment to his secretary only to begin blaming him again. His "almost affair" as Anne called it, had happened during a period in which Anne was in a midlife crisis and doubting her commitment to Ed. Though Ed was sorry and had told her so, now he insisted he could not tolerate this back and forth business. He had trusted Anne when she said he was forgiven. "Do you forgive me or not?" he now asked. "I won't be forgiven one day and `unforgiven' the next."

Loving Ed, Anne listened to and respected this limit he set, and she could see how much she'd hurt him. She thought about where she was in the process of forgiveness and realized she did, indeed, forgive him. But, as she explained to him, "I still need to talk about what you did and about both our parts in that low point in our marriage."

The two of them decided they could discuss his mistake and the dynamics of what happened, but that she would be responsible for not slipping into throwing it back in his face vindictively. Gradually her need to talk about the past subsided. Meanwhile he knew she had forgiven him even though she had not forgotten his mistake.

Once we're ready to take this last step, we can be dramatic or down-to-earth. One woman says she knew she was forgiven when she mentioned her mistake to her husband and he smiled, saying simply, "What mistake?" One wife took her husband to a gourmet restaurant and at a candlelit table, told him she was ready to be "as one" again and open to suggestions about how they might best proceed.

Would your partner like to have a formal ceremony to reinstate your relationship? Ask. We know one couple who renewed marriage vows in a little church after a period of estrangement. There was no minister present. Just the two of them stood before an altar and told each other how they intended to express their newfound love.

Show and tell your lover he or she is forgiven. Think about what your partner likes. Tailor your "I forgive you" to your lover's tastes: greeting cards; little gifts; a long hug; an offer to do a chore he hates; an "I love you"; an empty house one Saturday, with the kids off at a friend's place and you two alone. Formalize your forgiveness in some way.

At first, when we forgive our partner, she or he may not believe us, especially if our blaming has continued for some time. Be prepared to wait for acceptance. We have convinced our partner she or he was unlovable; it may take a while for her or him to believe otherwise.

Though the forgiveness process demands courage and love from the forgiver, and though the one we forgive won't always instantly or easily accept our forgiveness, it is the only reliable tool we know of for reestablishing an intimate relationship. We can pretend we forgive our partner. We can complain to friends forever and get a lot of sympathy—it's easy to evoke if we have any skill at all at painting a negative picture of our partner. But we will never get back with our mate in this way; only forgiveness will forge a new bond of love between us.

Meet with a therapist, clergyperson, or support group if forgiveness eludes you. It will be well worth persisting until you grasp it and can again invite your spouse back into your life. The following story illustrates how this reunion can happen.

You Do the Best You Can

At age fifteen, Marge and Peter's daughter Eileen entered a rehabilitation facility because of cocaine addiction. Now, two years later, Eileen is a freshman in college and continuing a day-by-day recovery. Five years before, her older sister, Cindy, also underwent treatment in a rehabilitation program for alcohol addiction. Married and the mother of a baby girl, she too is recovering.

Marge, a friendly, witty woman in her mid-forties, is

the curator of an art museum. She also paints part-time, specializing in impressionistic pastel watercolors of flowers. Gradually, her work has gained recognition. Next month she'll have a one-woman exhibit in a prestigious gallery in New York City.

Peter, a shy, quiet man who just turned fifty, owns a combination bookstore-espresso bar, which keeps expanding. More interested in books than in making small talk with customers, Peter has hired gregarious clerks to work out front while he handles behind-the-scenes business details. Marge, with her easy banter, occasionally fills in there on her days off.

Like many couples these two are a study in contrasts, and by and large they feel their differences have enriched their relationship. Each has fulfilling work. Each allows the other space and respects their different temperaments and interests.

But when it came to raising their two daughters, Marge and Peter agree—they unwittingly fell into a pattern that made them less-than-ideal parents. Marge, who grew up on a farm with parents who enforced a strict regimen of chores each day, vowed her daughters would have an easier life than she did. She wanted to provide them with a loose, casual home in which they could be creative and free. She saw schedules and chores as restrictive and unnecessary.

Peter, with an alcoholic father and a depressed mother, virtually raised himself. Since his was a chaotic home with no consistent rules, he thought he'd like to set some firm limits and also require his daughters to help out around the house each day. He suspected that knowing what to expect each day and having a list of chores, for instance, would make his daughters feel secure. They wouldn't have to guess what would be happening from one day to the next the way he did growing up.

Marge and Peter never clearly articulated how each of them felt about these parenting-lifestyle goals. Each assumed his or her position was "right." Both had evidence, gathered in their own childhoods, to support their positions.

Today these two see all this, but they didn't until they talked at length recently during the two months when Eileen was in rehab. They've realized that though Peter made attempts at disciplining, he gave up when Marge criticized him. In essence, he left Marge in charge and much of the time, just watched from the sidelines. And Marge, at the time, liked "running it all."

When I talked with Marge, she shared parts of her journey out of guilt (aimed at herself) and blame (directed at Peter). "I never felt Peter related right to the kids. He always could relate to me, but it was different with them. When he tried to discipline them, he did it at the wrong time, for the wrong things, with too harsh a punishment for one thing or not a harsh enough punishment for the other.

"But I took over for both of us. I had all this empathy and sympathy, 'cause I remembered how hard life was for me growing up. So our kids had a dad who would just holler and scream but not follow through and a mom who was too permissive.

"Recently I told Peter I shouldn't have taken over like I did. He comforted me and made me realize that no matter what you do you do the best you can. I forgave him too for bowing out. He's a compassionate person. He loves our daughters dearly. We both do. It's too bad we couldn't see what we were doing sooner.

"You have to forgive each other for not being perfect

or the relationship would just be all over."

As an outsider looking in, I imagine their daughters are now noticing their parents' honesty and new patterns of relating. Even now, at this late date, these two have a chance to model forgiveness and move on in spite of the knowledge that they, like all of us, made mistakes along the way. Their relationship, cleared of blame, is anchored in the present.

Reflection Opportunities

1. Do you find yourself blaming your partner? Are you blaming him for his part in the crisis? For how she is handling the crisis? For his differing perception of the crisis?

2. Have you tried to go through the steps of forgiving your mate? Can you still love him even though he isn't perfect?

3. When you decide you want to go through the process of forgiving your mate, here's one way to begin: Write a letter to your partner, only let it be for your eyes only. In it, pour out everything you blame him or her for. Don't hold back. Put down all the small or huge offenses. If past mistakes or future fears pop into your mind, add those too. Don't censor anything.

Next, write a second letter to yourself. Get as close to your feelings as you can. Begin, "This is how I feel about what she has done." You may find yourself recording feelings of betrayal, disappointment, horror, rage, or deep sadness. Put both letters aside (and in a safe hiding place). Be open now to listening to the wisest part of yourself or to your Higher Power to help you stop blaming and start forgiving. Periodically refer to the letters to get back in touch with your feelings. Finally, when you've come to a place of forgiveness, let your partner know he or she is forgiven of *all* this.

4. Once you have forgiven your mate, keep acting as if you have! Each day say or do something to let him or her know, or simply be there for your partner. Though occasional feelings of blame will most likely recur, be careful how you handle them. If you feel the need to discuss your mate's part in the crisis again, ask yourself, How can I bring up this subject in a loving, not judgmental or condemning manner? When would the best time be?

Chapter 11

Accepting the Altered Situation

Everything precious including our dignity can be taken from us but the one thing that cannot be taken away is our power to choose what attitude we will take toward the events that have happened.
Viktor Frankl

Their voices are loud and angry, interrupting the tranquility of my Sunday afternoon walk on a tree-lined street in an old neighborhood in Denver.

"I want that balloon."

"No, it's mine."

A wild scuffle between two little kids erupts. She tries to grab the balloon. He tries to pull away. *BANG!*

"I wanted that balloon," she screams, staring in disbelief at a never-to-be-a-balloon-again tattered piece of red rubber hanging from a string he still clutches.

Minutes later, a half-block away, I pass a frail older woman who pulls along an oxygen bottle, wearing the accompanying breathing apparatus and a smile. A spray of yellow daffodils decorates her bottle.

This chapter is about how we can go on when a crisis has left some part of our life as impossible to restore as that red balloon. It's about taking a step-by-step journey to a spiritual and psychological spot that we can decorate with daffodils, even though we might give anything to go back to where we were before a crisis. It's about forging an new intimate relationship with our partner by choosing to accept the changes in our lives and live in the present rather than taking up residence in the past.

Here, we won't be addressing the types of crises that come with a built-in momentum that helps sweep us into acceptance. If our crisis is facing an addiction to alcohol or work, for instance, once we acknowledge our addiction and begin recovery, though we may relapse on occasion, we don't usually believe our pre-crisis condition was better than our current recovery. In fact, we celebrate weekly, monthly, or yearly "anniversaries" of our new life.

Though we may joke about the brand of gin we liked the most; though we might recall the highs we experienced working until midnight then getting back to our desk by 7 A.M., though we might miss our addiction intensely at times, we still want to be who we are in the post-crisis state more than we want to return to the old habits. Some psychological crises are like this too. After we pass through a midlife crisis, after we've been through postpartum blues— we don't look back longingly at the bad old days.

However, there are other types of crises that require us to acknowledge some tough new reality, making us wish we could return to a time of rosy innocence that no longer exists. Some examples: "My husband has multiple sclerosis"; "My son is addicted to drugs"; "We have to leave the home and community we love and move across the country"; "My daughter was killed by a drunk driver"; "My wife was raped while I was on a business trip"; "My husband will never walk again"; "Suddenly—out of the blue—my husband and I have custody of his four children"; "My wife and I both retired at the same time, and for the first time ever, we're home together *all* day"; "Our grown daughter needs a roof over her head and it's going to be *our* roof"; "The company that employed me and provided retirement and medical benefits is bankrupt and I may get nothing promised me."

Three Paths to Choose

We cannot stay in the same spot as we were prior to a crisis. After our initial shock and disbelief, after we're able to say, "This really did happen to me (or us)," we embark on a journey for a crisis takes us someplace. But where? There are only three paths. The first two may look more appealing than the third, but in reality they lead away from acceptance and toward more pain. To complicate matters, often while we're trying one path our partner is heading down a different one. The paths can be described like this:

Path One

We try to run from the pain of a crisis. Like a recent makeup commercial, we proclaim: "I've had it with reality, I want illusion."

The lengths we go to avoid real suffering and to replace it with an illusion of pleasure or numbness are varied and creative. Here are a few examples: to stop thinking about our loss we have sex with a stranger or a friend; get drunk; sniff cocaine; begin smoking or start smoking again; sleep all day; take tranquilizers; work sixty hours a week; watch tv all day; eat too much or too little; run away; or contemplate suicide. We may pick more than one of those options or concoct still different escapes. We're capable of great ingenuity when we're desperately trying to avoid suffering.

Path Two

We allow the crisis to take over our lives and become "us." This path is the polar opposite of running from our pain. Instead of trying to escape, we become engulfed in a crisis so fully that we have no time for ourselves or our partner.

"We can make our crisis so special that it becomes our life," says Dr. Patrick Malone. "Say a child is slowly dying of cancer—that tragedy consumes huge chunks of your family time, energy, and resources. But even in a situation like this, you can't let the special consume *you*. You have to remember that you never gain anything by giving away your personal identity and taking on the crisis as your whole reason for living. This is such a stark, hard way to put it, but it's the truth. It's the truth until the last breath you take. No matter what's wrong in your life, you need to take responsibility for preserving something of yourself and some time and energy for your relationship with your partner. Or it's all over for you and your partner."

Path Three

We choose to accept our altered situation, seek to understand, use the lessons the crisis is teaching, and say yes to our present lives. This third path is the only one that empowers us to grow as individuals and to rebuild a satisfying, intimate relationship with our partner. But how, even if we choose acceptance, do we go about implementing it?

Becoming Acceptors

"Acceptor" comes from a Latin word meaning "one who admits a thing is true." In English today it is usually used in the context of chemistry and means "an atom that receives a pair of electrons from another atom to form a covalent bond with it."

By combining the old Latin meaning with the chemical definition, Marilyn and I have coined this new one: *an acceptor is one who by admitting a loss is true, receives a new identity and is structurally changed and bonded with the loss.* Accepting the altered situation of a crisis involves becoming this kind of acceptor.

When we become acceptors we recognize that we're no longer who we used to be, pre-crisis. From the inside out, something has changed—even our basic structure is different. When we lose something we value or someone we love, we're handed new insights, new heartaches, new handicaps, and new challenges. Like an atom receiving a pair of electrons from another atom, when we bond with our loss, we're more stable. In fact, to try to break that bond takes more energy than to accept it.

Martha came to accept her sixteen-year-old son's addiction to heroin one afternoon she'll never forget. We offer her insights here, not as a formula, but as an example of how one individual found her solitary way into acceptance.

"Jimmy had been good at hiding his addiction and I'd only found out about it a short time before he asked to be placed in a rehabilitation facility. During the two months he was there, for the first few weeks, I fantasized about being hit by a large truck. I thought about crossing a busy street, just not looking, and being put out of my pain. After a while, I realized I didn't really want this to happen, but even staying alive, I thought I could never really live again. If Jimmy doesn't recover, I kept thinking, I don't know if I can ever make love or laugh or ever do anything of value.

"One afternoon I visited Jimmy at the hospital and he asked me if we could pray together. He led us in the Serenity Prayer—`God grant me the serenity to accept the things I cannot change, the courage to change the things I can, and the wisdom to know the difference.' His hands were shaking. He had stubble on his cheeks. He said, `Mom I'm going to try and shake this.'

"I came back home and cried for a couple of hours. I prayed Jimmy would stay in recovery and win over his addiction. Then I thought about the words in the Serenity Prayer. I visualized the worst—Jimmy overdosing and dying; and almost that bad—Jimmy keeping on with his habit. I felt an immense sadness that I could not protect him. I felt angry that he had gotten hooked on heroin. I felt guilty, too, knowing he could have benefitted from more discipline from me growing up. Then I affirmed my love for Jimmy, a love that had been there since he was born prematurely and I had to view him in an incubator, behind the hospital glass wall, the first few days after his birth. I couldn't hold him then nor could I shield him from harm now.

"Somewhere in my thinking, I came up from the bottom and saw just a glimmer of sunlight. I felt the presence of a Higher Power that day. My acceptance came in the form of a message from deep within my soul. It was this: `You'll go on no matter how Jimmy's life turns out. You'll go on no matter what happens.'"

That decision carried Martha through some rough months. Her son relapsed three times, and though each time tore her apart, Martha didn't go back on her decision to continue living her life the best she could. Jimmy's been clean and sober for three years now. No matter what happens, Martha says she's come to know these three things: Jimmy's day-by-day recovery is his responsibility and she has no power or control over it; her acceptance of her son's addiction is her responsibility; to live a loving, productive life is also her responsibility.

"My husband accepted Jimmy's addiction more quickly than I did. I believe if I'd never come to the point of acceptance, ongoing depression and fear would have sapped all my energy. There would have been nothing left for my marriage, for my other children, for my work, for anything.

"I still have to renew that acceptance when I get fearful that something could happen that might turn Jimmy back to using. I rely, not on willpower, but on my Higher Power to help me keep doing this."

Living in Acceptance

The following six ideas for coming to accept the changes a crisis has demanded of us are like a six-room structure we decide to take up residence in. One day we may spend most of our time in one room. Another day, we find ourselves hanging out in a different one. All six have different functions. After we've spent some time in each one, if we're patient and compassionate with ourselves and our spouse, not demanding perfection, but simply committing ourselves to becoming an acceptor, day-by-day, eventually we'll feel at home in this new place we reside, the place called acceptance:

1. Open yourself to the grieving process and keep telling your partner "where you are" in the process.

2. Connect with your spirituality.

3. Alter unworkable beliefs.

4. Seek support.

5. Take small steps and make necessary practical changes.

6. Help others.

Open Yourself to The Grieving Process and Keep Telling Your Partner "Where You Are"

When we've suffered a loss, instant healing is applauded. If we emerge from a crisis wearing a smiling face, never once folding under the weight of our pain, family and friends reward us with comments such as: "She's one strong woman"; "He never missed a day of work after the tragedy"; or, "He never complains—he's such a saint."

To accept the worst, post-crisis circumstances of our lives, we need to resist the culturally approved habit of glossing over our losses. "Hurtful, angry, or guilty feelings that we try to deny stay with us for years and years," writes Ann Kaiser Stearns in *Living Through Personal Crisis*. "If we resist what we feel, we continue to have our troublesome feelings . . . ."

A crisis hurt us in some significant way or we would not be calling it a crisis! We need to admit that it left some part of our lives empty or damaged and to grieve our losses no matter what they are.

Grieving is an important segment of the crisis process. Dr. Elizabeth Kubler-Ross, a pioneer in identifying the grieving process, notes that we enter it when we lose a loved one or when we lose our health. Unless we resist the process, it also unfolds when we lose our livelihood, our home, a cherished image of ourselves, our peace of mind, or anything else of significance.

The stages of grief Kubler-Ross outlines are: denial and isolation, anger, bargaining, depression, and acceptance. "Some will go through all stages, others will skip some, and all will go back and forth between stages," Kubler-Ross noted in *Lupus Life*.

When we're in a committed relationship and are trying to go on together after a loss, it is crucial that we enter the grief process individually. We can take comfort from our partner's support and presence, but we can't ask our partner to do our grief work for us.

Speaker and newspaper columnist, Dottie Lamm, who is married to Richard Lamm, a former governor of Colorado, underwent a modified radical mastectomy in August 1981, while she was Colorado's First Lady. In her book *Second Banana*, Dottie writes about her surprise and pleasure when Richard "who doesn't write poetry" penned a special one for her two days after her surgery. In it he reflected on what life would be like without her, writing in one stanza, "So/Let me say simply/That without you/The days would be longer—the nights/Eternity."

Richard's heartfelt poem made Dottie feel loved and needed, but she still had to face her own grief. After her surgery, Dottie had tried to concentrate only on the positive, staying away from negative statistics or negative thoughts. But after a well-meaning person sent her a depressing article about cancer and she read it, she found herself "no longer in a positive place but in limbo.

"All my energies were tied up in not dealing with that article," she writes. "Two sleepless nights ensued. During one I tried to rid my fears by reading novels; the other I tried writing on subjects unrelated to my illness. But work, the great panacea for depression, failed. Finally I knew I must draw close those sheets of paper with sad stories and negative statistics. So I did, at 2 A.M., shivering under a night light. I cried.

"I went to the kitchen, huddled on a stool, and cried

some more. Panic-stricken, I entered the tunnel of my own death—I saw my weeping children, heard eulogies at my funeral—and came out the other end. As I wrapped my flowered flannel hospital robe around me tightly, the shivering and the crying suddenly stopped. I'd seen the worst. I'd encountered my possible demise. I'd been as far down as I could go. Now there was only one way: up.

"I reached for milk and cookies. I filled the tub and took a long, luxurious bath in the glow of the night lights and the sound of classical music. I was no longer depressed, not even `positive,' but just plain happy. Happy I was as well as I was. Thankful for my family and my friends. Sobered only by the realization that others in my situation had neither medical care nor love. Concerned, finally, about someone besides myself."

We can, as Dottie's experience illustrates, best free ourselves from our own pain, by entering into it. Feeling it. Facing it. Then, once we've opened ourselves to our personal feelings, we can be more available to our partner.

The story of a young Indiana couple, Tim and Donna Ray, poignantly illustrates how one partner who goes ahead and grieves, can then help the other enter the same healing process. Writer Leslie Dreyfous, visited the Rays right after a devastating tornado changed their lives forever, then returned one year later. Each time, in an Associated Press feature story, she took readers into their lives, and in particular, into their grieving process. The information and quotes that follow are taken from her moving accounts.

In June 1990 the Rays lost their only son, fifteen-month-old Benjamin, when a tornado blew out the four walls of their trailer home. One moment Donna was holding Benjamin tightly. The next moment, when a wind which sounded like a locomotive swept through the room, he was literally ripped out of her arms. Tim found Benjamin a few feet away from Donna who was unconscious. She awoke dazed. They strapped Benjamin, who showed no sign of breathing, into his car seat and took him to the hospital, but their son was dead; his skull had been crushed.

Besides dealing with their raw grief, the five surviving family members had all been injured. Donna had a broken collarbone; Tim a badly broken leg; their three young daughters, lacerations and bruises. After Benjamin's funeral, Tim lay on the living room sofa and cried. Unable to do much with his leg in a cast, he let himself feel the terrible, wrenching grief.

Meanwhile Donna, after expressing her anguish initially, coped by staying busy and locking her hurt inside. She wouldn't talk to Tim about Benjamin's death. "I couldn't stop long enough to talk about anything. I just wanted to stay on the go all the time, stay busy, keep running. I knew if I stopped, I'd just break," she says.

In her mind, she kept reproaching herself with "if onlys." Surely a mother could have held on more tightly to her son. Surely a mother's strength should have been greater than a 250-mph wind. That first summer and on into the fall, Donna carried around her confusion, rage, and guilt. Tim knew she was struggling and said, "I just didn't want her carrying it around alone."

"So one day we were in the car," says Donna, "and he was practically begging me to talk about it. And I just kept telling him I couldn't, even though it was putting a strain on us at the time."

Finally, Donna's tears came. She began to cry and Tim did too, while their little daughters sat quietly in the back-seat. "It started the healing," Tim said.

As we open ourselves to the grieving process, separately and together, the single most difficult stage for most of us is to allow and handle anger. Denial may come naturally. Most of us go ahead and try bargaining. Most of us get depressed over our situations or feel sad. But angry? As we explored in Chapter 10, we often don't do anger very well.

When we can no longer maintain our denial, what can we do with feelings of anger, rage, envy, and resentment? If you are afraid to get mad, you might want to read Dr. Theodore Isaac Rubin's, *The Angry Book*. At the end Rubin asks 103 questions designed to help the reader "to open up and to extend angry and loving ability." Question #22, for instance: "Are you an angelic phony or are you anesthetized? If you never get angry, you must be either one or the other or suffering from severe brain damage."

Once we're dealing with our own anger, we can help our partner get in touch with the source of his or her anger. When author Madeleine L'Engle's husband was battling cancer, she writes in *Two-Part Invention*, her book about their marriage, his illness, and ultimately his death, "Hugh has to work through all the anguish and frustration and denial and acceptance himself. The lonely valley is just that: lonely. Jesus walked that lonesome valley. He had to walk it by himself. Sooner or later we all do. There are no shortcuts through the place of excrement."

Madeleine knew too, however, that she could help a little. One day sitting at Hugh's feet, she said to him, "Darling, we've always promised to be absolutely honest with each other, and I don't think we are, right now. I'm very angry at everything that has happened. It isn't fair. It shouldn't have happened. You've got to be angry too."

Then, Madeleine writes, Hugh could acknowledge his anger and they held each other and cried.

Connect with Your Spirituality

Tony Award-winning actor Ben Vereen lost his six-teen-year-old daughter, Naja, in an auto accident in 1987. For a while, Ben, who'd used drugs before, turned to them again. "There weren't enough drugs or alcohol to take away the emptiness and pain," he recalled in an interview in by Claire Carter in *Parade Magazine*.

Ben considered suicide and kept on using drugs and alcohol, running from the grieving process until he hit bottom. Finally months after Naja died, he found himself broke, unshaven, and unkempt; with his life out of control, he sought psychiatric help, and then checked into a drug treatment center. "I reconnected with my spirituality," he said. "I realized that it had never turned from me. I had turned from it. It motivated me and became my rock."

Clean and sober now, Ben speaks to children across the country with an anti-drug message that emphasizes not only saying no to drugs, but saying yes to God and to ourselves as well. Ben says he and his wife Nancy went through "an emotional separation" after Naja's death and that they are still in the process of healing.

Ben Vereen's reconnection with his spirituality is help-ing him to mend his marriage and reach out to other people. But some of us find it hard to make that reconnec-tion. Jenny, in her lifelong battle with lupus, remains open but says, "I know all of us have four components—physi-cal, mental, emotional, and spiritual—but the spiritual is the hardest for me to tap into." Brad, who is filing for bankruptcy and feeling the stress in his marriage as he and his wife Annette are forced to move out of the home they built, says, "I don't know what `spiritual' is anymore."

Both Jenny and Brad were scarred by childhood expe-riences. Jenny, who grew up attending a strict Baptist

church in a small Southern town, remembers "the hypo-
crites at church, saying one thing and doing another."
Brad, now fifty-five, attended Roman Catholic Mass with
his parents from the time he could walk. Just after gradu-
ating from college, he taught English at a Catholic high
school for two years. It's been close to thirty years since he's
had a spiritual dimension in his life. Brad is angry about the
guilt and shame the church instilled in him. He's emphatic
that he wants nothing to do with anything remotely religious anymore.

Our purpose in this section is not to point a judgmental
finger at any organized religion or to list good and bad
ways to make a spiritual connection. Rather, we wish to
encourage you, if you are like Brad, to be open to modify-
ing a belief that spirituality can never have a place in your
life.

Many men and women who had decided, for one
reason or another, that spirituality was not for them, often
change their minds in the midst of a crisis. One dramatic
example, which involves millions worldwide, is the rapid
growth of twelve-step groups. Over fifty years ago Alcoholics Anonymous sprang up with its unique spiritual
approach to recovery from alcoholism. Other twelve-step
groups such as Emotions Anonymous and Co-Dependents
Anonymous have followed, using AA's original twelve
steps with slight modifications to fit the different circumstances.

Though Marilyn and I both attend twelve-step groups,
we're not endorsing any group or suggesting such programs are the only way to make a spiritual connection. We
bring them into our discussion of spirituality only to illustrate that in these groups, diverse people from many religious backgrounds are finding hope and help to go on with
their lives by opening up to the spiritual aspect of life. Some

do not believe in a God "out there," but discover the holy within themselves.

None of us, however, can force a spiritual connection. It comes to us only if and when we're ready. When Deborah and Jeff went through bankruptcy, they had to move away from their hometown to take new jobs far from family and friends. Deborah, an agnostic at the time, began to think, "There's got to be a reason for this life more than the moment-by-moment experiences. I wanted to unite with some force greater than myself." Those initial thoughts led her into a faith she still claims five years later.

As Marilyn and I write this book together and face our separate daily challenges, we both seek a spiritual connection not because we're holy, but because we're often helpless. Life has dealt us enough blows that we've found we can use some extra assistance. Through different routes, we have found, and continue to find each day, that the process of healing, of coming to accept harsh, tragic, inconvenient, or aggravating realities, though never easy, is possible in partnership with a Higher Power.

In *Two-Part Invention*, Madeleine L'Engle notes that her theological reading for several years has been in such areas as astrophysics, particle physics, and quantum mechanics. "These disciplines are dealing with the nature of being, and I find that much theology founders over peripheral things, gets stuck on a limited literalism. But the amazing discoveries in the world of physics reveal a universe which is enormous beyond comprehension."

L'Engle admits that she does not know how the creator works, but she does know this: ". . . when I cry out `Help!' the fact that I am crying out affirms that somewhere in some part of me I hope there is someone who hears, who cares."

In our seeking for a spiritual connection, one reward is what Aldous Huxley called "the reception of grace." In his book, *The Perennial Philosophy,* he claims that when we choose union with God, when we stop trying to suffer alone, we receive grace on the spiritual level, that is, we get connected with the love of God and we start to get a knowledge of God. And that's not all. Grace comes to us also on mental and psychological levels, "in the form of a diminution of fear, self-concern and even of pain."

Seldom does our suffering automatically teach us. Seldom do we find acceptance of our altered situation all by ourselves. As we're processing "why me, why us?" questions the best we can, we can also begin to ask ourselves, What are the lessons hiding in this crisis? As we pose all these questions, it helps many of us to have a spiritual connection.

"Blessed are the poor in spirit," Jesus says in the New Testament. Elaborating on that theme, author-psychiatrist M. Scott Peck, M.D., added in a lecture: "Blessed are the confused, searching, open, growing." As we struggle to accept the losses of a crisis, often that's us.

Alter Unworkable Beliefs

Though we may not be able to instantly list them, our beliefs are our underlying assumptions about life—rules, philosophies, and attitudes that comprise us and influence our behaviors and emotions. Some of our beliefs are rational, others irrational. As we discussed in Chapter 4, in a crisis, the irrational ones are often exposed and found faulty. A crisis forces us to uncover our assumed truths about the world, dust them off, and ask, Does this really work for me? Is it a rational belief? Is it at odds with my goal of becoming an acceptor?

Kathy, a vivacious woman with a soft Georgia drawl, who emanates such warmth and caring that you feel better just talking to her, found she had to revise her beliefs after a crisis. Five years ago when her son Mark was fifteen, he tried to commit suicide by swallowing a bottle of sedatives. He was, at the time, also experimenting with other drugs. Today, at twenty, Mark is a sensitive, kind young man who has a stable job and a dedication to ongoing recovery. Kathy says not a day goes by that she's not grateful for Mark's recovery, but she'll never forget finding him unconscious on his bedroom floor late one night.

Kathy believed that loving her two children would keep them away from drugs and any other kind of serious trouble. Looking back, she says, "I never dreamed I wouldn't have total control of my life. I had a picture of what marriage and husbands and families were. I thought my picture would come true. And I had all these wonderful ideas about raising our children. As it turns out, we made every mistake in the book."

In therapy, Kathy and her husband, Bob, began to revise their beliefs about how much control one has over life; about "ideal" families; and about how parents can best show love. Their changes in beliefs have helped them become acceptors. Kathy and Bob no longer assume that even their best efforts will necessarily be a shield against another crisis. And they've come to accept life and themselves with gratitude instead of focusing on imperfections. "My family, just as they are, are `ideal,'" says Kathy.

Peggy, who in Chapter 8 related how she and her husband, Stan, have depended on an ongoing dialogue to help them through a number of crises, says she's in the process of revising her beliefs since Stan lost his executive post at an oil company. "I believed—I expected—that when I reached age fifty I could do some traveling and have some fun. I've worked part-time and raised five kids and now finally, I thought this time would be my time. I went through a lot of rage, ostensibly at Stan's company, but really at Stan. I believed a husband would be my `security,' that a husband kept on being the primary breadwinner until retirement.

"I'm very disillusioned and I've been asking myself, what's more important to me, the security or my marriage? Can I let go of the security if need be—even lose this house we built ourselves—and still retain the marriage? Or will I be so angry if we lose the house that the marriage won't survive? I don't know. I really don't know."

Peggy, not at all liking this need to revise the belief that Stan would provide her with security, faced her rage head-on. As it has turned out, after admitting to and allowing all these feelings and reactions, Peggy recommitted herself to Stan. Instead of buying luggage, she found a full-time job.

Facing a belief and exploring its ramifications requires courage, for looking at our beliefs will not always ensure that our relationship stays intact. One thing, however, is certain. When a crisis forces us to acknowledge a belief and alter it to fit our new circumstances, that altering process can take place only when we are honest enough, patient enough, and resourceful enough to "see" our beliefs.

Peggy could have refused to alter her belief that marriage equals security, deciding, this stinks—I'll divorce Stan and go on alone or look for a husband who will provide me with a secure life. Or Peggy could have pretended she had another belief, such as, Good wives stand by their men no matter what without complaining or being disappointed. Instead, she discovered one of her core beliefs which was: I have to think about huge disappointments like this and then decide what to do.

A postscript to their story: A few months after our interview, Stan found a new well-paying executive position. Peggy decided she liked her full-time job and continued working. Now, two years later, both Peggy and Stan have decided to quit their jobs, rent out their house, and serve a year in the Peace Corps. Their openness to changing their values and goals and allowing their relationship to grow and evolve has taken them through many crises. Now they're both packing their bags, getting ready for a new adventure together.

Seek Support

To accept the altered situation of a crisis, we can use a little help. Several years ago, after his patrol car had been found abandoned with the engine idling and the door open, it appeared a city cop had been abducted or murdered. His wife and seventeen-year-old son were frantic with worry. A few days later, however, the police officer turned up in a neighboring state, at first maintaining he'd been kidnapped, but later confessing he'd staged the fake abduction and fled his present life by taking off on his motorcycle.

This middle-aged man had a lot to worry about: his home had been forced into foreclosure and would be sold at public auction unless he made up back payments; he was late repaying a smaller loan; and there was also the ongoing care of a second younger child who was handicapped.

In explaining why he left he said he was under so much pressure he couldn't handle it anymore. "I should have got some help somewhere. I didn't know where else to turn," he told a newspaper reporter.

I do not know the aftermath of the story, except that

this seventeen-year-veteran of the police force lost his job. At the time, a newspaper editorial sympathetically noted that if this man's saga has a moral, "it is that any human being—even a tough, street-smart cop—may act irrationally under extreme stress. That's why it's important for individuals to seek help when they're besieged by psychological, financial, or family problems."

No matter who we are, even if we're in a "helping profession," we all need support to accept the losses and stresses of a crisis or multiple crises. Theoretically, the natural place to start is with our spouse. Often we automatically look to our partner for practical support during a crisis. We call on our partner to drive to the hospital, feed the cat, do the grocery shopping, or cook dinner.

But in the area of emotional nurturance, our relationships are often unbalanced, with women doing most of the work. Women don't lean on their male partners to shore them up emotionally during a crisis as often as we might think. In 1987 when fifteen thousand women answered a Friendship Survey sponsored by *Family Circle*, 69 percent of those responding said they would discuss "feeling unhappy" with a friend instead of their husband or boyfriend. One woman commented, "With a best friend you share yourself inside, outside, upside down. Best friends never divorce you."

Most women seem to concur—female friends *are* easier to talk to. "With my friend Mary, I can let my sentences dangle—she finishes them for me," says Tina. "But with my husband—he stares at me with this `well, what next?'look!"

Men often depend solely on women for emotional comfort, too. Mother used to fix our hurts with Band-Aids, hugs, and soothing talk so it seems natural for adult men and women to seek solace from females. In short, females are the sex of choice when it comes to intimate sharing.

Lately, however, men all over the country are challenging the practice of saving in-depth sharing for women's ears only. To talk, really talk, to other men is a goal of newly forming men's groups, groups that include masculine rites such as drumming and using a talking stick that, passed to each man, gives him the floor to speak without interruption. In most groups, talk about automobiles, work, or football is discouraged as men are encouraged to talk to other men about a range of feelings and frustrations.

During a crisis, if you are a man, whether or not you embrace the men's movement or join a men's group, you may accept your altered situation more easily if you find a male friend or colleague you can trust to share some of your feelings with. Another man may comfort you in a different way and help empower you to speak more openly and boldly as you then also look to the female in your life for comfort.

If you are a woman, instead of talking exclusively with your female friends, you can try to open up more to men. For women, communication with the man in our life may never be as easy as with our same-sex friends, but a male perspective can enlarge our coping strategies, not simply comforting us with an echo of ourselves, but enriching us with new ideas and skills.

In short, when men stop depending only on a female partner for support; when women open their hearts to men as well as to female friends, as emotional support conditions shift and become less rigid, our possibilities for intimacy will increase dramatically.

Drs. Jordan Paul and Margaret Paul in *Do I Have to Give up Me to Be Loved by You?* write about how intimate sharing of pain powerfully unites partners: "The touching of hearts that occurs when we share pain lifts us out of the essential solitude that is a condition of existence....As we share pain, the weight of our protection is lifted and we feel lighter and clearer. We see our partner with a heart that is so full of love it wants to burst. We want to be as close as possible, to be one with, to be inside of. Our entire being comes alive with the intensity of our passion. Letting go of these feelings is wonderful: it feels orgasmic—whether it brings sex, laughter, joy, or even tears . . . . We rarely experience this passion because most of us have been so busy protecting ourselves that we have lost touch with our natural selves."

To attain that coveted level of sharing, we need to be clear about our motives. Sometimes we approach our partner saying, "Could I share this pain with you?" when we mean, "Could you fix this hurt for me?" When we share our pain, we first need to clarify to ourselves and then to say clearly to our partner, "I don't want you to fix anything. I'm not asking for solutions. I just need you to listen."

This takes practice if our relationship has been solution oriented. Be patient and gentle with each other as you experiment with growing in this kind of interchange. And be prepared for resistance in yourself and from your partner.

Sometimes we can comfort without words, by just being there for each other. After Arnold's office supply business failed and he and his wife, Joan, were facing bankruptcy, they commented on how much it meant to just sit close to each other. As Arnold expressed it, "I felt a great need for the comfort of Joan's touch even though I didn't have the emotional energy for intercourse. I just needed to know she still needed and trusted me."

"We are touchers and cuddlers," Joan adds, "and that helped greatly."

Sometimes we think we can't share our pain with our

partner because we're too tired to make passionate love, because our words come out wrong or we have no words at all, or because our partner reminds us of our pain and it's easier to pour it out to someone else. To get back into an intimate relationship, or to build one out of the rubble of a crisis, seeking emotional support from our partner is an option we may overlook—a choice so obvious that we don't see it.

But our partner can't be everything to us. Almost always when we're in a crisis our partner is in it too to some degree, so while we seek comfort from the one we love and live with, we also need to look for additional support from friends and family, in support groups, or in therapy.

The kinds of friends and relatives who can support us emotionally as we try to accept our altered situation are those who will allow us to talk about our feelings and will listen reflectively. The processing aloud to another is invaluable in moving us along through the stages of grief or acceptance of a loss.

Dottie Lamm, in *Second Banana*, describes true support this way: "It does not say, `I hear where you are hurting and failing, and how awful!' Nor does it say, `I hear where you are hurting and failing and you shouldn't.' Instead it says, `I hear where you are hurting and failing, and you will rise from that place and move on.'"

As we're attempting to accept the altered situation, we need to avoid those who give excessive advice, tend to place blame, see everything in a negative light, or see everything in a positive light.

Over the past twenty-five years, Jenny has gotten lots of advice about dealing with lupus, the incurable disease that has sapped much of her energy and put her into the hospital multiple times. "I have an aunt who believes that if you have the right mental imaging, you won't have any health problems. Hearing that used to make me feel guilty or inadequate that I couldn't conquer lupus."

Going through bankruptcy, Arnold noted, "There had been many men I knew who had sought me out for advice in personal or business matters and now they acted like I was no longer capable of giving any." His wife Joan adds, "Some friends were critical and snoopy. Some were extremely judgmental. Others just seemed to avoid us. The ones who questioned the way we spent our meager funds were the worst."

War stories about how friends and relatives mean well but make us feel bad, mean the worst and make us angry, or just react to us in fear when we're in a tough situation, could fill an entire book. We share these few examples to let you know you're not alone.

During a crisis, our self-esteem is sometimes low. Our lives are chaotic or out of control. In such a context, it's easy to feel even more down on ourselves and to doubt our judgment when we're misunderstood by the very people we'd hoped we'd be able to connect with for soothing comfort. In a crisis we're more susceptible than at other times to doubt the validity of our own perceptions. So, when friends and relatives come along with armloads of advice or criticism, we may believe them and turn away from the process of acceptance. Remember, you come first right now and so you have the right to stay away from these "advice experts."

We are, however, able to recognize the voices of those people who can really help us grow. They may not be eloquent, but we know they care. One woman, whose daughter was in a rehabilitation center for chemical dependency, was feeling like a total failure as a parent when a friend said spontaneously and warmly, "You must have done something really right to have your daughter come to you and tell you about her problem."

Arnold remembers the kindness one couple showed just after his business went under. "Joan and I had, for four or five years, gone to Aspen on the Fourth of July with Brent and Sandy, but we could no longer afford it. They said, `We're going and we're paying for the condo. You can take us sometime when we're broke.' That generosity enabled us to return to one of the fun things we did before the crisis without feeling obligated to them."

When we seek support from friends and relatives, we can't expect them to be mind readers. Ask yourself, Who could help me with what? Then ask for specific help. Each individual you're close to has the potential to help in a unique way. Often our loved ones, not knowing exactly what to do for us, may welcome our input. One may have time to go for a walk. Another may be available for a regular phone session. One might say yes to keeping your toddler while you and your partner go out for an evening. Another might recommend a helpful support group.

Throughout this book we point to therapy as a viable source of support. As you and your partner seek to comfort each other and as you ask friends and relatives for help, might individual, couple, or family therapy be an additional resource to help you through the hard task of finding acceptance? If, after many months, either or both of you are feeling farther and farther from acceptance; if your altered situation is making you feel as though life could never again be worth living; if your relationship with your partner is crumbling under the pressure; if friends and family seem far away and you feel as if you're in a tunnel looking out at them; if your partner is stuck in denial and showing no signs of moving through the grieving process—these "ifs" and others like them signal that support in therapy is not a luxury, but a necessity, like air, food, and water.

Ask friends for a recommendation; search out a suitable therapist who would be good at working with you in your particular set of circumstances. Therapy is not just for when we're feeling hopeless. A crisis may nudge us into spiritual and psychological growth and, liking it, we may decide we want more. Sometimes a crisis illuminates some of our previously hidden weaknesses. Sometimes a crisis puts our relationship's flaws up on a billboard. Now we see! But what do we do with our knowledge? Therapy can nurture these beginnings and give us direction and momentum to keep going.

Interview prospective therapists. A competent therapist should be open to and gracious about answering such questions as: What is your training? How long have you been a therapist? How much do you charge for each session? Is your treatment usually covered by insurance? Will I pay you first, then submit insurance forms to be reimbursed or will you handle that, allowing me to pay my portion later? What psychological approach do you draw on?

It's particularly important to ask, What's your philosophy of life—how would you summarize your beliefs about how a couple finds intimacy and how a couple can best make it through a crisis? Tell me a little about how you conduct a session.

Those and/or any other concerns can be addressed over the phone or in a preliminary visit. Ask the therapist if he or she is open to meeting for a consultation that you don't pay for. Connecting with the right therapist is invaluable for most people; it can save us when we're sinking. Or, when we're paddling along but want to improve our strokes, therapy can help us increase our skill, endurance, and strength.

Finally, don't overlook an invaluable resource for help—the many free support groups that meet regularly around the country. Newspapers often have listings; hospitals often sponsor groups; a clergyperson may also help you find the right one.

In the movie *Tough Love* about an organization of parents who are confronting their kids' out-of-bounds behavior, a character sums up the benefits of a support group. "I don't think people who are living through the same hell are ever strangers." We trust the input of those who've stood in the same spot as we are standing.

As support groups spring up everywhere, so do comedians' jokes about them. But don't automatically discount these groups. Often simple but profound means of help are misunderstood, feared, and ridiculed. Drowning our troubles in a bottle of Jim Beam may be more acceptable in some circles than regularly joining a circle of people who are going through a similar crisis, but it's not a healthy choice.

Our point is, don't overlook seeking out a support group when you're faced with accepting a significant loss or an upsetting change in your life. See for yourself what they're all about by attending at least three or four meetings. The first couple of meetings won't always give you a realistic feel for what's going on. You may be ill at ease, in denial, or something else may keep you from fully "being there."

Take Small steps and Make Necessary Practical Changes

We come to accept our altered situation by taking small steps: we change an attitude; we try to reach out to our partner even when we're exhausted; we call a friend and say "thanks for being there"; we listen to a soothing tape, or read an inspirational or entertaining book. These small steps indicate we're beginning to give up a portion of our suffering and we're beginning, at whatever pace is comfortable for us, to go on.

Arnold outlines small important steps he and Joan took after he'd lost his business and they'd lost their home. "We found cheap ways to be together—long walks in the snow, reading on the same sofa, sharing a movie. We'd look at old photos that reminded us of all we'd been through together. We learned to laugh again."

A few weeks after her son Mark's attempted suicide, Kathy remembers, "I was somewhere between the horror of the initial shock and the beginning of dealing with the reality of how to work through this. Bob and I had been through a few weeks of agonizing counseling sessions and heartbreaking visits to the hospital, and we had started to feel real sorry for ourselves. Why us? Why our kid? Why had tragedy hit us and no one else? I started to hate God. Then I started to hate every person I saw who had a smile on their face.

"Our lives had fallen apart and suddenly it was prom time for our daughter Kim. Somehow I had to help her shop for a gown. At the time it seemed almost impossible. A very bitter hateful person accompanied her to the mall that day. Finally, we found a dress but it was wrinkled.

"I remember standing in the store wondering, How can I take this home and iron it? Would my problems never end?

"A sweet, soft-spoken saleslady offered to press the dress. But I lashed out at her anyway. In a really ugly tone I told her that I could not deal with anything more! The dress *had* to be ready to wear in the next half-hour or I would not buy it! I told her I did not expect her to understand, but my son was ill and I did not have the mental strength to go home and iron that dress.

"The smile never left her face. She looked around, as if checking for privacy, and said, `I understand. I felt the same way when my son died.'

"My heart stopped. My whole life stopped. The self pity stopped. In that instant I realized that if I were going to ever be happy again I would have to work hard at it.

"Smiling faces did not mean people were happy or that people were more fortunate than I. Self pity only cripples you and it never gets better without pain and hard work.

"I wish I could thank that lady. She taught me the first step is to smile."

What small step might move you closer to acceptance? Often we don't even plan them, but when we're open to moving toward acceptance they happen.

Sometimes it's the practical changes we have to make that etch the reality of a crisis into our consciousness. We have to install a wheelchair ramp. We're forced to sell our house. We have to move our brushes, paints, and easel out of the spare bedroom because our frail father, alone now that our mother has died, is moving in with us.

For one family a necessary practical change was learning sign language. Fifteen years ago when Don and Linda's youngest son, Matt, was twenty-two months old, he contracted spinal meningitis which damaged his ears, leaving him deaf. Today this bright young man's speech is clear, he can read lips, and he's an honor student in a public high school. Don credits Linda with making these accomplishments possible. She spent long hours with Matt, teaching him to read and to speak words aloud.

Linda also insisted the entire family learn sign language. Linda came to this decision after speaking with a number of deaf adults. "Every single one of them who grew up in families that never learned to sign said they had felt left out—that they simply couldn't communicate that well without signing," she remembers.

She and Matt took a sign language course in a parent-child program. Don and the three other children learned in a community-sponsored class. When Matt is present the family signs, period! "Linda's always been very strong to insist that all conversations in the home be signed so that Matt could be included in all aspects of family life," Don says.

Necessary practical changes tie us to the reality of a crisis and move us into acceptance. Sometimes so sadly we can hardly speak of them. Sometimes with the relief that at least we can do something.

Help Others

In coming to a place of acceptance, it helps us to help others. After Jim and Helen Kilroy's son, Mark, was murdered by a drug-smuggling cult, they established The Mark Kilroy Foundation (MARK), a nonprofit foundation dedicated to attacking the widespread problems of drug abuse. As the Kilroys' struggle with the question they say they've asked many times—Why Mark?—their work helps turn a senseless tragedy into something good.

After his office supply business failed, Arnold, a skilled carpenter, set off on a mission trip to Guatemala to build houses for the poor. "After seeing the poverty of the people there and the joy in life they had, I came home thinking how fortunate I was to have three or four jackets to choose from rather than none at all."

Since Marilyn donated her kidney to her daughter in 1989, she's related her experience to other parents facing the decision of whether to give a child a kidney. She sees her sharing as an opportunity to be supportive to them. She is also active in the National Kidney Foundation.

Laura, who lost her son in a drunk-driving accident, went back to get her teaching certificate and now teaches high school English. "I have a captive audience of 150 students," she says. "As prom night approaches I share the story of my son's needless death and urge my students to keep the evening safe by not driving drunk or getting into a car with anyone at the wheel who's been drinking. Nothing will bring my son back, but I may be able to save someone else's son or daughter's life."

Elizabeth Glaser, wife of "Starsky and Hutch" star Paul Michael Glaser, has collected millions of dollars for pediatric AIDS research. Her dedication to this cause was born out of the death of their daughter Ariel, who died of AIDS complications at age seven. Both Elizabeth and their young son are infected with the HIV virus. Only Paul Michael has not been infected. Besides her fundraising efforts, Elizabeth has also written a moving book, entitled *In the Absence of Angels.*

Many of us won't travel to a foreign country, start a foundation, or raise lots of money in response to our crisis. But all of us can give of ourselves in ways impossible before. "Be a friend to someone else with problems. Help someone needier than you and you will feel some of your needs dissolve," says Arnold. "It works."

"Once you have been beat up, you look at life through a different pair of lenses," writes Robert Veninga, in *A Gift of Hope*. When we hug someone who's hurting, we may notice our hug is genuine and heartfelt. When someone shares their pain, we may now listen more empathetically than we ever could have before. As we move toward acceptance of our altered situation we find we can read the fine print on the bottom line of the suffering chart. And seeing it accurately now, we can use our sensitized vision to reach out to others.

If You're Still Resisting

If you're still resisting the changes acceptance requires and feel as though becoming an acceptor is about as likely for you as winning a million dollars in a sweepstakes, it's possible you've "scripted" yourself for unhappiness.

At some point in your past, did you decide that being unhappy was your lot in life? A friend's mother told her repeatedly as she was growing up that she was "emotionally unstable and probably never would be able to be happy." Somewhere along the line, did you adopt a "poor me" attitude and begin to grow comfortable seeing yourself as a victim? Do you set yourself up over and over again for avoidable crises? (For instance by spending too much money; taking on too much caregiving; not planning for inevitable transitions such as children leaving home or retirement; or not eating a healthy diet or exercising regularly.) Did a series of unavoidable rough blows—illnesses, accidents, deaths of loved ones, or other random tragedies—make you think God or fate intended you to suffer continuously and permanently?

Sometimes to stay in our suffering is to get rewards of

sorts. So long as we're stuck we can be lazy; maintaining the status quo requires no effort. So long as we're stuck we can be special too; by staying in mourning we get a lot of attention. Sometimes, in fact, being a victim gets us more attention than being a survivor. People may give us special consideration because of our crisis. We become known as the mother of the son with leukemia; the husband of the wife in the terrible car wreck; the partner of a man with AIDS; the couple whose house burned down; the woman who gave up her career to take care of her sick father.

Often we find out we can get more attention from our partner by staying stuck. Especially if he or she feels responsible for and guilty about a crisis, we can manipulate him or her into feeling sorry for us. With tears in our eyes, we can say things like, "Sweetheart, you knew you shouldn't have been driving that fast" or, "If only you'd have listened to me" or, "It's okay. I'll never forget what happened, but I know your intentions were good." We need to face these types of gut-wrenching self truths if, after a long period of time, we remain stuck in unacceptance.

Perhaps as you read this you find this section applies not to you, but to your mate. Sometimes your silent example—your modeling of acceptance as you go about your daily life—will inspire your beloved to join you. But sometimes, partners who refuse to go on after a reasonable period may also need to be confronted in a caring way. They need us to reflect back what we see. Instead of confronting the one we love with "Darling, it's time to go on," be more specific. For example: "It's been a month since you've been out of the house, except to go to the grocery store. You're leaving the answering machine on and not returning friends' calls. I feel you're shutting me out too, by watching TV the whole time I'm home. What's going on?"

Ask your partner to respond to your concerns. If he or she gets angry or defensive or shows no signs of moving toward acceptance, make specific requests, such as, "I'd like you to meet me for lunch next Wednesday. Would you be able to?" or, "I'd like to talk tonight, without the TV or any distractions. Could we set aside from 7 to 8 P.M.?"

If your partner continues to resist acceptance, tell him or her you feel the need to set a deadline. After you decide on a date, mark it on a calendar. This is the day on which you expect your partner to move forward. Ask for only an inch of movement: getting dressed, making a necessary phone call, attending one support group meeting, having one session with a therapist, or reading a particular book. Ask your partner to fulfill just *one* such suggestion.

Use all the creativity you can muster. What one activity or responsibility might lure your partner back to the present? Aha! Once you've got an idea try it out.

If, however, your mate keeps on refusing to budge after you lovingly and persistently confronted him or her, intervention from a third person—a professional or caring friend—may now be necessary. When our mate shows a prolonged inability to get back on course it strains our patience; we're lonely, wanting the companionship back in our relationship; and we may grow frightened about his or her predicament. Resist blaming or chastizing your partner for hitting bottom and staying there. Your best plan of action is to continue to keep your own life on course and to use gentle, consistent confrontation, coupled with outside assistance when necessary.

Back to the Present

There is a bittersweet feeling of triumph couples share when both separately and together they commit themselves to becoming acceptors.

Looking back to when her son tried to commit suicide, Kathy says that for a time her life seemed like a surrealistic horror movie. Calling 911. Traveling seventy miles-per-hour in an ambulance to a hospital emergency room with their unconscious son. Visiting him in the hospital as often as was allowed, for three months. Both parents hoping, praying he'd stay in recovery and want to go on living.

"It's the first time either one of us had experienced pain like that. It's just like first love—`first pain' is not going to be forgotten either," Kathy explains. "It wakes you up to an entire world you didn't know existed before . . . . We learned a lot about ourselves. We don't judge people so harshly anymore. We're more patient. People who have never felt such deep pain, who have miraculously been spared that kind of pain, are never going to understand 100 percent, never. But we know we're part of a large company of sufferers."

During the height of their crisis, Kathy says they did not philosophize like this—they fought, over every imaginable subject. "Even where to eat dinner out," Kathy laughs now. Divorce crossed Kathy's mind "daily" for a while. "But even at the absolute worst times, I would still honestly tell myself this man is what I basically want. Bob is faithful and hardworking. He includes me in his life. But during this crisis with Mark I also felt like, I hate him and he's horrible!"

In therapy, Kathy and Bob faced a number of crucial issues. One was that much of their dissatisfaction with each other was misdirected anger over their son's suicide attempt. Another was that two people can love each other and still disagree about all kinds of things. "We've learned when a disagreement's not important, to let it go," Kathy says. "We've stopped fighting about *everything* and save our energy for big issues, where we need to come to an agreement or compromise."

Having gone through the worst together, after acting their worst toward each other, Kathy and Bob are taking the lessons of this crisis and using them to build a stronger relationship. They no longer resemble the individuals or couple they were pre-crisis. They feel an immense gratitude for their son's survival and for their survival as a couple. They now do their best to live in the present.

"Intimacy . . . depends on your being in the space you are really in now, related to whatever and whoever is in that space, as they are now, and at the present moment—not time traveling in the past, or future, or space hopping to other places," write the Malones in *The Art of Intimacy*.

If we choose to run from a crisis, refusing to become acceptors; if we decide to become so engulfed in a crisis that it continues to be the central focus of our lives for months, even years—we miss out on the joy of becoming an acceptor. We never feel the transforming power that comes by admitting a loss is true. We never claim our new identity that comes from being structurally changed and bonded with a loss.

The big reward for becoming an acceptor is that once we're transformed by our loss we then can live in the present moment and not in the past. And being *all here* increases our capacity for the joy of personal growth, for intimacy with our partner, and for contributing to our larger world.

Reflection Opportunities

1. Are you in the process of becoming an acceptor? Have you admitted your loss and allowed it to begin changing and re-forming your identity? What tough realities have come into your life as a result of the crisis? Make a list using the following categories as appropriate: new insights, new heartaches, new handicaps, new inconveniences, and new challenges. On that list, what is the single hardest reality to accept?

2. Who or what might help you accept this hardest-of-all reality? Your partner? Your Higher Power? A friend? A therapist? A combination of people, plus more time and a belief in the healing process? An ongoing attitude of taking one day or one moment at a time?

3. Where are you in the grief process: denial and isolation; anger; bargaining; depression; acceptance? Where is your partner? Have you both entered into your own personal pain, felt it, spent time with it, and shared it?

4. Are you "doing" anger in your relationship? Can you share your anger about the crisis with one another? If not, do you need a objective third person to facilitate the process?

5. Has this crisis caused you to ask, What's life all about anyway? In your questioning and searching have you reconnected with your spirituality? Have you tapped into the holy within yourself? Have you reached out to a Higher Power? Or are you discovering both? Can you and your partner search together or do you prefer to do it individually? Are you headed in similar or opposite directions? Ask yourself now: What are the lessons hiding in this crisis?

6. Have you made the practical adjustments necessary

to help you cope with the changes? Have you adjusted your schedule, rearranged your living space, realigned your values, altered your beliefs? Take a close look at which adjustments are most pressing, most necessary. Have you discussed these with your partner?

7. Have you shared your personal pain with your partner? Have you asked not for solutions or advice, but for understanding? Do you empathize with your partner's pain?

8. Where might you share the skills and coping strategies you've learned?

Chapter 12

Something in Common: Traits of Couples Who've Made It Through

When the heart weeps for what it has lost,
the spirit laughs for what it has found.
anonymous Sufi aphorism

My brother Philip collects old books. Recently he showed me a charming 1926 title, *How To Find Happyland: A Book of Children's Stories*. If there is an antithesis to those glossy pages full of whimsical illustrations and happily-ever-after tales, it is this for-adults-only book you're now reading. "A fairy tale is the child's myth," wrote Joseph Campbell in *The Power of Myth*. "There are proper myths for proper times of life. As you grow older, you need a sturdier mythology."

The women and men who share their survival-through-crisis stories in these pages provide a sturdy mythology of survivors. We believe that their examples and insights can inspire all of us who are trying to survive a crisis alongside our partner.

Throughout most of this book we use a telephoto lens to view different aspects of crisis in detail, thoroughly probing one area of crisis management and couple survival at a time. In this chapter, however, we are deliberately using a sweeping wide-angle lens on the same picture.

Here we're taking a panoramic view of couple survivors to give you a look at the big picture, the overall landscape of these people's lives. We believe that by observing their particular collection of attitudes and behaviors, you can tailor them to fit your particular situation. When you're feeling particularly discouraged, when you're bumping into the trees, but the forest is a big blur, we trust this chapter will guide you.

The "couple survivors" you have met in these pages felt the pain, then ultimately discovered the deep, hidden joy of going through a crisis *with* a partner. They made their way through disappointments and losses to reconstruct new lives in the company of old partners. They are not grim survivors, but rather heroic individuals who went through the crisis process and came out altered—sadder and wiser—and glad still to be alive and to be together.

The couple survivors whom I've interviewed and Marilyn has seen in therapy all share at least seven common traits. They are not the traits of supermen or superwomen—not traits we read about and say "I could never be like this." So take notice and take heart. The traits they share are attainable for any of us who choose them.

They Have a Commitment to Each Other and Honor It

In one form or another, commitment is basic to a couple's survival. How and when did their commitments take hold? We found no unanimity. Some started their relationships with a firm commitment in place. Said one, "Divorce has never been an option." Others stumbled into their relationships, or more accurately into each other's arms, because of raging hormones and a red-hot attraction to each other. They thought about, then decided on, a commitment months or years later. One couple, married over thirty years, renews their commitment yearly, much like renters signing a lease on an apartment. They review their relationship, before deciding to renew it again, remaining open to the possibility that one year, they might not remain committed.

What does this commitment *feel* like?   Susan M. Campbell, Ph.D., in *The Couple's Journey*, describes it best. "We're on this roller coaster 'till the end of the ride, and we intend to stay on it, but that doesn't mean we don't experience the ups and downs in ways that often make us feel like getting off!"

When she and Jeff went through bankruptcy six years ago, Deborah recalls, "At the time, all kinds of thoughts passed through my mind. The doubt that we ever should have gotten married, that we ever should have gone into business, that we ever should have filed for bankruptcy, that we ever should have had children—everything. You are so hurt, so down. But the thought of copping out on our marriage—even though I felt like it at the time, I couldn't. You know where you are, you have a place you belong, when you find a relationship then keep it by working at it. So many people take the easy way out."

Jenny, who continues to battle lupus with her husband Merv by her side, when asked, "What would have happened to your marriage if you'd gone with your `feeling of the day'?" answered with an instant, "We . . . nobody would last!"

Three years ago Mary felt like splitting up with Rod when their daughter went through a rebellious "drinking and drugging" period. "We `do' normal times together better than crises," she explained. "In a crisis like the one with our daughter, we teach each other. I see in him a tough resiliency; he sees in me more depth. I get down into a crisis and feel the pain more. But frankly, at the time, this teaching is about as welcome as one more bill in the mail. It's one more thing to have to deal with!

"With thirty-two years together," she continued, "I can say this with certainty: 75 percent of the time I love my husband a lot. The other 25 percent is divided into times when I wish I'd never laid eyes on him and times when I feel neither positive nor negative, but rather blah about us. The way I see it, our 75 percent time, when we find joy, passion, and quiet contentment together, that percentage isn't bad, not bad at all . . . ."

They Value Their Individuality

Couple survivors are two wholes, not two halves. During a crisis either we maintain our individuality or we become engulfed in each other. To illustrate this, here are two statements which sound almost the same, but which represent vastly different attitudes:

"Honey, I've learned I can go through hell and back and survive—hold me, just hold me."

"Honey, I can't face any of this without you; just keep holding me forever and take the fear and pain away."

Statement number one reflects the attitudes of the majority of couple survivors we encountered. The second depicts an enmeshment in which one partner is attempting to become stronger by dissolving the boundary between himself and his partner. As we've seen, we can best survive a crisis together as independent individuals who care for each other but who also take responsibility for ourselves.

After Tom's construction-site accident which left him paraplegic, Cynthia, tired of running a catering business, decided to take night classes to earn a degree in environmental science. Unable to continue working as a builder,

Tom returned to school to pursue a degree in architecture. After learning to negotiate his wheelchair expertly, going up and down stairs and "popping wheelies," and after mastering driving a car with special hand controls, he's able to come and go without Cynthia's assistance.

Tom and Cynthia have turned a spare bedroom into a study. Tom's computer is on one wall; Cynthia's desk is on another. That room is an appropriate metaphor for the kind of individuality/interdependence couple survivors possess. Both Tom and Cynthia depend on each other in many ways. But each is also depending on himself, on herself, to go on living and growing.

As the Malones wrote in *The Art of Intimacy*, "Simply put, when you can be in your own personal space while you are also in the space you share with another, you are being intimate."

The couple survivors we encountered also validated each other's individual rights by acknowledging that there were two ways to view a crisis. Though they often fought initially to get their partners to view a crisis as they did, though at first it may not have dawned on them that there could be a second viewpoint, survivors sooner or later saw the futility and the destructiveness of trying to convert a partner. Though not always easily, they came to accept and respect one another's reality.

Fifteen years ago when Don and Linda's son Matt became deaf, Linda started doing volunteer work for organizations that help hearing-impaired children. Don sensed that her work was helping her deal with Matt's tragic, unexpected impairment. Don, a devoted husband and father, learned to sign and spent time playing with Matt, trying to help him adjust to his silent world. But Don had no desire to do volunteer work. His best way of handling the extra stress was to build a new garage. Hammering, sawing, and pouring concrete was his therapy.

Though Don is exceptionally proud of what Linda has accomplished in implementing improvements in education and other areas for deaf children, he has at times wished she hadn't stayed quite so busy with it all. He would have liked more time off together. At times Linda has wished she and Don could have tackled the volunteer work as a team. They have, however, respected each other's choices and been flexible. Don helps out occasionally in fundraising events; and every so often Linda sets aside time to take off for a week away with Don.

They Practice Their Love

A few years ago I read in a self-help book that in "happy" marriages, couples refrain from saying certain terrible things to each other. They never hit below the belt, the author reflected; they never used the knowledge of a partner's weakness to inflict hurt.

That criterion for a "happy" relationship did not hold true for most couple survivors. They were not habitually verbally abusive to each other, but sometimes they said those terrible things they wish they could have gone back and erased. Couple survivors echoed an anonymous Spanish proverb that says, *"Quien bien te quiere te hara llorar,"* whoever really loves you will make you cry.

Often crises brought out the worst in partners. For many, there were periods of blaming each other. Often they had difficulty deciding what to say aloud to a partner and what to keep to themselves. "I had not wanted to go into the aluminum-siding business, but Jeff insisted we try it," Deborah says. "And when we went bankrupt, for a while I held it against him. Finally I felt I had to be honest enough to tell him I was blaming him—but then when I did, I knew I had hurt his feelings. I couldn't live with myself not telling him, yet he felt worse when I did."

However "right " or "wrong" her words were, when she spoke her truth, the healing between them began. We suspect their underlying love and commitment outweighed awkward or ill-spoken words. And they didn't stay in this difficult spot. Deborah did stop blaming Jeff. Both started rebuilding their lives, finding work, and trying to use the lessons of the crisis. "Whatever mistakes I make, Jeff is there for me," Deborah says. "Even though we don't always agree, he tells me his true feelings and I tell him mine."

In writing about those people who love each other well, Teilhard De Chardin in *Human Energy* points out, "How many disasters, ups and downs or, to put the best complexion on it, how many misunderstandings and estrangements take place even in the most successful unions!"

Couple survivors know that practicing their love does not make them perfect. They also know that practicing their love, however imperfectly, is the only way they will maintain a satisfying relationship. What we saw in these couples was a dedication to practicing again and again, despite the hurt and pain, and to keeping on forgiving themselves and each other.

They Trust Themselves

A couple in a crisis may as well be wearing a sandwich board with bold print that reads "NOW'S YOUR OPPORTUNITY TO GIVE US ADVICE AND HEAP JUDGMENT ON US." These couples reported receiving advice from virtually everyone—friends, relatives, experts, even strangers. If the crisis is infertility, someone knows what you're doing wrong while someone else knows a magic cure or marvelous new procedure. If the crisis is a child's substance abuse, someone is willing to tell you, the parents, exactly where you went wrong and will be willing to pray for you. If the crisis is a struggle with an addiction to work, someone will tell you exactly how to break the addiction, and someone else will assure you your dedication to long hours is praiseworthy, not compulsive.

Out of the cacophony of voices, couples who survive develop their own philosophy for handling a crisis. Sooner or later, couples who stay together find a core trust in themselves. Usually not at the beginning of a crisis and often after months have passed, individually and together couple survivors eventually begin to trust their own reality.

After Tom's accident Cynthia was not sure she would remain in the relationship. Did she want to? Did she have the commitment, the energy to live with a husband who was paraplegic? A beautiful woman who presumably could easily attract a new mate, Cynthia, keeps hearing from friends and acquaintances either one of two comments, "I don't know how you do it—I think you're great," or, "I don't know how you do it, why don't you leave?" After going through the process of sorting out her beliefs, Cynthia withstands outside influences and honors her own judgment.

Ultimately Cynthia's answer was "Yes, I want to stay," based on this belief: This isn't perfection, but then all the options I have aren't perfect either. As she explained, "I look at life as all ups and downs. You always like the ups, but you've got to pick the down that you like the best. Tom

and I have been together ten years—I ask myself, do I want
to grow old by myself or do I want our kids to come home
to us at Christmas? Do I want to stay with this man who's
known me most of my life even if he can't walk? We have
a lot in common. We like the same foods, the same music.
Where am I going to find a guy that I get along that well
with?"

Other couples reported the need to keep believing in
themselves in the face of professional advice that conflicted
with their perceptions. When Don and Linda's son lost his
hearing, Don remembers his frustration. Initially psycholo-
gists and social workers they were referred to seemed
intent only on finding out how he and Linda *felt* about their
son's deafness.

"My *feeling* is," Don remembers telling them emphati-
cally, "the boy is deaf and he needs some professional
help—where do we go to get it?!" Don and Linda started an
independent search for appropriate help for Matt. By talking with other parents of deaf children, by visiting support
groups, by contacting deaf adults—in short by following
their own gut-level beliefs that they needed to seek help for
their son first, then address their feelings and needs second—they accomplished this, their primary goal.

Today at eighteen, Matt, an honor student, reads lips,
speaks clearly, and is proficient in sign language. Many
times, says Don, he and Linda were told their son would
never attain this level of functioning. Many times they
heard, "Nothing can be done. That's just the way it is."

"We spent time and effort researching on our own,"
Don says. "As you face any situation in your life, my advice
to other couples is this: Don't be content with pat answers.
Look for solutions rather than just accepting what's handed
to you."

Marilyn, in counseling couples about how they develop trust in themselves, says, "We must have self trust in order to trust our partner. We foster the growth of trust by openly sharing our feelings, perceptions, truths, and beliefs. The more we understand our partner's mode of seeing the world the more we can predict his or her reactions. That predictability also fosters trust because the world seems organized and we know what to expect."

In the chaos of a crisis, couple survivors seek to restore and build trust in themselves and in their partner.

They Accept The Altered Situation and Evolve Together

Couples who stayed together were gutsy people who found the courage to face a crisis, then to accept whatever ways it altered their lives. "You've got to say yes to this miracle of life as it is, not on the condition that it follow your rules," writes Joseph Campbell in *The Power of Myth*. The couple survivors discovered this belief and integrated it into their lives.

The drugs Jenny must take to control lupus have caused her to gain weight. "I have these chipmunk cheeks now," she says. "I've gained one hundred pounds. I never had a weight problem before. I tried dieting and ended up in the hospital. I'd rather be fat than gravely ill. You have to make choices."

Jenny says many marriages break up when a partner with lupus is no longer as physically attractive as before. Jenny and Merv don't like the physical changes the disease and its treatment have inflicted, but their gratitude at being alive and together overpowers bitterness about what might have been. They take leisurely strolls together. In the late afternoon, after the sun is low enough—Jenny must avoid exposure to midday sun—they swim and relax together.

They enjoy too the stream of grown children and young grandchildren who visit them often.

Couple survivors resist staying stuck in self-pity. They process their losses and step-by-step they return to the present, sometimes sadder, often wiser. They courageously open themselves up to living life as it is right now.

They Develop Support Systems

Couples who survive crises together never do it totally alone. They reach out for and eventually find support somewhere. They get together with friends or relatives, they read books, listen to tapes, attend lectures, join support groups, or find a therapist. Or they find support in other less obvious, but equally effective ways. Some take an adult education class and meet students who will talk about ceramics and not about the death of their son. Some sign up for a judo class, releasing physical tension and making new friends.

Besides seeking help by connecting with people and interests, often couple survivors seek spiritual support from a Higher Power through prayer, meditation, or worship. "Support came from faith in God—that there would be a way out—that he would provide housing," said one woman remembering going through bankruptcy with her husband. One couple, whose son committed suicide on his sixteenth birthday, recommitted themselves to their Christian faith and have found warm support and empathy in their new church "family."

When Sarah's daughter was in a resident treatment program for drug abuse, she recalls entering the hospital lobby and seeing the familiar face of an acquaintance. Both are award-winning poets who occasionally found themselves scheduled to read their work in the same locations on the same evenings. "What are you doing here?" Sarah asked Tanya.

"My daughter's in rehab on the fourth floor," she answered. The two wordsmiths were speechless, but their hug lasted a long time. They exchanged phone numbers and called each other when they were feeling down.

Sometimes individuals found support through such serendipity; sometimes they searched methodically for it until they finally found an appropriate connection. The only consistent thread in the theme of finding support was that every couple we know about who has survived a crisis had outside help in one form or another. Were any of us to depend solely on ourselves or on our partner, the stress of that load would most likely break us apart.

They Inspire And Influence Others

By their attitudes and by their actions, these couples make a difference in other's lives. Men and women who survive a crisis, who grow individually and together, exude a different aura than those who have sailed through life as yet untouched by any great loss. Couples who've been through a crisis together no longer try to look perfect. The imperfection that life has handed them has shown them clearly that perfection and control were only illusions anyway.

Kathy, whose son Mark tried to commit suicide five years ago and survived, no longer makes a big deal of small problems. She says her sister still gets upset when her daughter "leaves three spoonfuls of green beans on her plate. I say to her, now wait a minute—let me explain—this is *not* a big problem."

In gentle confrontations like this, in role-modeling a set of deeper values found during a crisis, in sharing their survival stories, in showing their children ways to confront loss or grief, in ways as diverse as they are, the couple survivors inspire and influence others by their attitudes.

"Dealing with a crisis is not easy," says Dr. Patrick Malone. "Acceptance is hard work—most people run away. Every time life gives them a chance to grow they run from it." You can join the courageous minority of couples who simply refuse to run. Cultivating the traits mentioned in this chapter will make your decision to grow together at least a little easier.

Chapter 13

Inventing a New Relationship

*Developing truly intimate relationships is
an activity that lasts a lifetime. Great
changes don't happen overnight . . . .
There's no shortcut for learning how to love.*
E. Edward Reitman, Ph.D.

For five weeks, Evelyn and Richard Shanklin had been on a dream honeymoon, island hopping in the Bahamas. But late one night, aboard their thirty-foot sailboat *Go For It*, there was a bang and the boat seemed to be dragging. Alarmingly quickly, they were standing in knee-deep water.

They may have hit a coral reef. Whatever happened, enough damage had occurred that they had no choice but to abandon ship. They followed an orderly plan—gathering up supplies, radioing "mayday," and preparing the dinghy. But as Evelyn was walking toward Richard, carrying some of the things they needed, suddenly she got tangled in the mast's rigging. Richard struggled to free her, finally getting her loose. By then, the boat was beginning to sink, their supplies were floating off, and it was too late to untie the dinghy from the boat.

Thus the honeymooners found themselves in the dark water, wearing orange life vests and clinging to a boat bumper that had floated by. During their twelve-hour

ordeal before being rescued by the Coast Guard, Evelyn
and Richard talked and talked. One thing they faced right
away was their anger. Richard was fifty-one and Evelyn
forty-nine. After finally finding love together, they had
expected a long life as a couple. "When we married, I had
made her promise me forty years of her life," Richard said
in an interview by T. M. Shine in the Fort Lauderdale *Sun-
Sentinel*, "and she still owed me thirty-nine." But now their
survival seemed questionable, especially when sharks
began circling.

Despite their situation, Richard articulated a new way
of relating that he wanted to try out if they had the privilege
of resuming their life together. Before they got married,
Richard had promised Evelyn she could yell at him once a
day. Out there in the water Richard pledged he would start
yelling back. "I never did that before," he reflected later.

Instead of just murmuring sweet nothings, Richard
did the hard psychological and spiritual exercise of isolating a pattern of passive behavior, and out there in that scary
situation, vowed to make a radical change. During that
crisis, some gut-level wisdom told Richard that being
yelled at without the right to yell back would sooner or
later damage the relationship with the woman he loved.

Usually not with sharks literally surrounding us, but
often as they symbolically circle us during a crisis, we can,
like Richard, see our relationship clearly and are able to
change what needs changing. We see an unhealthy way
that we treat our mate; we see an unacceptable way he or
she treats us; we see habits we've fallen into or promises
we've made—and we have a chance to sort out the ones we
want to keep from the ones we'd like to discard or modify.

When we survive a crisis together, we have the opportunity to use our new perceptions to change our relation-

ship—to invent a new healthier and sturdier one out of the pieces of our crisis-shattered lives.

Like Humpty Dumpty

After his great fall, "all the king's horses and all the king's men" tried to put Humpty Dumpty "together again," but couldn't. To put the pieces of our individual or couple lives back together as they were pre-crisis, is just as impossible. Often, however, we refuse to believe it. We try to sweep up the pieces of our individual and couple lives. We get out the super glue. We think if only we're diligent enough, we can put ourselves back together again and be exactly who we were before.

The problem is, when we are faced with a significant loss or a change serious enough that we call it a crisis, we are changed. We are not the same individuals. We are not the same couple. All the pieces of our old selves and our old relationship are not there anymore. We've been broken by a crisis—not to be repaired, but to be transformed.

We can't simply patch things up after a major upheaval in our lives. A crisis creates chaos. But, as science writer K. C. Cole points out in *Lears*, "Even though things fall apart, they fall into interesting patterns." How to take the interesting new patterns of our lives and invent from them a new relationship is the challenge we face.

This is not easy, for in addition to the disarray a crisis brings into our lives, both during and after, two people face each other looking at a familiar visage, but feeling like strangers. Anxiety, fear, sadness, disappointment, anger, and rage over losing our old partner and our old self can easily engulf us.

Though we cannot undo the damage or loss of a crisis, there are two ways we can create a new intimate post-crisis relationship with our spouse. The first is to reach for courage. "One man with courage makes a majority," said Andrew Jackson. One couple, sometimes even one partner within a couple relationship, with courage can invent a new relationship. While friends and family predict your demise, while statistics offer a grim reminder that "it ain't easy," gather up your courage.

Second, take small steps to get to know yourself and your partner anew. The rest of this chapter is a compilation of suggestions for you to use. We're providing the ideas; you'll have to provide the courage to implement them!

We wish you well and say bravo! Bravo for those of us who are determined to invent a new relationship. We are pioneers as we dare to learn how to put loving our partner ahead of loving and longing for our old circumstances.

As we go forward together, we are, in effect, saying to our mate, "I love you more than I love what we once had. I love you enough to go on instead of looking back. I love you in the present tense even though we've lost a lot, and I'll dedicate myself to finding out just how to practice my love." With such attitudes in place, more often than not, a new love for each other can take hold and grow strong.

The suggestions that follow fall into three categories: communication, comfort and consolation, and celebration. They will serve you best when you adopt this mind set: Any of the suggestions you decide is worth doing, is worth doing imperfectly!

When we keep on trying, again and again, when we don't expect perfection from ourselves or from our partner, we'll find joy in making small changes. We'll be able to forgive ourselves for regressing, for not getting the hang of how to sustain the deeper relationship we're seeking, and for being inconsistent.

Losing then regaining the will to keep on trying is the way most of us zigzag upward. Instant change happens on the pages of romance novels, but in real life, several months of calendar pages, usually more, will have to be turned before we make enough small changes to effect a new relationship.

Communication

Express Your Intentions

Your partner may be anxious, fearful, angry, confused, or uncertain about the state of your relationship. If you're ready to invent a new relationship with your mate, let him or her know. Think about your intentions, decide what the truth about them is so you can speak about it honestly and without exaggeration. Promise your partner only what you intend to give.

Statements like these tell our spouse our intentions: "Honey, we'll never be the same, but we still have each other and I don't want to lose `us,' ever"; "I was used to our old life. I'll miss our house, but I want to be with you even more than I want our old lifestyle"; "I'm ready to stop blaming each other and life and start learning how to move closer again. I've missed you desperately"; "I'm not sure who you are now or who I am either. I'm not sure we'll be together forever, but I'd like to try my best to make things work for the next six months."

Ask your partner if he's ready to express his intentions. Don't expect an instant "I feel exactly the same way, sweetheart." She may need to mull things over. State your reality lovingly, making it clear that after all that's happened, you too need reassurance and confirmation of the status of your relationship.

Set New Goals

When our lives are as smooth as silk, when our dreams haven't been crumpled up like a piece of paper tossed into the trash, we may think grand thoughts, and set big goals. Often a crisis forces us to modify some of our goals, a task that seems as inviting as going to a used-car lot to pick out a two-hundred-dollar clunker after our shiny new Taurus has been totaled. When, however, we face the necessity of setting new goals, we can move ahead with our lives. As we set new goals we increase our capacity to live in the present.

Before Stan lost his executive position, Peggy, finally finished with raising their five children, was ready to kick up her heels. Specifically, she was trying to decide if she'd rather fly to Paris to see the Mona Lisa and dine in the open-air cafes or if she'd prefer taking hiking boots and a backpack to Australia to trek around the outback.

With a drastic drop in their income, the question became academic. Peggy had to stop reading travel brochures and start looking for a full-time job. In fact, most of Stan's and Peggy's old goals and dreams had to be put on hold. Just after Stan was laid off, they decided a necessary new goal for their relationship to survive, was, as Peggy put it, "to allow each other the freedom to deal with the crisis in the way we are best able to handle it, and to come from our own point of view."

Stan was pessimistic. He was pretty sure they'd lose their house. He wasn't going to be convinced otherwise until he and Peggy secured new jobs that brought in enough to cover the mortgage and other set living expenses. Peggy, on the other hand, was optimistic. She felt sure "something" would happen.

Both Peggy and Stan were doing everything they could to secure employment. Neither could fault each other's efforts. If, however, they had not discussed their underlying opposing viewpoints and made it a goal to allow them, they most likely would have expended energy on bickering. Peggy might have said something like: "How could you be so glum? You know we've always made it before." And Stan could have answered: "Optimism like yours is about as realistic as imagining China will become a democracy next week."

However, instead of putting each other down, Stan set up a consulting business and Peggy completed a real estate course, which led to a job selling residential and commercial properties. As it turned out, they were able to keep their house.

Setting goals is as regular a part of Peggy and Stan's relationship as paying bills. They emphasize that their lives evolve and change so quickly that they regularly need to revise their goals. Not just in crises, but in the more routine flow of days, they set personal goals and relationship goals.

Setting goals together during and after a crisis, can be bittersweet. As we go forward we may reminisce about the losses and changes, the parts of our lives we miss, but cannot retrieve. Our memories can console us so long as they do not substitute for forging a new life together in the present.

Think about a variety of arenas of your life—financial, vocational, social, spiritual, emotional, physical, psychological, philosophical. Sometimes a crisis illuminates one of these aspects we'd previously ignored or given only minimal attention. What are your goals in each of these areas?

As you and your partner set new goals together, here are some questions for each of you to answer: What are my immediate (for the next month) personal goals? What are my long-term personal goals? What are my immediate couple goals? What are my long-term couple goals?

Revise Unworkable Parts of Your Anger Contract

On a recent television talk show one man described how he and his wife interact. "We don't fight . . . as in a sense of beating and hitting. It's like, you know, I piss her off, she goes that way. She pisses me off, I go the other way."

In effect, this couple has an anger contract—they've agreed to be mad in certain predictable ways. Anger is a part of every crisis. By discovering what our relationship's anger contract consists of and by consciously trying to revise it into a more workable one, we can use our anger to build instead of destroy intimacy.

To begin to understand the anger contract in your relationship answer these questions alone, then ask your mate to answer them too, so you can discuss them together. Write them down or record them on tape to make sharing easier.

Look first at current anger transactions with your partner. How do you express anger to your partner? (For instance, do you grin and bear it? Explode uncontrollably? Both, depending on the situation? Or do you allow your anger, feel it, then express it?)

How about your partner? When he or she is angry, how do you usually know?

Next, look back at the anger environment in which you grew up. What happened when you expressed anger to a parent? (Were you spanked, sent to your room, lectured, shamed, ridiculed? Or was your expression re-spected and allowed?) How did your parents express their anger to each other? (Did they fight? Pout? Get violent? Minimize each others' feelings as in, "Don't be angry; there's no reason to be"? Or did they allow expressions of anger and validate each other's feelings?)

Finally ask: In this crisis exactly what is making me angry? Don't censor your thoughts as you list the sources of your anger. For instance, "I'm angry that my friends won't talk about my loss, and act as if our little boy never lived. I'm angry that God let that drunk driver loose on that street at the exact moment my son was crossing. I'm angry that my husband goes on playing golf every Saturday as if nothing happened."

Here are highlights of how one couple, through ther-apy, began to understand their relationship anger contract. Mary, now in her forties, recalls hearing her parents curs-ing and yelling at each other and watching them push each other around during arguments. By the time she was four years old, she routinely tried to physically separate them, begging first one and then the other to "say you're sorry." For a long time in interactions with her husband, Jim, she responded in one of three ways when she was angry: (1) She suppressed anger, that is, she never voiced it aloud to him; (2) She repressed anger, that is she denied it even to herself. ("Everything's just fine!" she'd sometimes snap, believing she meant it!); (3) Occasionally she exploded, making irrational statements, exaggerating complaints, and dragging out smoldering resentments.

Jim grew up in a home in which he seldom heard an angry word spoken between his parents, except on very rare occasions when his mother would "fly off the handle" about some little thing, then apologize. Jim seldom showed his anger to Mary or to anybody. But over the years, in three or four arguments when Mary lashed out at him about something, he'd thrown objects across the room, one time smashing a crystal vase against the bedroom wall.

Mary has learned her angry feelings are, as her therapist pointed out, "not good or bad—they just are." Now instead of attempting to bury her anger instantly, she feels it, then expresses it. Sometimes just silently acknowledging her anger to herself is enough. When she feels she needs to address her anger with Jim she uses "I" language: "I get angry when you forget to call our son when you'd promised you would." (Instead of saying "You sure don't follow through on your promises like you should.") Now that Mary is not alternating between being a "nice lady" bothered by nothing and a "bitch" who rants and raves irrationally, Jim has stopped being either ultra-cool or mad-enough-to-throw-something angry. Mary's modification of her part in their anger contract, plus couple therapy, is helping Jim to show his anger more appropriately too. (For more insight into the dynamics of women's anger, read Dr. Harriet Goldhor Lerner's, *Dance of Anger* in which she named and defined the "nice lady" and "bitch" extremes and explored the consequences of using them.)

Most couples could use some large or small revisions in their anger contracts. Revising an anger contract takes time, both to figure out what needs revising and then to keep making repeated efforts to establish new habits.

As you work on this, meanwhile, here are two specific thoughts to put to use right away. First, these wise words from Dr. Theodore Isaac Rubin in his book *Reconciliations*: "Consciously feeling anger is an expression of anger, even if it is expressed only to self." Rubin makes the point that we can never soothe ourselves, never deal with our anger unless we feel it. Especially in a crisis we need to acknowl-edge our anger and allow it. Anger is not dangerous. Suppressing it, repressing it, exploding over it, converting it into depression: all these choices hurt us. But when we can feel our anger, we can process it, then decide what to do with it. If we skip the "feeling" we invite the deadening of both joy and pain because we can't disallow one emotion and allow the others.

Second, allow your partner to feel his or her anger. "Too frequently we get angry at our lovers for being angry," writes Dr. Alan Loy McGinnis in *The Romance Factor*. He suggests asking these two questions "'Honey, have I done something to make you angry?' If the answer to that is no, the second is 'Then is there anything I can do for you?' If not, you are free to leave your lover alone. And by giving him or her the right to an occasional funk, you have transmitted a wonderful gift."

A crisis, with the anger it inevitably stirs in us, gives us an opportunity to learn about our anger contract with our partner and to revise it. We have an opportunity to look at what evokes our anger. If we discover too much is making us angry too often, we can look at why. If we discover we've lost our ability to feel angry, we can enter therapy to uncover the sources of our loss and eventually thaw our frozen emotions.

Confront Each Other Lovingly

During a crisis, we may see parts of our partner previ-ously hidden. We may find out that our partner is brave at the onset of a crisis but folds during the long haul. We may find out that our wife avoids facing a situation, escaping into work, sleep, or alcohol.

We need to confront our partner lovingly when he or

she is either self-destructing or putting us or our relationship under excessive pressure. Actress JoBeth Williams'
experience was told in a *Parade Magazine* article by Larry
Barton. JoBeth married in her early thirties in 1982, hoping
she'd get pregnant in a few months. When she didn't, she
consulted eight doctors in the next eight years. Finally, she
became pregnant in 1986, but had a miscarriage ten weeks
later. In 1987, she had an ectopic pregnancy.

At this point, with no diagnosis about the cause of
their infertility, and little hope, JoBeth began to think of
herself as "an inadequate wife, a difficult woman, a simple
failure." As her self esteem plummeted so did her energy.
She stopped reading most of the scripts sent her. She was
hitting bottom emotionally, when her husband, director
John Pasquinn, confronted her as they were talking late one
night.

What John expressed "shook" and "bothered" JoBeth.
"He said he couldn't reach me anymore and that I was the
only one who could pull myself out of this before I de-
stroyed everything," she remembers.

"At that point I decided to talk openly about infertility
to our friends and acquaintances. And they began to open
up to us! All of a sudden, we discovered that couples we
thought we knew well were also trying to have a baby in
vain. Why hadn't they mentioned it to us earlier? Why
hadn't we?" Late in 1987, they became parents through
adopting their first son, William. John's words had helped
nudge JoBeth into going on.

". . . Loving spouses must repeatedly confront each
other if the marriage relationship is to serve the function of
promoting the spiritual growth of the partners," writes M.
Scott Peck, M.D. in *The Road Less Traveled*. "No marriage
can be judged truly successful unless husband and wife are

each other's best critics."

Few of us like to have a reality we've been denying pointed out to us. So as we employ the gentle art of confrontation, often we will have to brave our partner's initial resistance. As we dare to confront each other, however, our trust in the process and our courage to try it again can grow. Often our mate's icy "How dare you say I'm doing that" will the next hour or next week melt into a warm "Thank you sweetheart for caring enough to say what you said."

Edit What You Say

Recently when I served on a jury in a civil case, I was impressed with the discipline, respect, and politeness the jurors extended to each other. As we deliberated our verdict, at first we were split six to six. Each side believed strongly in its conclusions, but we spoke without attacking each other and without wandering off into areas that were not pertinent to the case. We edited our words. We took turns speaking. As a result, even though two jurors never agreed with the majority, we all left the room respecting each other and feeling that the process had an inherent integrity.

In a crisis and even in everyday communication with our partners, we don't always resemble polite, disciplined jurors. We let our words rush out like lava flowing down the side of a volcano. Or we indulge in unfocused thinking, rambling all over the place expecting surely our spouse will mentally delete what's not important. And sometimes when we're angry at life, but not at our partner, we spit out hateful words so indiscriminately that it's hard for our partner to know where our anger is directed—at him or her, or at the situation itself.

The art of editing—cutting out impoliteness, vague-
ness, put-downs, and irrelevant old resentments—takes
determined effort. Instead of saying "Damn it, won't you
shut up so *I* can say something?" try "I know you have a lot
on your mind, but I'd like a turn too. Could I interrupt for
just a moment?" Instead of "You think you're the only one
who's discouraged," try "You look really down. I am too.
Maybe we could talk about what's bothering both of us
right now." Instead of "You're a selfish SOB to spend that
money without consulting me first. Your carelessness is
wrecking the budget," try "I'm upset about that big bill that
just came in the mail. I'd like to come up with an agreement
we can both live with, some plan to communicate with each
other before we make such large purchases."

By editing our words, by extending the same politeness and kindness to our partner that we routinely extend
to friends and even strangers, we gain control over what
flows from our mouth, we spend less time in regret, and we
have a firmer foundation on which to build intimacy.

"When there are many words transgression is unavoidable. But he who restrains his lips is wise," says
Proverbs 10:19 in the Old Testament. Though we often err
in not saying enough to our partner, at other times we say
too much with too little regard for the impact.

Practice Patience

When we love this man or woman who is our partner,
invariably we take turns. Our spurts of growth, our regres-
sions, are seldom synchronized. As Joyce explains, "After
twenty years married to the same man, I know this. Sometimes he waits for me. Sometimes I wait for him. We're in
a financial crisis right now due in large part to his faulty

judgment. But he waited for me to outgrow a midlife crisis. And so I'll wait now. He's a good man I don't want to lose though I'd like to strangle him right this minute!"

Often we may need to exercise patience with a partner who has, under extreme stress, returned to primitive beliefs. We can be less judgmental with our partner when we realize that old beliefs, dragged back out and dusted off in the anxiety of a crisis, are in operation.

Here's how one couple survived one partner's regression. Frank, after his wife, Rita, came down with an undiagnosed viral infection, tried to ban her from ever working again. He was convinced she had picked up the virus from one of the fifth-grade students she taught. For awhile, he believed it was his job "to protect her by keeping her home and safe." When, after three weeks in the hospital, she recovered, he returned to his more rational way of relating. He supported her decision to get back into the classroom. He apologized for his overreaction, which was grounded in the sheer terror of thinking he might lose her.

During the weeks before Frank came back to his senses, Rita could have decided that she, an independent, able woman, wanted no part of a union with someone so dictatorial. But Rita sensed that Frank was overreacting more out of fear than out of disrespect. She knew Frank's behavior was not typical, but was a radical deviation from his usual egalitarian manner.

It wasn't easy, but though Rita felt hurt and angry with Frank, she resisted accusing him of being a throwback to pre-liberation dark ages. Instead she questioned him about his fears. She listened to them, thinking, though never saying: How ridiculous. After he shared his fears, she reassured him she'd take good care of herself. She pointed out gently that it's possible to pick up a virus in the supermarket or anyplace. When she validated his concerns, when she noted that viruses do lurk everywhere, Frank began to let go of his rigid stance. Later, he told Rita he was not only sorry about trying to take over her life, but that he was also embarrassed that he had been sounding more like his father (who *had* tried to restrict and run his wife's life) than himself!

Start Sharing Feelings Instead of Making Presumptions

Dr. Patrick Malone had just finished a therapy session with a couple on the afternoon I interviewed him. He seemed elated at the outcome. "By the end of the hour, this husband and wife were able to arrive at the position in which they both understood that they did not understand what the other was talking about at all!" he said. "They simply had no experience that allowed them to comprehend what the other person was really feeling or saying. And today they stopped pretending that they knew. Often, we presume we understand our partner and act on our presumptions. It makes us feel more secure to think we define our world."

When we spin our own scenarios of what our partner is really like, what he or she is really up to, really feeling, we block any possibility of intimacy. When we say, "I don't want to listen—I already *know*," we are, in effect, saying, "I trust my own perceptions, but I don't trust yours and I see no reason to listen to you."

When we make presumptions, we prejudge our partner, causing him or her to feel unworthy, unloved, devalued. In turn we stir up resentment and anger. When, however, we ask for and listen to our partner's reality, we build trust.

Here's how spending a small amount of focused time

together can let us in on each other's feelings. Over breakfast or at another regular time early in the day, take five
minutes to find out how your partner is feeling, then share
your own feelings. In the evening, again spend a few
minutes talking about what happened during the day to
intensify or change the feelings you began the day with.
Use the list of feelings on page 30 to help you to pick out the
exact words that reflect each of your states of mind.

A morning exchange might go like this:

She: I'm feeling lethargic and lifeless. I'd give anything if I didn't have to go to work. I'd just like to go back
to bed and blank everything out for awhile. Would you
pour me another cup of coffee please?

He: I'm feeling hopeful. I'm feeling a little frightened
about being hopeful! I thought I'd never be able even to
smile again after what we've been through, but maybe
there's a way to go on....I'll think about you at work and
hope your day gets better.

That same couple, regrouping in the evening might
say:

She: I got through work okay. I'm feeling proud of
myself for not giving in to my desire to stay home. On break
this morning I shared what had happened to us with
another teacher. I couldn't believe it. She and her husband
went through the very same thing a year ago. She hugged
me and I started to cry. I'm going to meet her on break again
tomorrow. I feel a little more hopeful now.

He: I guess hope and sadness sum up my day. This
morning I hoped I was over feeling any more intense
waves of sadness. I hoped the pain was over. But a guy at
work was passing out cigars tied with pink ribbons and I
remembered all over again burying our baby girl. The
sadness sometimes feels like a sword's being thrust into

my heart again and again.

Twice-a-day sharing of feelings with your partner gives each of you a "crisis update." Instead of guessing, you know how your partner feels. Simply listening without attempting to change, judge, or modify each other's reality, creates a strong bond between two hurting partners. As an old love song says, "To know you is to love you—and I do."

Comfort and Console Your Partner

To comfort and to console have slightly different nuances of meaning. Our beloved will appreciate both. When we comfort our partner we help lessen his or her pain by cheering, calming, or inspiring with hope. *Comfort*, as the dictionary explains, means "to soothe in distress or sorrow; to ease the misery or grief of." Essentially, we become a "fort," a strong place for our partner.

When we console him or her we do little to actually change the situation; rather when we console we try to quiet our partner's fears, calm her nerves, or encourage him to go on in spite of. "Consolation is a spiritual undertaking," writes therapist Daphne Rose Kingma in *True Love*, a wise little volume about how to practice the art of loving. "It begins with the state of grace that accepts we are all suffering and that it is one of our highest callings to move into the vale of tears with one another."

Find Out What Kind of Comfort or Consolation Your Partner Needs And Wants

Ask your partner directly what he or she considers comforting. Observe your partner's behavior for clues. When is he or she most discouraged? What situations or times of the day seem to be worst? One couple facing a dramatic loss of revenue in their small, previously thriving mail-order business, came in for counseling because Esther, who was in charge of the personnel department, felt that her attempts to comfort her husband, Frank, who was growing increasingly discouraged, were being rebuffed. She'd been offering him back rubs each evening and trying her best to find words of consolation, such as, "I'm sure, dear, that things will get better." But Frank was growing irritable and starting to say, "Just leave me alone."

In joint therapy sessions, Frank expressed that what would comfort him the most would be to share a weekly report of profits and losses with Esther. He emphasized that no words of caring from her would help as much as updating her on how the business was faring. After they initiated that ritual, Frank relaxed more and the two of them could talk openly about their fears and anxieties about the business.

We're often wrong when we assume that we know best how to comfort our partner. As Marilyn says, "When I have PMS, I want to be left alone. When my husband Bill is in a deep funk, he wants me to put my arms around him and tell him how much I love him. If he used that strategy with me, thinking I wanted the same thing he wants, he might find himself in danger. Somebody joked that the only difference between a pitbull and a woman with PMS is that the woman may be wearing lipstick. Mine is like that! It's best to stay away."

Console an Imperfect Partner

The tag on a denim skirt I ordered out of a Land's End catalogue tells me my skirt has been through a lot to become so soft and comfortable: "After it's made, your garment is actually tumbled in a huge vat filled with water and stones," it says, then instructs, "Please don't consider the rough texture and variations in color as imperfections—they merely add to its spunky personality."

After we've been tumbled around by a crisis, we're not so perfect either. Neither of us. We console each other best when we embrace our imperfections.

In a film documentary about a fortyish man about to receive a heart transplant, there was a poignant scene apropos of this. His wife is with him in the hospital room the day before the scheduled surgery. He lights a cigarette, inhaling deeply. She looks at him, a mixture of "How could you?" and "I love you anyway" on her face.

"How do you put up with me?" he asks, seeming to read her mind. "I think we kind of put up with each other," she answers. "That might be the secret of our success, putting up with each other."

"Just hold me, hold on all the way," he whispers.

We comfort each other best when we hug a flesh-and-blood partner not a slick, one-dimensional fantasy. The feeling of being cared for, for who we are, right now, unites us in a solid, deep way.

Don't Offer Comfort or Consolation That Is Insincere or Less Than Loving

Sometimes consolation rings with insincerity, is patronizing, or even cruel or sarcastic. In my early teens, I or one of my friends might say a sympathetic "you poor thing" to someone we didn't like and then turn around once she was out of earshot and zap her with our holier-than-thou judgment. "Did you see that tacky dress she was wearing? No wonder she's having trouble with her boyfriend," we'd hiss seconds after our spurious cordiality. In the jargon of the 1950s, what we did was "two faced." It was also mean.

In our relationship with our mate, offering two-faced comfort--casually offering comfort when we don't mean it--is potentially devastating to our relationship.

When we're angry with our partner, when we're still in the process of sorting out guilt and blame, when we're hurt over his or her part in bringing this crisis into our lives, we need to console one another with words that reflect where we are emotionally, spiritually, and mentally. We can say perhaps, "I love you darling and I'm sorry about all this," when we cannot say, "Sweetheart you don't deserve this." We can say perhaps, "I'll be here beside you," when we cannot say "I like being here with you." Our consolation will inspire trust when we speak honestly and kindly.

Take Care of Yourself

Even if our partner is ill; even if our partner is hitting bottom emotionally; even if our partner has been affected by a crisis much more than we have—we lose our capacity to console or comfort when we lose ourselves. When author Madeleine L'Engle's husband was ill with cancer and in the hospital, she continued her morning regimen of swimming and reciting poems and prayers to herself. "The movement of the body through water helps mind and heart to work together," she reflected in *Two-Part Invention*.

When the need to console our partner is greatest, we especially need to renew our own energy. Take a walk. Phone a friend. Go to a support group. Get up a half-hour early to read inspirational material or listen to tapes. Find moments in the day to meditate or pray. When we burn out, we give up our ability to console.

Hold Each Other

In many crises, our friends, our relatives, even strangers, upon hearing what's happened to us, may act as if we're contagious. When our son or daughter is battling a drug addiction; when our child dies; when one of us is very ill; when we lose a job or go bankrupt—others may shun us, fearing that by being near, somehow our affliction might spread to them.

In a crisis we can put our arms around each other, knowing that if the crisis—whatever it is—is catching, it's too late! We've been exposed; we're in it together, two against the world. Just holding each other can bring immeasurable comfort.

The initial step back into each other's arms after a crisis has driven us apart is comparable in intensity and ecstasy to our first hugs, our first embraces. We return to each other as new people, influenced and changed by a crisis, yet longing for the comfort of the same familiar arms.

Celebrate Together

On the popular TV game show, "Wheel of Fortune," one contestant has a chance at the big prize. By filling in enough of the missing letters to solve a word puzzle, he or she can walk away with $25,000, a sunny vacation in Mexico, a red Corvette, or something worth big bucks. If the contestant can't solve the puzzle in five seconds, a buzzer sounds and the audience collectively wails an "ohhhhhhhh" of disappointment. But when a contestant *wins?* Family and friends swarm onto the stage and light on the winner in a breathless flurry of hugs, screams, and congratulations.

In our society, it is usually the "winners" of prestige, money, or status who bask in the celebration spotlight. When we've lost something in a crisis—our health, wealth, or control over our daily lives—we may feel slightly apologetic or out of place. What can we celebrate? Plenty actually. Surviving a crisis is a great accomplishment, worthy of celebration.

In quiet talks or on walks together; over a candlelight dinner; snuggling in bed; in any way or any place you and your partner choose, here are some things to celebrate, some things you've won by surviving a crisis together. They're not glitzy and transitory; they are lasting and deep like the love you're cultivating.

Your New Values, New Selves, and New Skills

Celebrate the new wisdom that is leading you into more growth as an individual and spilling over in your relationship with your partner. What irrational beliefs have been discarded during this crisis? Do you smile sadly now remembering how you used to think you were smart enough to keep all harm from you or your family? Do you believe now that bad things happen for seemingly no reason at all? Do you finally see how one trait of yours, one you'd never acknowledged before, helped invite a crisis? Do you now accept crisis as a part of your journey through life together? What do you know now that you didn't know before?

Any new skills—spiritual, psychological, physical, practical, or intellectual—that we pick up during a crisis are worthy of our celebration. Perhaps we've learned to cook and manage the household while our partner was bedridden. Perhaps we've learned to reach out to others, offering hugs and help now that we know, first hand, what it's like to experience deep grief. Perhaps we've learned to tell our partner how much he or she means to us now that we know how tenuous life is. Perhaps we've learned to focus on what we have left. Perhaps we've finally made physical fitness, good nutrition, and regular relaxation a priority.

Sometimes, our learning shows up even in our work. Lynne, an artist, stayed with her husband Aaron after finding out about a short affair he'd had. After forgiving him, in fact just days after they reconciled and determined they'd keep making daily efforts to rebuild their relationship, their hundred-year-old house, which they had lovingly and patiently restored, burned to the ground. A month later, Lynne's mother died suddenly of a heart attack.

Two years after this traumatic period, Lynne looks back at all she and Aaron went through together and believes that not just their relationship, but her work, too, was strengthened. "Everybody says, `Your work's much tougher. It's got more to it.' They say it's more powerful compared to what I used to do. And the critics say it's `transcendent'! I like it that I seem to be showing up in my work."

Your Courage

In his 1975 classic, *The Courage To Create,* Rollo May points out that "the word *courage* comes from the same stem as the French word *coeur,* meaning `heart.' . . . Thus, just as one's heart, by pumping blood to one's arms, legs, and brain enables all the other physical organs to function, so courage makes possible all the psychological virtues.

Without courage other values wither away into mere fac-similes of virtue."

It takes courage to wipe away tears and greet a son or daughter in a rehabilitation center with a hug and encouraging words, and then to go home and not vent our anxiety and fear on our partner; it takes courage to go back to work when our heart is breaking over the loss of a newborn son and then to come home to hold a grieving wife in our arms; it takes courage to hold an ill partner's hand, to smile and be cheerful, to cry with him too, not knowing if he'll beat the odds and still be beside us next year; it takes courage to move into a new community and deal with our loneliness without attacking our partner; it takes courage to stay focused on making it through one day at a time when a crisis has put a big question mark in some crucial part of our lives.

Courage is the ability to resist the pull of the negative and to sculpt something positive out of our not-so-positive situations. Courage is the art of seeing each day as a new one and locating even a thin swatch of light to focus on and be thankful for. Courage is acknowledging and feeling the darkness, sadness, and uncertainty, but going on anyway. Courage is allowing our partner to grieve in his or her own time and way, and to gently en-courage them with our own courage. Courage is learning to manage our fears. "The trick," someone wrote, "is not to rid your stomach of butterflies, but to get them to fly in formation."

In a crisis, we should celebrate any and every form of courage we can muster.

The Power of Your Example

As we were raising our two sons, Matthew and Timothy, now young men, my paperback copy of Dr. Benjamin

Spock's *Baby and Child Care* was consulted so often that the cover separated from the pages and then the pages started falling apart too. I did my best to keep my sons physically and psychologically well, but I barely glimpsed one huge truth along the way. It was: How my husband and I handled crises spoke to our sons and keeps on speaking to them today more loudly than any childrearing techniques we tried.

In short, our children are watching us! As we make discoveries about ourselves in a crisis, our children have their binoculars trained on us. If we're childless, someone else is being influenced by our survival: our next-door neighbor; our brother or sister; a friend.

When we stop being drugged or drunk, when we refuse to run away, when we seek comfort in our partner's arms instead of embracing someone else, when we decide to learn and grow from the lessons of a crisis, we inspire others. If we have children, we may be changing and helping to halt the perpetuation of unhealthy family patterns to run away from or shun such lessons.

"Children tend to inherit *whatever* psychological business we choose not to attend to," writes Harriet Lerner in *The Dance of Intimacy*. By attending to the business at hand during a crisis, we've done the work not just for ourselves, but for others too.

Your New Capacity For Joy

In the late 1970s, in Colorado, high in a mountain meadow decorated with bright violet, red, and yellow wildflowers, my husband Jack and I attended one of the most emotionally moving weddings I can remember. The sun bathed the setting of quaking aspens and a gurgling mountain stream that June morning without even one cloud darkening the hour-long ceremony. The bride wore a flowing pink mumu; the groom, a tie-dyed shirt and jeans.

The couple had made up their vows and memorized them. Honoring each other's separateness, yet practicing devotion to the new "us" was spoken about sincerely that day, as the bearded young man and his fair-haired love stared into each other's eyes.

I went home feeling like a failure at love. Jack and I had already been through the crisis of infertility, followed by the adjustments of raising two little sons, followed by two cross-country moves. In addition, at the time of that wedding, I was working through a painful midlife crisis. My discontent with myself was large, my commitment to my marriage tenuous.

The purity of the love this couple seemed to possess in that heady mountain setting was the perfection I'd wanted in my marriage. However, what I've gotten instead is a far from flawless, but much deeper joy. My midlife crisis ended, and slowly and unevenly; with therapy and a renewed commitment to each other, Jack and I found healing together.

Since then, through a couple more tough crises, we've survived again. Not easily. Not perfectly. But we celebrate our doing it together. By going through it all, our joy is like finding the pot of gold at the end of the rainbow; it's a joy we wouldn't have discovered without the thunderstorms.

(A postscript to that meadow wedding: Within two years, they split up permanently. He, a psychotherapist, was having an affair with a client. She, a nurse, moved back in with her parents to raise her baby son alone.)

After couples have made it through a crisis, or a string of them together, if they've also worked at inventing a new relationship, an undercurrent of joy fills their days. It's more like a sonata playing quietly in the background than a brass band blaring down Main Street. We don't parade our joy, try to impress others with it, or even explain it so much as we experience it, together.

A Concluding Wish

On a window-shopping stroll through downtown Olympia, Washington, my first stop was a tiny gift shop with a "SORRY, WE'RE CLOSED" sign still hanging on the door. Inside were candles, sterling silver jewelry, pottery, and bright quilts artistically displayed, as was a Siamese cat who slept sprawled on her back, stretched out in the middle of the only sunny spot on a worn hardwood floor. As I watched her, she woke up suddenly, then roused herself long enough to move six or eight inches to the right. I'd cast a shadow on her, and instinctively she sought the remaining swatch of sunlight.

Like the cat, in a crisis, one of our first instincts may be to seek the sun. Not one of us likes it when a crisis casts its shadow over our lives. But the women and men who resist the impulse to run and who stay by their mates to make it through the dark night together wind up with new insights and courage, with a greater capacity for loving themselves, their partners, and others. In essence, we learn from a crisis how to give more to each moment and how to get more from each one.

Unlike a crisis, these rewards are predictable and certain—they are guaranteed bonuses we can count on collecting together when we take on the challenges of loving each other while coping with loss and difficulty. Meanwhile now, moment by moment as you are facing what you must, we wish you on-going fortitude and faith in yourselves, and we hope that ultimately you find great joy as you bask in the satisfaction of making it through the night—together.

Chapter 14

Other Helpful Reading

*More marriages might survive if the part-
ners realized that sometimes the better
comes after the worse.*
Doug Larson

U nlike our friends with answering machines that
tell us "we'll call you back just as soon as we can,"
a book is always there for us. We found the following to be especially helpful resources for individuals and
couples during and after a crisis. Some address how to
build a better relationship or offer ideas for individual
growth. Others look at the "whys" and "how comes" of
crises by delving into psychological, philosophical, or spiritual issues. A few deal with handling specific types of
crises. In vastly different ways, all offer valuable insights
and useful information.

Understanding Crisis

When Bad Things Happen to Good People by Harold S.
Kushner, Avon Books, 1983. When something cruel or
unfair happens to us, we wonder why, and we wonder
how we'll survive. Rabbi Kushner explores how God can
still be a source of comfort in "this less-than-perfect world."

Living Through Personal Crisis by Ann Kaiser Stearns,

Ballantine Books, 1985. This book emphasizes how we find healing by going *through* the crisis process. Stearns offers excellent advice about how to deal with guilt, anger, and fear. A short, highly readable book packed with hope and insights.

Necessary Losses by Judith Viorst, Simon and Schuster, 1986. Viorst examines the many losses we all must face beginning with birth and ending with death. If you're struggling with guilt, consult her chapter "Good as Guilt." If you're feeling ambivalence toward your partner, find out you're not alone by reading "Love and Hate in the Married State."

The Power of Myth by Joseph Campbell with Bill Moyers, Doubleday, 1988. Scholar Joseph Campbell, an authority on mythology, converses here with journalist Bill Moyers about subjects ranging from marriage to suffering. Campbell's ideas reflect a synthesis of world myths, philosophies, and religions from ancient to modern times. He believes that the hero "is the one who comes to participate in life courageously and decently, in the way of nature, not in the way of personal rancor, disappointment, or revenge." He helps readers in their quests to be heroes.

The Perennial Philosophy by Aldous Huxley, Perennial Library, 1990. This anthology, originally published in 1944, is a collection of quotes from many different saints and sages from diverse times and places interspersed with Huxley's own comments. From St. Theresa to Chuang Tzu, we learn about the nature of good and evil, suffering, faith, charity, and much more. For readers with a philosophical bent, for those seeking spiritual comfort, this classic contains immense hope and inspiration.

When All You've Ever Wanted Isn't Enough by Harold S. Kushner, Summit Books, 1986. Rabbi Kushner probes how we give our life meaning. In his chapter "Feeling No Pain, Feeling No Joy" he challenges readers who've felt they must anesthetize themselves during a crisis, to face and feel the pain. Then, he contends, we can also feel joy.

Understanding Each Other

Communication

That's Not What I Meant!—How Conversational Style Makes or Breaks Relationships by Deborah Tannen, Ph.D., Ballantine Books, 1986. In all our relationships, our conversational styles sometimes mesh, sometimes clash. Tannen's chapter "Talk in the Intimate Relationship: His and Hers" focuses on how this relates to communicating with our partner. "Male-female conversation is cross-cultural communication," says Tannen. Even though you and your mate may have similar values and goals, your conversational styles may be playing havoc with your relationship. Tannen sheds light on why and thus helps us know better what to do.

You Just Don't Understand: Women and Men in Conversation by Deborah Tannen, Ph.D., William Morrow and Company, Inc., 1990. In her latest book Tannen tackles identifying and understanding gender differences in ways of speaking. She concludes that women use conversation for rapport and men for report. Her development of that theory alone makes the book worthwhile reading for any of you in love but in the dark about your communication difficulties.

Getting the Love You Want: A Guide for Couples by Harville Hendrix, Ph.D., Henry Holt & Company, 1988. In this highly readable book, Hendrix delves into the nitty-gritty of common couple relationship problems, such as why we engage in power struggles and end up acting like children to get our way. Hendrix offers user-friendly, couple-tested exercises designed to deprogram us from ineffective tactics and teach us how to communicate with our partner lovingly and constructively. An excellent, helpful tool for couples to consult often.

Intimacy

The Art of Intimacy by Thomas Patrick Malone, M.D., and Patrick Thomas Malone, M.D., Prentice Hall Press, 1987. When we can be true to ourselves and also affirm our partner's separate self, these two freedoms can lead to intimacy, say these psychiatrists. They also point out that we tend to form long-term relationships with partners "essentially different from ourselves" and "to have brief affairs with people who are essentially like ourselves."

During a crisis, learning to be intimate with our partner is a challenge. This groundbreaking book explains why. It also offers inspiring, insightful ideas about the often misunderstood nature of intimacy and spells out what the art of intimacy demands of us. A wise, thought-provoking book.

The Dance of Intimacy: A Woman's Guide to Courageous Acts of Change in Key Relationships by Harriet Goldhor Lerner, Ph.D., Harper & Row, 1989. Instead of angry confrontations, instead of distancing ourselves, when we desire to see changes in an important relationship, Lerner suggests that we plan for "small, manageable moves based on a solid understanding of the problem, including our own part in it." A practical, sound book with concrete ideas for making those crucial moves that may lead to more intimacy, not just with our partner but all those we love.

Do I Have to Give up Me to Be Loved by You? by Jordan Paul, Ph.D. and Margaret Paul, Ph.D., CompCare Publications, 1983. We do not find intimacy by giving up ourselves or by trying to change our partner, say the authors-therapists. When we stop accusing our partners or predicting their behavior, we can discover more about them. The authors include many practical ideas about how we can overcome our anger and fears and open ourselves up to learning more about the person we love.

Super Marital Sex—Loving for Life by Paul Pearsall, Ph.D., Ballantine Books, 1987. If a crisis is affecting your sexual relationship for the worse, read this excellent book, which invites readers to care for and attend to each other more than they care about and attend to "the lawn, the kids, the job, the car, and the leaky sink." Pearsall also devotes an entire chapter to the effects of stress and loss on our sexual intimacy. "Must" reading to help us find our way back into each other's arms.

Notes to Each Other by Hugh Prather and Gayle Prather, Bantam Books, 1990. Back in 1965 this married couple made a commitment to each other to remain together for life. With unusual candor and clarity, through short diary notations, they take readers along on their journey. A sample: "Will the time come when we won't have to work so hard on our relationship? No, the time will come when there will be no lapse in our efforts. The time will come when it will be unthinkable for us to take a break from kindness." Tested by various crises themselves, this couple's insights ring with authenticity.

Guilt, Forgiveness and Regret

Forgive & Forget: Healing the Hurts We Don't Deserve by Lewis B. Smedes, Harper & Row, 1984. If in a crisis you are blaming yourself or your partner for something large or small you did or failed to do, this loving, wise book has many healing messages. "When you forgive the person who hurt you deeply and unfairly, you perform a miracle that has no equal," writes Smedes. His entire book is a manual for those of us who are not saints, but who aspire somehow to learn how to forgive.

Our Appointment with Life: The Buddha's Teaching on Living in the Present by Thich Nhat Hanh, Parallax Press, 1990. A short, simple, profound set of gentle instructions about living in the here and now. In a crisis we may want to flee the present; we may look back with regret; we may fear the future. "Our appointment with life is in the present moment. The place of our appointment is right here, in this very place," writes Thich Nhat Hanh, a Vietnamese Buddhist monk, poet, and peace activist who lives in exile in France.

Practicing Love

True Love: How to Make Your Relationship Sweeter, Deeper and More Passionate by Daphne Rose Kingma, Conari Press, 1991. Kingma, a therapist, offers more than sixty practical suggestions for ways to demonstrate love to our partner. Instead of focusing on why loving our partner is impossible, she shows us exactly how it is possible. A sample: "Reveal Your Fears"; "Console One Another"; "Walk a Mile in Your Sweetheart's Shoes"; "Your Sweetheart Isn't Psychic." When your relationship has been beaten up by a crisis, her wise ideas put into action will gently facilitate the healing process.

The Romance Factor by Alan Loy McGinnis, Harper & Row, Publishers, 1982. In this thoughtful and practical book, McGinnis examines romance from many different angles. Instead of including only the obvious "buy her flowers" tips, he also lets readers in on how commitment and kindness feed romance. Of particular interest to couples in a crisis is his chapter "Why an Affair Can Be Tempting." McGinnis also has on-target suggestions to help couples avoid affairs during stressful periods.

A Time for Love by Eugene C. Kennedy, Image Books, 1972. Father Kennedy, a Roman Catholic priest, filled this book with down-to-earth wisdom about the art and practice of loving. Kennedy explores some of love's attributes drawn from I Corinthians 13 in the Bible. These themes have much relevance for couples in a crisis.

The Road Less Traveled: A New Psychology of Love, Traditional Values and Spiritual Growth by M. Scott Peck, M.D., Simon and Schuster, 1978. "Life is difficult." With these three words Peck opens his groundbreaking book. For a couple immersed in the difficulties of a crisis, there is much wise advice about the art of loving in these pages. Peck emphasizes the discipline and effort love requires of us.

The Art of Loving by Erich Fromm, Harper & Row, 1956. Love is not a sentiment, but an art that requires knowledge and effort, says Fromm. To practice any art, he maintains, we need discipline, concentration, patience, and supreme concern. To practice love we need to overcome our narcissism, have rational faith in ourselves and the one we love, have courage, and be in "a constant state of active concern with the loved person and with the rest of life." The renowned psychoanalyst delves deeply into all this, leaving the reader with profound insights.

Married People: Staying Together in the Age of Divorce by Francine Klagsbrun, Bantam Books, 1985. The author points out that we experience a constant pull between loving ourselves and loving our partner. Drawing on interviews with happily married couples, she explores exactly how couples can find a satisfying union. Everything from sex to fighting is covered, and a chapter entitled "Crisis!" offers excellent insights into crisis survival.

Anger

The Angry Book by Theodore Isaac Rubin, M.D., Macmillan Publishing Company, 1969. When we accept our anger and feel it, we can then decide whether to express it only to ourselves or, in addition, to the one who stirred our anger, says this eminent psychiatrist. This little classic is like an owner's manual—since we all own anger we'd be wise to read here all about its various guises, distortions, and consequences. In clear, mostly one-to-three-page chapters, Rubin covers anger from many helpful angles. An excellent handbook especially during a crisis.

The Dance of Anger: A Woman's Guide to Changing the Patterns of Intimate Relationships by Harriet Goldhor Lerner, Ph.D., Harper & Row, 1985. For women who struggle with being so nice they never show their anger, for women who explode, alienating others with their out-of-control anger, Lerner offers step-by-step help in learning how to identify the true sources of our anger, communicate our feelings, "observe and interrupt nonproductive patterns of interaction," and "anticipate and deal with `change back!' reactions from others." Invaluable, workable material that men as well as women can benefit from reading and implementing.

Understanding Ourselves

Second Banana by Dottie Lamm, Johnson Books, 1983. This book is a collection of Lamm's most popular columns and diary excerpts and includes a section written in 1981 when she underwent a mastectomy and chemotherapy. Lamm, a longtime *Denver Post* columnist and former First Lady of Colorado, translates her emotions, opinions, hopes, and dreams into words that make us say, "Yes I've felt that way too." For those struggling with recognizing and feeling their emotions during a crisis, for those who might like to begin keeping a journal, Lamm's words serve as a model and an inspiration.

Reconciliations by Theodore Isaac Rubin, M.D., The Viking Press, 1980. Here Rubin challenges the premise that "success deserves self-acceptance and that failure deserves self-rejection, self-hate, and depression." Rubin believes our culture's value system is destructive in its glorification of materialism and ambition. This book can help readers who have suffered a loss to redefine their values and affirm themselves. Rubin's mellow approach to living ends up sounding more inviting than collecting trophies in a "rat race."

Celebrate the Temporary by Clyde Reid, Harper & Row, 1972. In this eighty-five page book the author says, "I invite you to breathe into your pain and celebrate that instead of sealing it off. I invite you to be more aware of the gifts of breath and water and food..." A thoughtful, beautiful book that extols the virtues of right now and invites us to learn how to embrace the present.

Alcoholics Anonymous: The Story of How Many Thousands of Men and Women Have Recovered from Alcoholism by Alcoholics Anonymous, World Services, Inc., 1976. Originally published in 1939 and commonly called "The Big Book" by AA members, this contains the powerful original text that is the basis for all twelve-step programs. Here the steps are outlined and explained, and many personal stories about the ongoing benefits and challenges of recovery are shared in poignant detail.

If you are battling an addiction of any kind or grew up in a dysfunctional family or if you are fighting to avoid sinking into self-pity and resentment in the aftermath of a crisis, this book offers hope and specific suggestions. Of particular help are guidelines for forgiving ourselves and those who have harmed us, and returning to the present to live one day at a time.

The Twelve Steps for Everyone by Greatful Members, CompCare Publishers, 1975. This book was originally written to interpret the AA program for Emotional Health Anonymous (EHA) members. Here readers find a clear description of the purpose of twelve-step programs as well as a commentary on each of the twelve steps. The twelve steps emphasize a one-day-at-a-time approach to problem solving and a letting go of problems in order to allow a Higher Power guide us. The author calls twelve-step programs "a nonreligious path of spiritual growth." If you are feeling powerless over a crisis, this is an excellent book to use either in conjunction with a group or alone.

Specific Crises

Young Alcoholics: A Book for Parents by Jack Mumey, Contemporary Books, Inc., 1984. Mumey, a recovering alcoholic and a professional alcohol therapist, wrote this book "to help parents deal with the day-to-day problems of living with an alcoholic child." Parents of a teenaged or young-adult alcoholic will find much compassionate, practical advice here. Mumey tackles such topics as enabling, guilt, setting consequences, and coping with relapses. His warm, conversational tone leaves readers feeling as though they've been visited by a well-informed, caring friend.

At Risk by Alice Hoffman, Berkley Books, 1988. In this novel readers meet Polly and Ivan, and their children, Charlie and Amanda. This family has an ordinary existence until the discovery that Amanda has AIDS. How Polly and Ivan move through their grief, how the crisis impacts their relationships with each other and their children is poignantly captured. Readers see the close-up realities of the grief process while being caught up in their tragic story.

Hour of Gold, Hour of Lead by Anne Morrow Lindbergh, Harcourt Brace Jovanovich, 1973. In these diaries and letters covering 1929-1932, Anne records the happiness and adjustment of her early married years to Charles Lindbergh. In 1932, however, tragedy struck when their toddler Charles Lindbergh, Jr., was kidnapped and murdered. Anne's detailed accounts of her grief and that of her husband resonate with comfort for any of us undergoing intense suffering. Anne and Charles went on to raise five children and to accomplish much in their respective lives. Their grieving process provides clues for anyone hoping and wishing someday to be able to go on too.

The Bereaved Parent by Harriet Sarnoff Schiff, Crown Publishers, Inc., 1977. The death of a child has been called "the ultimate tragedy." If a child of yours has died, this book by a journalist who lost her ten-year-old son will help get you through your grief and eventually back into the land of the living. With great compassion, Schiff assists readers in facing myriad emotional, spiritual, and practical issues. Her chapter "Bereavement and Marriage" will especially help those couples locked in their separate grief and feeling divided by their loss.

Love, Medicine & Miracles: Lessons Learned about Self-Healing from a Surgeon's Experience with Exceptional Patients by Bernie S. Siegel, M.D., Harper & Row, Publishers, 1986. *Peace, Love & Healing—Bodymind Communication and the Path to Self-Healing: An Exploration* by Bernie S. Siegel, M.D., Harper & Row, Publishers, 1989. These two books provide inspiration, hope, and solid information for those fighting an ongoing or life-threatening illness or disability or those who are well and want to learn about how to cultivate continued good health.

Bernie, as he asks patients to call him, is a surgeon who started Exceptional Cancer Patients, a form of individual and group therapy based on "carefrontation" that facilitates personal change and healing. He has observed that patients who dare to defy the statistical odds and beat cancer or other serious diseases, manifest the same basic qualities. They are: "peace of mind, the capacity for unconditional love, the courage to be themselves, a feeling of control over their own lives, independence, an acceptance of responsibility for decisions affecting their lives, and the ability to express their feelings."

Both books delve into how to cultivate such life-saving traits. Not all of us can find total healing, he says, but all of us can "make use of all illness to help us redirect our lives."

Index